MOTHERLESS *Tongues*

MOTHERLESS *Tongues*

The Insurgency of Language

amid Wars of Translation

VICENTE L. RAFAEL

Duke University Press
Durham and London
2016

Library of Congress Cataloging-in-Publication Data
Rafael, Vicente L., author.
Motherless tongues : the insurgency of language amid
wars of translation / Vicente L. Rafael.
pages cm
Includes bibliographical references and index.
ISBN 978-0-8223-6058-2 (hardcover : alk. paper)
ISBN 978-0-8223-6074-2 (pbk. : alk. paper)
ISBN 978-0-8223-7457-2 (e-book)
1. Philippine languages—Political aspects.
2. Translating and interpreting—Political aspects—
Philippines. 3. United States—Languages—Political
aspects. 4. Philippines—Colonial influence.
I. Title.
P119.32.P45R34 2016
30.44'9599—dc23   2015034666

Cover art: "The Escolta business street," from
Photographs of the Philippines taken by U.S. military
personnel (PHLK 173). University of Michigan Library,
Special Collections Library.

In memory of

Catalina Leuterio Rafael

(1925–2010)

CONTENTS

....

ACKNOWLEDGMENTS xi

INTRODUCTION The Aporia of Translation 1

PART I *Vernacularizing the Political*
....

CHAPTER 1 Welcoming What Comes 21
Translating Sovereignty in the Revolutionary Philippines

CHAPTER 2 Wars of Translation 43
American English, Colonial Schooling, and Tagalog Slang

CHAPTER 3 The Cell Phone and the Crowd 70
Messianic Politics in the EDSA II Uprising

PART II *Weaponizing Babel*
....

CHAPTER 4 Translation, American English, and
the National Insecurities of Empire 99

CHAPTER 5 Targeting Translation 120
Counterinsurgency and the Weaponization of Language

PART III *Translating Lives*
....

CHAPTER 6 The Accidents of Area Studies 149
Benedict Anderson and Arjun Appadurai

CHAPTER 7 Contracting Nostalgia 162
On Renato Rosaldo

CHAPTER 8 Language, History, and
Autobiography 173
Becoming Reynaldo Ileto

CHAPTER 9 Interview 189
Translation *Speaks with Vicente Rafael*

NOTES 203

BIBLIOGRAPHY 233

INDEX 247

The degree of the historical sense of any age may be inferred from the manner in which this age makes translations and tries to absorb former ages and books. . . . In the age of the Revolution, the French took possession of Roman antiquity . . . and the [the Romans], how forcibly and at the same time naively they took hold of everything good and lofty of Greek antiquity, which was more ancient! How they translated everything into the Roman present! . . . They seem to ask us: "Should we not make new for ourselves what is old and find ourselves in it? Should we not have the right to breathe our own soul into this dead body? For it is dead after all; how ugly is everything dead!" They did not know the delights of the historical sense; what was past and alien was an embarrassment for them; and being Romans, they saw it as an incentive for a Roman conquest. Indeed, translation was a form of conquest. Not only did one omit what was historical; one also added allusions to the present and, above all, struck out the name of the poet and replaced it with one's own—not with any sense of theft but with the very best conscience of the imperium Romanum.

—FRIEDRICH NIETZSCHE, *The Gay Science*

When I speak to you in your language, what happens to mine? Does my language continue to speak, but in silence? . . . Even to say that I speak to you is perhaps claiming too much, it's taking advantage of an illusory power, of a simple breath. . . . Madness of language, but how sweet, how tender in this moment.

—ABDELKEBIR KHATIBI, *Love in Two Languages*

ACKNOWLEDGMENTS

....

This book was made possible by the generosity of more people than I can recall, much less repay. Their names appear in the earlier versions of the chapters that follow. Still, I would like to thank those friends spread around the world whose help has been crucial in assembling the final form of this book.

My colleagues at the University of Washington have always been supportive, in particular Andrea Arai, Jordanna Bailkin, the late Stephanie Camp, Susan Jeffords, Sandra Joshel, Moon-Ho Jung, Linda Nash, Chandan Reddy, Laurie Sears, Cynthia Steele, Lynn Thomas, Adam Warren, and Kathleen Woodward. I am also grateful to colleagues in various parts of the world. In and beyond Manila these include Filomeno Aguilar Jr., Remmon Barbaza, Joi Barrios, Julius Bautista, Jonathan David Bayot, Walden Bello, Kiko Benitez, Karina Bolasco, Rica Bolipata-Santos, Jose Buenconsejo, Jose Wendell Capili, Jeremy DeChavez, J. Neil Garcia, Francis Gealogo, the late Francisco Guevara, Ramon Guillermo, Caroline Hau, Judy Ick, Reynaldo Ileto, Jazmin Llana, Resil Mojares, Ambeth Ocampo, Susan Quimpo, Lulu Reyes, Dinah Romah, the late Fr. John Schumacher, Vincent Serrano, Ed Tadem, Julio Teehankee, Lily Rose Tope, Von Totanes, and Cora Villareal. I am also grateful to the students from whom I learned a great deal when I served as a visiting professor in Manila during the summers of 2013 and 2014 at the University of the Philippines, the Ateneo de Manila University, and at De La Salle University.

Throughout the years the following colleagues and friends gave me the chance to present various parts of this book: Paul Bandia, Joshua Barker, Tani Barlow, Jonathan Beller, Simona Bertacco, Michael Cullinane, Lola

Elizalde, Alyosha Goldstein, Derek Gregory, Maria Constanza Guzman, Jeffrey Hadler, Susan Harding, Val Hartouni, Robert Horowitz, Vina Lanzona, George Lipsitz, Alfred McCoy, Bonnie McElhinny, Mary Louis Pratt, Florentino Rodao, Renato Rosaldo, Daniel Rosenberg, Danilyn Rutherford, John Sidel, Nikhil Singh, Neferti X. Tadiar, C. J. Wee Wan-ling, Jeff Wasserstrom, and Henry Yu. I have also benefited from Michael Meeker's careful reading of a number of these essays. My thanks to Mona Baker and Lawrence Venuti for being stimulating interlocutors, pointing me to valuable work in and around the field of translation studies.

For nearly three decades I've had the great fortune of having James T. Siegel and Benedict Anderson as teachers and friends. So much of my thinking has been shaped through theirs and those whose ideas they introduced me to, even as I am keenly aware of the distance and discrepancies between their works and mine. To this day their writings continue to be indispensable guideposts for my thinking. I thank Carol Dahl, who was always supportive during the writing of many of these pieces, while Craig and Cristi Rasmussen, Yoshiko Harden, and Leila Dahl Abe always kept me in the loop. Thanks too to Geri and Bob Haynes, models of compassion and true philanthropy. My gratitude goes to Abdi Sami, my brother from another mother, who taught me about living and dying beyond anything I could ever expect.

At the Nida Institute of Translation Studies in Misano Adriatico, I was lucky to find gracious and stimulating interlocutors: Stefano Arduini, Sandra Bermann, Edwin Gentzler, Valerie Henitiuk, Bob and Mary Hodgson, James Maxey, Siri Nergaard, and Sherry Simon. As always, Ken Wissoker at Duke University Press was unfailing in his encouragement, clearing a path for me during those moments when I could not see my way through this project.

I am especially grateful to Lila Ramos Shahani for the many valuable contributions and sharp-eyed suggestions she made as this book took its final form. I am thankful to Leticia Ramos Shahani for her hospitality in Manila. I also wish to acknowledge the friendship of Ranjit and Chanda Shahani and Cyd Sydney as well as the abiding support of Joselito, Rosemary, David, Malu, Enrique, and Menchie Rafael. Finally, I am grateful to the Lenore Hanauer Research Fund at the University of Washington for its assistance in completing this book.

The Aporia of Translation

Each time we express ourselves, we have to break with ourselves.
—**OCTAVIO PAZ**, *The Labyrinth of Solitude*

I don't know how, or in how many languages, you can translate this word *lécher* when you wish to say that one language licks another, like a flame or a caress.
—**JACQUES DERRIDA**, "What Is Relevant Translation?"

This book is about the vexed relationship between language and history seen from the perspective of translation practices in the Philippines, the United States, and elsewhere. Crisscrossing various colonial and postcolonial terrains, *Motherless Tongues* explores the ways in which translation has played an important, if overlooked, role in the unfolding and understanding of particular events in the imperial and national sites I examine here. Each chapter is a signpost for mapping those moments where linguistic exchange and historical imagination give rise to one another within the context of persistently uneven, and always contingent, relations of power. By way of introduction, I want to begin by offering a brief narrative of my own linguistic history that is mine by virtue of belonging to others. In a book on the historicity of translation, we might situate such an accounting by asking: who speaks and to whom? By what right and in what idiom? Who or what is the I that addresses *you*, whoever you might be, and how does it come about in this particular language that we share?

Speaking in Tongues

English is neither my first nor my second language, but serves as both. I speak it when I want to speak something else—that which I imagine to be my mother tongue. Thus is English my language to the extent that it comes from and belongs to someone else. This has to do with the accident of my birth, which has consigned me to a double relationship with English. Born in Manila a decade after the Philippines had gained formal independence from three years of Japanese occupation, nearly half a century of U.S. colonization, and about 350 years of Spanish colonial rule, I grew up inhabiting a complicated linguistic landscape where the mother tongue often seemed like the other's tongue. I went to Catholic schools in Manila where the medium of instruction was English. At home, neither of my parents spoke in their respective native languages to any of their four children. Coming from different parts of a country with over one hundred languages, they spoke mutually unintelligible tongues. They communicated with us in the only language they had in common, a second language that they had learned in school: English.

Both my parents had provincial roots and met in Manila after the war. Born in the mid-1920s, theirs was a generation removed from the Revolution of 1896 and the Filipino-American War of 1899–1902. Living under U.S. colonial rule *entre deux guerres*, they attended the colonial public school system, where English was enforced as the medium of instruction, while the vernaculars were repressed and denigrated.[1] My father spoke Ilonggo, while my mother Kapampangan, though she had become fluent in Tagalog, having gone to school in Manila. English was their lingua franca. When I was born in 1956, English had become far more entrenched in the wake of the American victory over the Japanese. Through a series of unequal treaties, the country remained firmly within the economic, military, and political purview of the United States that made it very much a neocolony. The widespread use of English in schools, businesses, and pubic life testified to the ongoing hegemony of the United States. In the midst of the cultural Cold War, American popular films, music, and television spread throughout the archipelago, increasing the spread of English while investing it with the glamour and power of modernity. In contrast, vernacular languages and Spanish were marginalized in schools and in the public sphere, associated with the uneducated and backward "masses," in the former case, and with a conservative Church and oligarchy, in the latter.

The dominance of English, however, was far from definitive. It was but one of the many languages that was spoken by my family, both immediate and extended. As the lingua franca for the postwar middle classes, it was spoken in a variety of registers and mixed with other languages and accents. By the 1960s, American R&B broadcast on radio and covered by local bands had insinuated Black English and countercultural slang into the "proper" English we were expected to speak. The very Americanness of English meant that it was itself creolized and pervaded by other modes of speaking. Indeed, early efforts by American schoolteachers and their Filipino successors to rid natives of their accents had consistently failed. English came to be spoken with distinctive regional accents, bearing the stigmata, as it were, of the vernaculars it had sought to exclude.[2] In our home, the help did not speak English, though they had some understanding of it. My father addressed them in Ilonggo, since they were all from the province of Negros. The kids spoke to them in a mix of Tagalog and English, while they replied in their native tongue, which we understood but could only haltingly speak. My mother eventually learned enough Ilonggo to give orders to the help and, just as importantly, to communicate with her mother-in-law, who, having only had minimal schooling, spoke no other language when she came to visit us along with other Bacolod relatives. With my maternal grandfather, after whom I was named, I would speak in Tagalog and English. Born during the year of the Revolution of 1896, he was fluent in Spanish, having gone to a Jesuit school and then law school where Spanish was required since it was still the dominant language of the courts and the Philippine legislature until 1941. With my mother and her sisters, he switched between Kapampangan, Tagalog, and English.

As a child, I recall spending humid afternoons reading the Ilonggo-language magazine, *Hiligaynon*, kept both by the help and my grandmother before I could even read Tagalog. In the middle-class subdivision where we lived, we also had Chinese neighbors. With their kids, we spoke in a mix of Tagalog and English, even as they would intersperse their conversation with Hokkien cuss words that all the neighborhood kids avidly learned. While Hollywood movies were predominant in the postwar era, the first film I remember seeing was in Tagalog, *Captain Barbel*, which starred the Chinese mestizo comedian Dolphy, with my Ilongo-speaking grandmother in downtown Manila. And while American shows like *Combat* and *Bonanza* dominated the early days of television in the Philippines, locally produced variety shows were just as popular, which, along with local films, radio, comics, and tabloids, trafficked in the rapidly evolving urban creole, Taglish.[3]

The linguistic scene in private schools in Manila was similarly complex. English ruled, but everyone was required to take several units of Spanish, which was taught badly so that very few learned it properly, while Tagalog—or Filipino, as it would be eventually to be called—was taught as a standalone subject and so effectively marginalized. Speaking the vernacular was still discouraged, and at some schools, it was not uncommon to be fined a small amount if caught speaking it on school premises. Yet the practice of rampant code-switching among the vernaculars, English, and, at times, Spanish, ran beneath and through the American English that was meant to be the standard medium of instruction. *Conyo*-speak, *collegiala* talk, Arneo accents, at times laced with Hokkien and Hakka terms that seeped out of Chinese-language schools, particularized the class character of the chatter that came out of these institutions.[4] By the 1960s, there also emerged a distinctive gay *argot* that found its way into popular culture, promiscuously coupling terms from the various vernaculars, bending the grammatical limits of English and Spanish, while occasionally spicing things up with bastardized words from French and German. Adding to this inter- and intralinguistic Babel was the Catholic Church. Attending mass before the days of Vatican II meant hearing it in Latin. As an aspiring—and ultimately, failed—altar boy, I memorized the liturgy in Latin but understood only fragments of what I was saying. I was fascinated by the sonorous syllables and grave tones of a language whose power, like the pig Latin inscribed on the *anting-anting* or amulets sold in stalls outside some churches, came directly from their otherworldly opaqueness.[5]

In high school, my economics teacher introduced me to Marx. He was then a member of the Communist Party youth group *Kabataang Makabayan* (Patriotic Youth) and led me to a world of left-wing activism that had its own set of codes. I encountered dense English translations of Marxist-Leninist-Maoist literature, full of weighty terms like *dialectical materialism*, *imperialism*, and *bureaucrat-capitalism*. Other words, like *puppets* and *running dogs*, were recodified as weapons of condemnation rather than terms of endearment.[6] At the same time, activist life also brought with it a whole new way of hearing and speaking Tagalog. Coming from the streets the vernacular took on an electric energy, spoken in ways that were lively, inventive, and full of trenchant humor critical of authority. A giddy sense of defiance connected youthful participants in demonstrations as they felt themselves traversed by chants like "Makibaka, huwag matakot!" (Fight, don't fear!). Chanting our slogans, we marched in the streets to their distinctive rhythm. Every demonstration would climax with the anthem of the global left, the "Internationale," sung with clenched fists in Tagalog, evoking deep feelings of solidarity.[7]

Such is a condensed inventory of my linguistic legacy: the privilege of American English punctured and punctuated by a variety of vernaculars: Tagalog, Ilonggo, Kapampangan, bits and pieces of Hokkien, Hakka, Spanish, and Latin. The garrulous and swiftly changing idioms of creole Taglish, gay-speak, private school talk, and Marxist-Maoist jargon woven into the black vernacular and bohemian lexicon of American pop culture of the 1960s—all of which were pronounced with different regional accents—further added to this dizzying diversity. Hence, whenever I am asked what my native language is, I always hesitate to respond. I cannot point to a single one without feeling that I might be betraying the others.

It is thus that I share the fate of many other Filipinos both in the Philippines and elsewhere in the world when I say—this I that now addresses you in an English that doesn't belong to it—that I have no mother tongue, or rather that I have many mother tongues. Whatever I happen to be speaking at the moment is always commingled and contaminated with a whole train of other languages I grew up speaking and hearing in the past and to this very day. Whenever I speak or write in what seems to be coherent English, it is only because I have managed to momentarily repress this history of linguistic pluralism. It is a repression that amounts to an act of translation, transforming a train of possible expressions into a grammatically correct and stylistically recognizable discourse. For to inhabit multiple mother tongues means that speaking any one language entails translating not only across different languages but also within the same language insofar as they are spoken in different ways in different contexts. Inter- and intralingual translation defines the condition of speaking any language in the Philippines— and perhaps elsewhere. My language is thus one that is already of and from the other.[8]

But who is this other? And who is the I that addresses and is addressed by it? How do they come about in the process of addressing each other, and how do they come apart?

Pronouns and Persons

Emile Benveniste many years ago wrote about the peculiarity of the first- and second-person pronouns. In and of themselves, they have no referents except in their actual use, for example, when I say I to refer to myself. In other words, I takes on meaning only at the moment that it is spoken or written by someone and, as Benveniste stresses, always in relation to the second person, you. A language without personal pronouns, he says, is impossible to imagine. By generating the category of persons, pronouns posit the sense of subjectivity—of one who speaks and is spoken to—and makes possible linguistic communication as a means for referring to the world:

> I use "I" only when I am speaking to someone who will be a "you" in my address. It is this condition of dialogue that is constitutive of the person, for it implies reciprocally "I" becomes "you" in the address of the one who in turn designates himself as "I." Language is possible only because each speaker sets himself up as a subject by referring to himself as "I" in his discourse. Because of this, "I" posits another person, the one who, being, as he is, completely exterior to "me," becomes my echo to whom I say "you" and who says "you" to me. This polarity of persons is the fundamental condition of language.[9]

Following Benveniste, every time I say I, it is to address a you who in turn addresses me as another I. Both are mutually entangled with and inhabited by one another. I express myself, as Octavio Paz says, only by breaking with myself. My identity comes not from being the same but from differing, drifting, and detouring, always intermediate and interconnected: always addressing, addressed by, and becoming, in turn, a you. It takes its singularity from the historically specific ways by which it has been doubled and bounded, repeatedly opened, and often violently dispersed, over time. The personal pronouns I and you designate not just the self who speaks and the other who is addressed; they also posit the dialogical relationship between the two. The "person" is that which is formed in and through this interminable dialogue. Put differently, the reciprocal relationship between I and you constitutive of the person means that I emerge as one who is always already in transition, on the way to being other than who I am. In this way I can say "I" by virtue of being an effect of translating within the same language, and between language and a social world, which, insofar as it is a world, must be historical in the sense of being constructed and contingent.

Language can exist as a means of communication, Benveniste says, only because it establishes "the category of the person," which, as we saw, comes from the reciprocal, translative relationship between I and you. If language without personal pronouns were unimaginable, then it would also be unusable without translation that characterizes the reciprocal relationship between the first and the second person.[10]

But what if, as in my case that is doubtless analogous to many others, I and you occur in two or more languages rather than within the same one? As Abdelkebir Khatibi asks, "When I speak to you in your language, what happens to mine? Does my language continue to speak, but in silence?" What happens to the I that says "I" across languages? How does it manage to reach a you, and can it always count on a response? What risks does it run, what debts does it incur? And what of the native tongue, if there is one? Left behind, how does it continue to speak, if it speaks at all, in the face and space of another language? Is there a certain "illusory power," even "madness" in thinking it is possible to speak as a different I capable of addressing a you and being addressed in turn across a linguistic divide?[11] Inasmuch as the I emerges by speaking otherwise under conditions of translation, is there ever a way that it can control the power that constitutes it? Can I, once it speaks, ever use the power of translation to step outside of it? How, in the first place, can we understand this power?

Translation and Power

To be constituted in and through translation means that one is compelled to address not just the topics or objects under consideration, but also the means for and modes of addressing them. Roman Jakobson once referred to this discourse on discourse as metalanguage. It is that which comes after the fact of speech in order to explain or interpret what one has just said.[12] "A faculty of speaking a given language implies a faculty of talking about this language. Such 'metalinguistic' operation permits revision and redefinition of the vocabulary used."[13] A metalanguage is thus a medium for meditating upon mediation and mediumship, allowing you to reflect on reflection. Metalanguage is, in this sense, not metaphysical at all. It is not the truth that precedes and transcends language, but precisely a kind of speech that comes after the fact of speech acts. It asks not only about the *what* of a statement but also the *how* and the *who*. It is in this sense secondary and belated, supplementing what has been said, but it is itself always liable to more explanation, generating more supplementation, and so on, around the hermeneutic circle.

Metalinguistic operations, according to Jakobson, are akin to the act of translation insofar as it supplements the original. Betraying, in both senses of that word, the original, translation exceeds or falls short of its task. It invariably proves incapable of providing the exact equivalence of the substance and style of one language in another. The translator thus always incurs a debt to the original. He or she is always seeking to make restitution to make up for what is missing in the translation, which, because of its inherent shortcomings, comes across like a "series of unfavorable currency transactions."[14] Just as metalanguage conveys what is said by deferring its full disclosure, so translation reconstitutes the original by shortchanging now its meaning, now its style, and usually both at the same time. "In these conditions," Jakobson says, "the question of translation becomes much more entangled and controversial."[15]

These "entangled and controversial"—which is to say, aporetic—workings of translation are what I hope emerge in the chapters that follow. Their geographical and temporal locus shifts between the United States, the Philippines, and elsewhere, beyond their national boundaries from the last decade of the nineteenth century to the last few years of the twenty-first. Written for separate occasions and diverse audiences, each chapter plays out a set of questions held together by recurring obsessions about the politics of language and the ethics and pragmatics of translation. These emerge in various locations and moments: chiefly in the imperial and nationalist languages of sovereignty, the war-making and interpretive protocols of counterinsurgency, the class struggles over technologies of communication with which to address a corrupt state, and in autobiography as sites for dramatizing cultural, as well as linguistic translation. The hegemony of American English in global wars and colonial classrooms is taken up alongside the linguistic predicaments of postcolonial nostalgia and nationalist anxieties over authority and authorship. In each case, acts of translation are further complicated by linguistic histories and social practices that exceed conventional limits: the agency of accident in area studies, the recalcitrance of vernacular notions of freedom, the play of slang under neocolonial conditions, the messianic discourse of crowds seeking justice, the highly unstable identities of interpreters in the midst of military occupation, and the inaccessibility of the dead to nostalgic and nationalist recuperations, among other things.

It is this play between translation and what resists, yet calls out for it, that runs through the entire book. Often forced to serve as the instrument of an imperializing or nationalizing power, translation in these pages is also underwritten by the recurrence of mistranslations and the persistence of untranslatability.[16] In doing so, histories of translation reveal not only the structuring logics of colonial powers; they also reopen the regions of linguistic pluralism that have been repressed. The responses to the reappearance of linguistic plurality and their speakers are as various as they are uneven. A dominant reaction has been to instrumentalize language as such: to use translation, for example, to domesticate foreign languages as well as the foreignness that inheres in language itself. Such entails the mastery of one language over others, and the regulation and standardization of the play of speech. Put differently, attempts at linguistic and social domination seek to recruit translation as a means for waging war on the complications within, as well as across, languages. But such wars of translation are never unchallenged. As I seek to demonstrate, there is an irreducibly insurgent element in every language that undermines such attempts at mastery. In the wars of, and on, translation, what emerge are multiply mothered and motherless tongues amid shifting zones of untranslatability.

What, then, does this insurgency of language consist of? And how does it figure in the relationship between translation and history? Let us return briefly to Jakobson. He says, "A faculty of speaking a given language implies a faculty of talking about this language." This "faculty" is, as I have suggested, the faculty of translation, allowing one to move within, as well as across, languages. It is the capacity to speak otherwise, to say what one meant to say after having said it, to explain what one had just tried to explain, over and over, if need be. It is thus an ability to translate repeatedly, to take hold of language in order to talk about language not just here and now, but into a future that eludes final determination.

It is worth noting that this faculty to translate "a given language" implies that language is already given. In other words, we encounter language as a kind of gift. It is there, available and waiting before one arrives to speak it inasmuch as it is always already being spoken by others.[17] This observation supplements and extends Benveniste's argument that it is "the condition of intersubjectivity that alone makes linguistic communication possible."[18] Subtending the social, language becomes historical only when it is spoken—translated by countless other speakers, who, in order to speak it, have to be able to repeat its structure and vocabulary, that is, to translate it from the start. And doing so means having already been subjected to the process of translation as the condition of possibility of speech. Coming before communication, language, once spoken, plunges its speakers into an "imagined community."[19]

One such enduringly powerful and globalized imagined community is undoubtedly that of Western Christianity. Institutionally and ideologically, it has arguably been an enabling and critical feature, along with capitalism, of Western imperialism. It is also an elementary aspect of "Western" civilization and civilizational discourse that, thanks to colonialism, has spread across the planet and affected even the most un-Christian and secular of societies.[20] In the context of Christianity, where everything has always already begun with the Word, the notion of language as a gift remains central. As a gift, however, language is neither free nor is its circulation unrestricted. Rather, it is imagined as the coming of a divine fire that is meant to burn and consume all other languages in the process of making them bear the language of God.

This imperializing theory of translation is perhaps most clearly exemplified in the event of the Pentecost. The Holy Ghost visits the Apostles in the wake of Christ's return to heaven, appearing as tongues of fire over their heads, empowering them to speak not just their language but all other languages in the world. "And there appeared unto them cloven tongues like as of fire, and it sat upon each of them. And they were all filled with the Holy Ghost, and began to speak with other tongues, as the Spirit gave them utterance."[21] Receiving the promise of the Spirit, the Apostles, and all the other missionaries—religious, colonial, national, and otherwise that arrive in their wake—come to believe in their authority to preach the Word in all the words of the world. Translation and Truth thus become irrevocably linked so that bearing witness entails speaking in tongues, but only insofar as the latter is believed to come from and return to the self-same Word. Endowed with the gift of translation, the Apostles can transfer and transport the Word of God across all the other languages. Thus does conversion always require translation.[22] Converts gain the "faculty of speaking" not just a given language but also the very gift of language. In so doing, they convert their speech into prayers seeking the mercy and blessings of God with which to gain salvation.

The given language brings with it the gift of translation (and vice versa) according to this still dominant Western Christian tradition and its various secular colonial and nationalist versions. As a gift whose origin transcends the world of its speakers, the faculty of translation is determined in a particular way: as that which reorders linguistic plurality into a linguistic hierarchy—the Word of God on top, followed by languages of rule, then all other languages on the bottom—issuing from and returning to its One True Source. Thanks to translation, all languages are conscripted to secure the relationship between signs and referents, bodies and souls, history and destiny, mortality and immortality, whereby the former is made to yield to the latter by the coming of the Word. The Word comes to conquer all words and remake them into aspects of the ever-repeatable promise of salvation retraced by the ever-renewable instruments of prayer and ritual that will bring down grace from above to those below.[23] Thanks to prayer, a social hierarchy is erected on the basis of a linguistic hierarchy. Prayer as the privileged form of address entails the ceaseless petitioning of God across the infinite distance that separates Him from His people. It is precisely the role of prayer and the language of rituals to translate—that is, to both bridge and maintain that divide—between God and man inasmuch as its definitive crossing is possible only upon death. Indeed, death itself is reconceptualized by the language of conversion, sanctified as the decisive translation of earthly life into an afterlife, of infinity into eternity, either in heaven or in hell.[24]

Translation in this Western Christian sense rehearses the transit from life to the afterlife. What lies beyond living, no one really knows. No one can speak of it except speculatively, in anticipation of what is to come: perhaps the final reckoning, the arrival of divine justice, the end of the world as we, whoever we are, know it. But whatever it is, it will no doubt bring the end of translation and linguistic transfers, since there will be no other there to transfer to. Thus would the end of translation bring about the end of the faculty of speech altogether. It would consequently be the end of the other from whom I derive and to whom I direct my speech. The tongues of fire would not only lick all other tongues, as Derrida's epigraph suggests, but also consume them in a holocaust of eternal conflagration.[25]

However, Jakobson also says that there are types of discourses that read-ily take exception to what I have characterized as Christianity's apocalyptic fantasies of translation. Such other discourses persistently defy direct an-nexation or conversion either within the same or across different languages and media. These include poetry, jokes, dreams, magic, and other sorts of "everyday verbal mythology."[26] In such cases, form and content are co-constitutive just as meaning and style are inseparable. Neither "free" nor "literal" translation will do, neither "word for word" nor "sense for sense."[27] Instead, what emerges is a condition of untranslatability, whereby the ques-tion of translation becomes ever more "entangled and controversial." Be-coming entangled, the faculty of translation is trapped by language that seems to yield to no definitive explication or just exchange. One who trans-lates poetry, for example, finds himself or herself immersed in "grammat-ical categories [that] carry a high semantic import," whereby, for example, *death* is gendered feminine in Russian but masculine in German. Similarly, efforts to translate metaphors and puns threaten to erect "skyscrapers of footnotes" as the translator endlessly seeks to restore the sense or the style robbed from the original.[28]Attempting to deal with the essential untrans-latability of these discourses, one is plunged into a sea of possible trans-lations, making any single one a betrayal of the original. Translation thus exposes us to the fact that "language itself is an ocean alive with aporia."[29]

Elusiveness Made Flesh

What could this mean, that language is "alive with aporia"? What kind of life, linguistic and otherwise, dwells in aporia? How is it different from the afterlife projected by Christianity and its secular avatars? From the Greek *aporos*, Latinized as *aporia*, the word is defined by the OED as "an irresolvable internal contradiction or logical disjunction in a text, argument or theory," as in, famously, "a Cretan declares all Cretans to be liars." But in Greek, it also means "impasse," "lack of resources" (that is, without *poros*), and "puz-zlement." Aporia is thus a site that prevents passage, blocks progress, and arrests movement from one place to another. As Sarah Kofman points out, Plato and other Greek philosophers have often referred to the sea as the aporetic space par excellence, with its "endless realm of pure movement, the most mobile, changeable and polymorphous of all spaces, a space where any way that has been traced is immediately obliterated, which transforms any journey into a voyage of exploration which is always unprecedented, dangerous and uncertain."[30] Hence to engage in discursive exchange is to risk drowning in the sea of its aporetic movements. It is to plunge into a "storm of difficulties" that threatens to erode distinctions and divisions, upend authority, and unsettle beliefs.[31] So, too, with translation, which draws one into a sea of languages, entrapping one in their multitude of referents and their ever-changing currents of meaning. Indeed, the only way out of this aporia of language is, ironically, language itself. One translates in the hope of finding a way out—poros—of the trap of language, but only by recourse to another language. One tries to get beyond aporia but, as in the metalinguistic scene described by Jakobson, ends up deeper in another aporia.

In Plato's work, the Sophists are usually blamed for being the chief purveyors of aporia, with their fondness for "techniques of disorientation" that threaten the authority of the philosopher. As weavers of enigma (from the Greek, meaning a fishing net, a woven basket) Sophists are accused of being "living snares . . . mottled, polymorphous and hydra-headed," who, as Kofman says, "cannot be placed in any category. . . . Their form is ambiguous . . . elusiveness made flesh, as bizarre and as dangerous as the 'mad becoming.'"[32] Just as worrisome to the philosopher are the youth, who, upon discovering aporia, rejoice and use it against their parents and other figures of authority. In Plato's *Philebus* we read:

> As soon as a young man gets wind of this feature of speech, he is delighted: he feels he has discovered a treasure-trove of ingenuity. He is in his seventh heaven, and he loves to worry every sentence, now shaking it to and fro and lumping it together, now rolling it out again and again, and tearing it apart. Above all, he confuses himself, but he also confuses anyone he ever comes across, be he younger, older or the same age as himself. He spares neither his father nor his mother, nor anything which can hear—not even animals escape, let alone men. He wouldn't have mercy on the foreigner, if only he could get hold of an interpreter.[33]

Like the Sophists, the youth delight in aporia. It affords them a way out of the trap of parental authority. It gives to them a language that is irreducibly material rather than an empty vessel for containing and giving out meaning: they can shake it, lump it together, roll it out over and over again. Aporetic language thus becomes an occasion for engaging in play, producing delight among the youth, especially when it comes at the expense of their parents. But they also target others, such as animals and foreigners, and do not spare even themselves. They, too, are ensnared in the movement of language and neither give nor ask for "mercy." Unlike the quasi-Platonic Christian notion of translation, which entails the Word transiting into all other words and converting them into ordered relays with which to ask for mercy from above, the youth, in seizing upon aporia, refuse to grant or plea for mercy.[34] Irreverent and free from guilt, they do not ask forgiveness from a higher figure. For the youth, then, playing with language is a way of translating it, not in order to escape it but rather to become ever more enfolded into it. Thus do they embrace the insurgency of language, its capacity to resist reduction and conversion into definitive meanings and authoritative intentions. Like the Sophists, the youth experience aporia as the joy of interminable translation, the experience of being in between different and incommensurable states. In this sense, both foreshadow some of the responses of other historical agents—colonized peoples, working classes, and other subordinated groups—who, as we shall see, had been enmeshed in the language of colonizing power even as they wove their own traps to reverse and displace this power's hold.

Entangled Motifs: Overview of the Book

Each chapter in this book takes up the constitutive, transformative, and often disruptive workings of translation within specific historical contexts. Part I deals mainly with the colonial and postcolonial Philippines, highlighting the plurality of languages—vernacular, Spanish, and English—that shape not only the representation of events but also their very enactment. Part II focuses on the United States and approaches linguistic plurality from another angle, by interrogating the putative monolingualism of the U.S. nation and empire, and by showing how American English is itself the effect of a history of translation practices. Linguistic differences in both places require translation as the process from which issue imagination and action. Filipino nationalists and revolutionary fighters inflect the notion of sovereignty and independence from the West, translating them into vernacularized Christian idioms of pity and compassion (chapter 1). The U.S. military and policymakers seize upon language as a weapon and reformulate translation as part of a Cold War liberal project of area studies or, in the midst of the "global war on terror," as part of a "complex weapons system" (chapter 4). In both cases, English plays an important role. In American efforts at counterinsurgency, it is installed at the apex of a linguistic hierarchy in reference to which all other languages become legible, while in Filipino nationalist writing, English is invested with a demonic power to enslave minds and distort the culture of a people to the point of hastening its death (chapter 2).

In other instances, the proclamation of Philippine independence in 1898 in Spanish—the language of the nationalist elite—shows not an iteration of the Enlightenment ideal of equality and fraternity but their retranslation into colonial notions of hierarchy and dependency, suggesting the beginnings of a counterrevolutionary regime (chapter 1). Other chapters (3 and 5) focus on the telecommunicative workings of translation, that is, its ability to communicate at a distance across social and geographic divides. It is this mediating power of translation materialized in cell phones and weapons, text messages and drones, that leads both the U.S. military and the Filipino middle class in the early twenty-first century to seek control of its workings for their own specific purposes. For the Filipino bourgeoisie seeking to oust a corrupt president at the dawn of the twenty-first century, controlling translation involved using cell phones and the language of texting to surpass and direct the crowds of Manila in order to speak directly to the state (chapter 3). For the U.S. military, attempts to develop automatic translation systems and mechanize the protocols for interpreters in the wake of the attacks of 9/11 led to destructive fantasies of direct communication with enemy insurgents and the population alike. And where the history of American area studies has privileged the role of foreign language-learning to gain knowledge of, and power over, the non-American world during the Cold War (chapter 4), Filipino vernacular languages extend the insurgent war against colonial education that was originally conceived as a counterinsurgent measure to end the Filipino-American War (chapter 2).

Indeed, the relationship between war and translation pervades many of the chapters in this book. Because translation is predicated on the inevitability of mistranslation, it spawns undecidability, ambivalence, and, at times, violent misinterpretations. By revealing the intractability of linguistic plurality, and therefore the radical irreducibility of languages to one another, translation tends to become a kind of war and, in the context of revolution and military occupation, to instigate and intensify conflict (chapters

1, 2, 4, and 5). However, this ongoing war of translation and the recurrence of untranslatability also occur alongside linguistic play and the proliferation of differences that cannot be politically or ideologically contained. We get a sense of this excess, for instance, in the sections that track the unstable workings of American English: its promiscuous mixing with Tagalog in Philippine postwar street slang (chapter 2), its uncanny idiomatic workings within the official discourse in a U.S. counterinsurgency manual, and its interlinear translation of Pashto in reports of civilian deaths caused by American missiles in Afghanistan (chapter 5). These chapters thus allow us to glimpse some of the ways language escapes the commands of empires and nations, resisting their reduction into mere instruments of domination.

The insurgency of language and the wars of translation thus produce unexpected and unsettling sociohistorical effects. These are further dramatized in (auto)biographical writing, the subject of part III. What is the relationship between translation and biography? The word *biography*, literally "the writing of a life," indicates something of the way language always figures in rendering the singularity of each and every life. Conventional biographies often regard lives as retrospectively meaningful: seen from the vantage point of the present, the fragmentary and uncertain progression of a life can be redrawn to seem as if it had always followed a certain design, leading up to the moment of its recollection. But one can also think of how lives unfold according to a series of accidents, of events unforeseen and unmotivated, which remain resistant to explanation, yet beg for explication. It is this radical contingency at the foundation of each and every life that spurs the transformation—we might say, translation—of one into something other than what one had anticipated. One encounters others at the same time that one discovers in oneself the workings of a certain otherness—of a difference that calls for expression and acknowledgment if it is to take on a social reality. How do we know this?

The discovery and expression of otherness are evident in the flow of desire. Entwined with desire, this otherness—the *you* that, in its response, constitutes the I and which the I seeks, in turn, to address—never quite arrives. It is precisely this otherness, both inside and outside of oneself—indeed, one that comes before there is even a sense of the inside and the outside, much less of a self—that translation promises to bring forth. But just as every translation is essentially incomplete, the arrival of otherness will always be deferred, disguised, and displaced. Although the word *translation* rarely appears in chapters 6 and 7, it is in fact implied throughout my discussion of the accidental formation of agency in and through encounters with alterity. In the last two chapters, 8 and 9, the link between biography and translation in relation to untranslatability and contingency becomes more explicit.

The contingent workings and unexpected outcomes of translation are clearly evident in the practices of area studies. In the personal accounts of those who have engaged in a study of other places and peoples, we hear histories of suddenly becoming foreign. For example, Benedict Anderson and Arjun Appadurai retrace the origins of their scholarly interests in accidental encounters with unknown peoples and imported objects, decisively recasting their lives into one of ongoing translation, both cultural and linguistic (chapter 6). They show how autobiographies are about self-becoming only to the extent that they entail being and speaking otherwise while relying on some narrative about translation that obscures as much as it reveals the enduring recalcitrance of language as such.

In Renato Rosaldo's and Reynaldo Ileto's respective recollections of the political and cultural conditions of their lives and works, they, too, find themselves enmeshed in the aporias of translation. We see this in the various accounts of Rosaldo as he navigates between the rhetoric of a colonial-popular discourse on "savages," the recovered notes of his late wife's ethnographic description of Ilongot mourning, the unspeakability of his own grief conjoined to the memory of loss, and the sudden mechanical return of the voices of natives preparing to hunt heads after the practice had been outlawed (chapter 7). In Ileto's magisterial account of Tagalog popular movements, we witness how English and Tagalog are juxtaposed in a relationship of translation, indicating how attention to linguistic complexity and the politics of language can shed light on aspirations for freedom emanating from mid-nineteenth to early twentieth-century peasant groups (chapter 8). These linguistic matters, however, are deflected in his later autobiographical writings into generational and gendered anxieties regarding nationalist authority and authorial control over the history of the "unfinished revolution." Finally, my own interview in chapter 9 reprises many of these questions about authority and biography in the context of the interminable demands of and for translation. It returns us to the question of the I that speaks and stutters its responses to *Translation*, both the journal, as well as the phenomenon.

Taken as a whole, *Motherless Tongues* seeks to contribute not only to a history and theory of translation studies but also to the comparative understanding of historical imagination, especially in the midst of what remains of post–Cold War area studies and the endless "war on terror." Such is possible to the extent that we think of imagination itself as both the agent and effect of translation practices broadly conceived. At the same time, the ongoing process of supplementation—those "metalinguistic operations" constitutive of translation—suggests that the commerce among languages prepares for, and permeates, the coming of events. By allowing us to say more about the eventfulness of events, it also brings us to say something other and different from what is given, including, for example, the authority of imperial gifts—whether from Christianity or its secular avatars such as the U.S. military—and the hierarchy of signs and indebtedness they bring. Put differently, acts of translation that register the untranslatability of language allow us to reckon with ideologies that reduce translation and languages into mere instruments of conversion, colonial conquest, and social control.

Here then lies the larger, though largely implied, stakes of *Motherless Tongues*. It is arguably this linguistic commerce, at once powerful and insurgent, that keeps open both our understanding and experience of what is historical, of what it means to live on, to survive in view of the radical contingency of what comes. Like the sea of discourse that Plato at once welcomed and feared, it underwrites ongoing interpretations where no one has the first or last word. What emerges in the aporias of translation is a kind of semantic *bouleversement*, the sense of upheaval whereby the endlessly enfolded meanings of particular events will always make any discourse feel unfinished and incomplete. They thus persist as sources of continuous bewilderment in need of further explication, calling forth imaginative revisions. It is the imperative for such revisions, I hazard, that lends to a historical imagination steeped in translation an irreducibly democratic aspect. Just as the insurgency of language ensures the future of translation, so the contradictions and contaminations of translation hold out hope for democratizing historical imagination. Both, as I try to show, make room for dissenting voices, counternarratives, and alternative interpretations from unexpected and often repressed sources speaking in a variety of tongues. And in addressing us, perhaps such tongues, at once motherless and mutant, might help us, whoever we are, find a *poros*—some way out of the aporetic violence, the endless wars, and the tortured lives of this common imperial moment.[35]

Figure P.1 (*overleaf*) The scene of translation:
Mary Cole and her class, Palo, Leyte, 1901.
Courtesy of the Bentley Historical Collection.

....

CHAPTER 1

Welcoming What Comes

Translating Sovereignty in the Revolutionary Philippines

Beyond need, the object of desire is, humanly, the miracle; it is sovereign life, beyond the necessity that suffering defines.
—**GEORGE BATAILLE**, *The Accursed Share*

After more than three hundred years of colonial rule, Filipinos began a revolution against the Spanish regime in August 1896. Through a complicated chain of events, by 1898 they succeeded in defeating the Spanish forces with the aid of the United States, declared independence, and soon formed a Republic under the leadership of Emilio Aguinaldo along with the wealthiest men in the archipelago. But by February 1899 Filipinos were engulfed in a new war against an emergent U.S. empire that lasted until 1902 and paved the way for U.S. occupation until 1941.[1] During these turbulent years Filipinos sought to account for the event of the Revolution as the struggle to regain, if not enact, their sovereignty. But given the class divisions in colonial society—divisions that were violently disturbed and nearly overturned in the course of fighting—sovereignty came to mean and, perhaps just as important, be experienced differently by different groups.

What were the idioms of sovereignty that circulated between and among the Filipino elites who sought to assume control of the Republic and the people who fought and supported the Revolution? Given the recent surge of scholarly interest in the question of sovereignty as it relates to power and freedom in the making of Western modernity, is there something that the history of the Revolution in the Philippines can contribute to our comparative understanding of this topic?[2] In particular were there ways the Philippine Revolution, especially in its Spanish and vernacular articulations, opened up alternative notions of sovereignty and other ways of experiencing freedom distinct from imperial notions of self-determination and absolute mastery?

Sovereignty and the Political Theology of Empire

Like many other nation-states the Philippines bears an imperial inheritance. More than three centuries of Spanish colonial rule have left behind a certain idea of sovereignty rooted in Christian thinking. It is an idea of sovereignty that gives the ruler the freedom to take exception to the law. Whether embodied by the king, by the state, or, in its nationalist revolutionary moment, by the people, sovereignty is the power to define and decide upon what is exceptional, so exceptional as to warrant the breaking of laws in view of either preserving or destroying the existing order and establishing a new one altogether. In Carl Schmitt's oft-quoted definition, "Sovereign is he who decides on the exception."[3] It is the sovereign who, in founding the law, gives to himself the license to operate both inside and outside of it. The self-legislating and self-granting agency of the sovereign is precisely what allows him to decide who will live and who will die and what forms such living and dying are to take; who is the friend and who is the enemy and the terms of such friendship and enmity; and who is the citizen and who is the foreigner and the laws of citizenship that allow for the assimilation or expulsion of the foreign. The power to decide on the exception—to break with the norm, rupturing the precedents and processes of deliberation and debate—gives to sovereignty an absolutist nature. Jean Bodin, writing some three and a half centuries earlier, foreshadows Schmitt in saying, "Sovereignty is not limited either in power or in function or in length of time. . . . For he is absolutely sovereign who recognizes nothing, after God, that is greater than himself."[4] Sovereignty as absolute power is thus absolutely free of any obligations and conditions. This makes it a kind of impossible power, truly exceptional because it is beholden to no one and nothing else but God. However, rather than serve as a limit, God here figures an infinite force, exceeding any attempt at codification into positive human law. Like a pure gift it can neither be calculated nor reciprocated. True sovereignty, freed from the limits of human laws, is beholden only to God's laws. The sovereign comes to be the sole agent of Divine power. He thereby embodies the impossible possibility of a thoroughly nonhuman, immortal power manifesting itself in the world.[5]

This awesome conception of sovereignty, however, ran into insurmountable difficulties in the case of the Spanish Empire in its efforts to rule the Indies. The assertion of the king's power always required its representation and delegation. His absolute power to decide was undercut by the recurring need to channel his will through the mediating institutions of colonial bureaucracies, courts of law, the movement of armies and missionaries, the coercive collection of tribute and labor, periodic inspections, and annual visitations to the colonies that generated endless cascades of paperwork, all of which distorted and deformed even as they sought to convey the shape and substance of royal authority.[6] Imperial sovereignty, if there was such a thing, was thus split between an absolute prerogative to decide and take exception, and the necessity to divide and partition itself among its various representatives and representations, rehearsing and exhibiting its capacities in spectacles whose meanings and dissemination it could not always control. Less than absolute, sovereignty was always other than itself.

We can see the animating contradictions of Spanish imperial sovereignty, for example, in one of its important institutions, the Patronato Real (Royal Patronage) of the Catholic Church. Emblematic of the vanguard role of the Spanish Crown in the Counter-Reformation, the Patronato Real obligated the monarch to supply the material and military needs of the Church and further its planetary project of evangelization. It grew out of the imperative to conjugate colonialism with Catholic conversion. Beginning with a series of papal bulls between 1486 and 1493, the Crown received the Indies as a papal "donation," a gift for which it would assume the responsibility of converting native peoples.

The Patronato also granted the Crown the right to all tithes collected in the Indies and, more important, the privilege to appoint bishops and assign parishes that fell vacant in all the colonies beginning in 1508. Evangelization in turn legitimized conquest as a supremely moral undertaking designed to liberate the very subjects it subjugated, filling them with the Word of God that resonated with the will of the Spanish king. Acting as the "vicar of Christ," the king enjoyed what some Dominican theologians described as a "supernatural sovereignty" over the Indies. Unlike the "natural sovereignty" that local princes exercised to ensure the earthly needs of their people, supernatural sovereignty meant that the king was obligated to act in ways that would ensure the salvation of the souls of all colonial subjects. He was thus expected to use everything within his power to intervene and protect Christian converts against the threat of non-Christians. This included waging "just wars" meant to secure the submission as well as consent of natives to the king's protection. Imperial sovereignty was thus meant to generate the global conditions necessary to spread the Word of God.[7]

We can see, then, how Spanish imperialism was sustained by a political theology. State power was understood in ideal terms not merely as a means for the accumulation of wealth but also as the expression and extension of Divine power. Human laws were thus regarded as the instruments for the actualization of natural and Divine law.[8] In this context sovereignty possessed what we might think of as a magical quality owing to its transcendent source. Because it rested on that which was immortal and nonhuman, its force was such that it could break with and thereby free itself from every human norm and custom so as to pave the way for the emergence of a new social order under God's name. Colonial intervention in the name of Christian conversion was thus construed as an act of liberation. It was a means for establishing the king's supernatural sovereignty to free native peoples where before only the tyranny of paganism and demonic practices existed. Not surprisingly this proto-modern conception of imperialism was predicated on an order constituted in and through a hierarchy that reached down from heaven to earth: God, king, colonial officials, and missionaries ruling over local elites and the mass of male and female natives.[9] It was an order that was further articulated through a linguistic hierarchy: Latin as God's language and Castilian as the idiom of the king and his officials on top, local vernaculars as instruments of conversion and colonial command for native subjects below.[10]

But as I have indicated, Spanish political theology was far from seamless. In practice the sovereign could never be fully sovereign.[11] Imperial sovereignty was always fraught, mired in the material complications of historical contingencies: ambitious merchants and corrupt officials, for example, or foreign pirates and rebellious natives. In the case of Spain, church and state relations were as mutually dependent as they were antagonistic, as each sought to gain absolute authority over the other. Symptomatic of these tensions was the essential yet odd position of the missionary priest.[12]

The key importance of evangelization made the Spanish missionary an indispensable relay in the transmission of God's Word and the king's will. Often the only representative of empire in the farthest reaches of the realm, the missionary enjoyed considerable influence and great latitude in interpreting or, more often, setting aside the laws of the king in the name of preserving and furthering God's laws. The missionary's position was further enhanced by his knowledge of native speech. It allowed him to stand as the indispensable mediator between colonizers and colonized, translating between the demands of one and the responses of the other. Capable of traversing different political, social, and linguistic realms, the missionary occupied a position at a remove from all these. In this way the clergy constituted a critical force within colonial society. Intimately, at times oppressively involved in the day-to-day affairs of the people, he came to possess the power to decide on the exception—for example, abusive colonial officials, accused sorcerers, heterodox ritual practices, or subversive nationalists. This capacity for deciding not only what was an exception but how to deal with it turned the priest into a kind of sovereign power himself, often undercutting the authority of the king's colonial representatives in Manila. The missionary was thus a sort of double agent, simultaneously enacting and limiting, enabling while challenging the absolutist vocation of the king's supernatural sovereignty.

The contradictions of Spanish imperial sovereignty became more acute in the aftermath of the Napoleonic invasions and the momentous loss of Spanish possessions in the Americas during the first two decades of the nineteenth century. The rise of a liberal constitutional regime in Spain was meant to repudiate monarchial absolutism. Yet it sought to consolidate what was left of the empire after the 1820s by redeploying the economic and political mechanisms of its Bourbon dynastic predecessor. Throughout the nineteenth century both liberal and conservative governments rationalized and broadened the exercise of state power in what remained of Spain's imperial possessions—to make that power, in a word, more, not less, absolute.

In the Philippine colony this meant, among other things, strengthening the functions of the governor general, extending colonial control to areas previously outside of Spanish reach, launching military offensives against recalcitrant Muslims and other non-Christians, consolidating the state monopolies on tobacco and alcohol, introducing a new tax code, revising the penal code, regularizing native names to ease tribute collection, attempting (and failing) to secularize parish churches and public education, and liberalizing foreign trade. But it also meant denying Filipino representation to the Spanish Parliament, even as Puerto Rican and Cuban creoles were given seats. Deemed to be racially inferior and far more culturally heterogeneous by virtue of the presence of sizable non-Christian populations that had long resisted Spanish rule, Filipinos—creole, mestizo, and indio alike—were consigned to live in a state of exception, subjects of Spanish sovereignty but ineligible for Spanish citizenship. And despite liberal animosity toward the friar orders whose properties had been despoiled in the Peninsula, in the Philippine colony the liberal state redoubled its reliance on the regular orders so as to protect the regime against the rising tide of *filibusterismo*, or subversive thinking, and the frequent outbreak of peasant revolts.[13]

These contradictions would be discerned most acutely by the *ilustrados*— the emergent, Spanish-speaking, Philippine-born, university-educated, racially mixed colonial bourgeoisie. Influenced by liberal ideals that professed equality under the law for all citizens of the Spanish imperial nation in the wake of the Cádiz Constitution, they felt simultaneously entitled to and excluded from a share in colonial power.[14] Desirous of tapping into the sovereign power of the state by way of assimilation into Spanish society and gaining representation in the Spanish Parliament, ilustrado nationalists as self-styled sons of the nation targeted the friars in particular for blocking the path of their political ambitions. They blamed the *soberania monacal* (monastic sovereignty), as Marcelo H. del Pilar put it, for all the colony's ills.[15] The friars responded by threatening ilustrados with imprisonment and excommunication. Calling each other *filibusteros* (subversives), and thus traitors to the *patria*, Spanish friars and Filipino ilustrados sought to portray the one as the negation of the other. In doing so each claimed the right to call themselves the real patriots and thus sovereign citizens, while casting the others precisely as the exception to be expelled from the body politic. Given the racial logic of imperial rule, it is not surprising that the Spanish liberal state, despite its disdain for the friars, would side with them against the growing militancy of Filipino nationalists.

As separatist sentiments took hold over assimilationist aspirations, there arose in 1892 a secret revolutionary society called the Katipunan, literally "the gathering," dedicated to gaining freedom from imperial rule. With the Spanish discovery of its secret cells, colonial authorities were seized with terror at the prospect of a mass uprising and a race war. When the Revolution erupted in August 1896, imperial sovereignty entered into a prolonged period of crisis. But rather than disappear it continued to exist in displaced form, informing revolutionary discourses on "popular sovereignty."

Revolution and Popular Sovereignty

What was the Revolution, and how would it come to reappropriate Spanish sovereignty? According to the Proclamation of Independence of 12 June 1898, written in Spanish and declared from the window of Emilio Aguinaldo's house in Kawit, Cavite, the Revolution was the people's response to "the ominous yoke of Spanish domination" that included "the arbitrary arrests and cruel treatments conducted by the Guardia Civil," the "executions by firing squad . . . the unjust deportations of eminent persons of high social position, all at the instigation of the Archbishop and the friars." Thus did the people (el pueblo) begin a "revolutionary movement [un movimento revolucionario] . . . with the purpose of recuperating the independence and sovereignty that Spain had taken from them" when Spain began colonizing the archipelago in 1565.[16] Revolution from the perspective of the Proclamation is the restoration of a precolonial sovereignty. It signaled the inauguration of a new era as a return to an ancient one.

What is curious about the Proclamation, written by one of the members of Aguinaldo's elite advisors, is that nowhere do we actually hear the "people" as the source of this document. The "we" that speaks in the declaration is not "we, the people" but "we, the representatives of the people": "And summoning as a witness to the rightness of our intentions the Supreme Judge of the Universe, and under the protection of the powerful and humanitarian North American nation, we proclaim and solemnly declare, in the name and authority of the inhabitants of the Philippine Islands that they are and have the right to be free and independent; that they are totally free from any obedience to the Crown of Spain."[17]

Though it claims to speak in the name of the people, the "we" that speaks in the Proclamation is one that is beholden to the recognition of two higher powers: God and the United States, which was responsible for bringing Aguinaldo, the leader of the Revolution, back to the Philippines from his exile in Hong Kong. The people are referred to instead in the third-person plural, as a "they," as if they were apart from the "we." The Proclamation was written by Ambrosio Rianzares Bautista, one of the elite members of Aguinaldo's revolutionary government, in Spanish, the lingua franca of the ilustrados but barely understood by the overwhelming majority of the masses. It is perhaps no surprise that the people figure neither as witnesses nor as guarantors to the Proclamation. As a "they," they are spoken for and about and do not speak for themselves. Neither are they expected to claim authorship retrospectively for the Proclamation that conjures their existence, as in the case, most famously, of the American Declaration of Independence.[18]

The Proclamation proclaims the success of the Revolution in restoring the people's lost sovereignty while at the same time restoring the social hierarchy that places "them" below "us," the latter being the ilustrado elites who had earlier rejected the Revolution and would, after Aguinaldo's return in 1898, seek to control it for their own purposes.[19] Independence here means the restoration of a chain of dependencies stretching from God to a foreign benefactor, then on to an "enlightened" and wealthy minority, and finally to the mass of people. The Proclamation thus already contained the seeds of a counterrevolution that would undo the sovereignty of the people even as its ilustrado author and signers drew upon it to legitimize their postrevolutionary authority.[20]

The ambivalent regard for the unstable force of the Revolution runs through much of the writing of the largely ilustrado leadership of the revolutionary government. Filipino elites sought to capitalize on, yet contain, the sovereign power of a people it claimed to represent. We can see this ambivalence, for example, in Apolinario Mabini (1864–1903), widely regarded as the most astute theoretician of the Revolution. He served as the chief advisor of Emilio Aguinaldo, president of the revolutionary Republic formed just north of Manila in Malolos, Bulacan. Mabini was born in the Tagalog province of Batangas of *indio* parents of modest means and educated in philosophy and law in Manila. Contracting polio that left him paralyzed from the waist down in 1896, he had to be transported by hammock during the Revolution as the revolutionary government sought to elude the advancing American forces. He was popularly known as "the sublime paralytic" and, unlike other prominent nationalist leaders, never traveled outside the Philippines except when he was exiled to Guam by the Americans for refusing to take the oath of loyalty to the U.S. occupation government. It is remarkable that Mabini's modest background, lack of travel, and pronounced disability allowed, rather than impeded, a robust and sophisticated formulation of a

Figure 1.1 Apolinario Mabini, 1864–1903.

revolutionary theory, certainly one far more nuanced than that propounded by the Proclamation of Independence.[21]

Filipinos fought, Mabini claimed, to attain independence, but not as an end in itself. Rather it was to be the means to arrive at a "moral government" with which to secure the conditions for the general "well-being" and "happiness" of the country. Such conditions required, furthermore, a popularly elected and truly representative government that would, as he told the U.S. military commander, General Joseph Wheeler, "assure all Filipinos of the freedom of thought, conscience, association; privacy of their persons, houses and correspondences; popular representation in the drafting of laws and imposition of taxes." While the Revolution, according to Mabini, may have started out as an act of vengeance in 1896, by 1898 it had become transformed into something else: a manifestation of the irresistible movement of Reason around the world.[22]

In his writings Mabini repeatedly situates the Philippine Revolution as a continuation of the American and the French Revolutions, inspired by the same ideals and moved by the same aspirations for liberty, equality, and fraternity. Such, he argued, lent to the Philippine Revolution a cosmopolitan character, in contrast to Spanish and American insistence that it was merely a Tagalog uprising. For Mabini national history when seen through the optic of the Revolution was in fact an aspect of universal history that placed Filipinos at the vanguard of a global anticolonial movement.[23] It is this shared history of revolutionary beginnings that Mabini reminds Americans of in the aftermath of the Treaty of Paris and in the midst of the Filipino-American War. Indeed in fighting the Americans, Filipinos "show to the United States that they possess sufficient culture to know their rights. . . . They hope that the war reminds the Americans what their forefathers had to sustain in their past against the English for the emancipation of their Colonies and what is today the free states of North America. At the time [of their own revolution], the Americans were in the place of the Filipinos today. . . . The fighting is not due therefore to race hatred, but [to] the same principles sealed by the blood of their forefathers."[24]

From Mabini's perspective, then, the Revolution was neither a race war nor a criminal act of uncivilized people, as both Spaniards and Americans had claimed. Rather it was the most compelling evidence of the people's enlightenment, suggesting thereby an emergent historical kinship between revolutionary Filipinos and civilized Americans and Europeans. This is underlined by the fact that, as Mabini points out, the Filipino people fought to recover and protect their "natural right" to be free, and in so doing joined their fate to that of all civilized peoples in the world. Indeed it was because they were willing to sacrifice and die for their rights that Filipinos showed themselves capable of self-rule.

For Mabini it was never the Proclamation of Independence of 12 June 1898 or the establishment of the short-lived First Republic at Malolos and the Constitution that proved Filipino capacity for independence. In fact he had repeatedly criticized these institutions as premature, and early on saw how they were being used by the ilustrados to put an end to the Revolution, in effect recolonizing the nation under their rule. Rather it was the very fact of risking their lives to fight injustice that filled a people with what he called "virtue," the capacity to place the common good above one's self-interests, a capacity he felt was scandalously lacking among the elite leaders of the Republic. For Mabini, then, sacrifice born of virtue was the essence of the Revolution, the basis of its legitimacy, and the proof of its modernity. Founded on Reason and stemming from "natural law," it was propelled by a virtuous people simultaneously enacting the very thing it sought to restore to itself: its own sovereignty.[25]

In Mabini's account of the history leading up to the Revolution, he cites a common theme in nationalist historical thinking: that a bond of friendship and mutual support characterized the initial relationship between *indios* and Spaniards sealed by the blood compact, or *pacto de sangre*. This originary social contract was betrayed by Spanish duplicity and oppression, and Filipinos would respond by rebelling.[26] By breaking the social contract, the Spaniards had broken the natural law. So too had the Americans, who, in signing the Treaty of Paris (1899), assumed sovereignty over the Philippines from Spain in exchange for the sum of US$20 million. For Mabini such an act amounted to treating the Filipinos as if they were slaves to be bought and sold, and so represented a barbaric regression on America's part. In using the instruments of positive international law, the Americans gained legal title to the Philippines, but did so by violating natural law that forbade slavery and the usurpation of another people's sovereignty.[27] In rising up first against the Spaniards, then against the Americans, Filipinos were seeking to restore what justly belonged to them. "Then and now our battle cry remains to be natural law, the eternal foundation and regulator of justice and of all human laws. It is God's law promulgated in men's conscience." Natural law in turn "recognizes no other sovereignty except that of the people. . . . Their precepts are orders from Divine Reason dictated to the human conscience."[28]

Popular sovereignty derived from natural law is thus a function of Divine sovereignty and so shares in its unassailable and absolute nature. As with the Proclamation of Independence, Mabini frames the Revolution as a kind of restoration to the extent that it also marks an exceptional event: the recovery of the people's natural right as the providential revelation of God's will. In breaking with the politics of empire, he also reiterates its political theology. In attempting to undo imperial claims, he resorts to a language of rights that finds its ultimate sanction in the Christian notion of natural law.[29] Sovereignty in this case rests on the people, but only insofar as they are infused with Divine Reason and thus become the privileged instruments of His will. Their freedom, if it exists at all, is indissociable from their subordination to and assimilation of His awesome power. In this sense Revolution as the recovery of a people's right to be sovereign is also paradoxically the restoration of God's unending rule over man.

It is important, however, to stress that Mabini's texts do not merely occasion the return of the imperial specters of political theology. There is another powerful force that inhabits all of his writings, and that is of course the Revolution, whose eruption points to other possibilities. The Revolution comes across not simply as the medium for the restoration of absolute sovereignty in a national body that would lead to rational institutions even as it restores social hierarchy. It can also appear as a radically new, profoundly unrecognizable and therefore thoroughly inhuman force. In one essay Mabini writes of the fear and trembling that the Philippine Revolution had struck in the hearts of other European colonizers, who saw it as "contagious, very contagious." For the Revolution "bears in its volcanic bosom the germ of yellow fever or the bubonic plague, which is fatal to their colonial interests. In the not so distant future, it could constitute the uncontrollable dike against their overwhelming ambitions." In another piece he writes, "The American authorities will understand that it is senseless to claim that the Revolution can be stifled by force because there is no human force capable of preventing the natural flow of things." And in addressing the conservative ilustrados Pedro Paterno and Felipe Buencamino he warns of the "dangers" that another revolution would bring should the Republic negotiate with the Americans without first securing the recognition of Filipino rights. Without justice there can be no peace, he avers, only an unending uprising beyond the Republic's—or any other regime's—control.[30]

In this and other passages the Revolution exceeds both human and, it would seem, Divine agency. Its "naturalness" leads not to the creation of new institutions, much less to the revelation of Divine Reason, but to sheer destruction. Like a plague it knows no boundaries and respects no rank, inflicting on everyone its relentless violence. Its effects are unforeseen and beyond anticipation, incurring losses beyond calculation. In this sense the Revolution becomes an event that cannot be recuperated for social uses inasmuch as it impairs the very mechanisms and agencies of social recuperation. Leading neither to restoration nor return, the Revolution here is imagined as escaping the sovereign determination of both the human and the Divine. In the name of justice the Revolution as such could just as easily sow injustice or, more precisely—and here is the source of real terror—confuse men's minds about the difference between the two. Such is the case, for example, when revolutionary fighters find themselves overcome with urges they cannot control. Mabini at one point imagines the following scenario:

> We took the enemy by surprise and made them prisoners. Our easily won victory made us conceited. We grouped the soldiers into two, assigning one to attend to the prisoners. We ordered the soldiers to tie the hands of the prisoners and shoot them after stripping them of their money, clothes, and jewelry. Immediately afterwards, we commanded the other group to go over every house and confiscate the money, jewelry, and clothes that they find inside cabinets and boxes. They were also ordered to take the prettiest women and then burn the town. The last words of the order had barely left our lips when a thunderous voice shouted: God, humanity, progress! We looked up at the sky and it was red as blood. We gazed at the sea and we saw it turning over, hurling foam and pounding the shore. It roared furiously and threatened to flood and drown everything. The mountains rumbled and the ground shook beneath our feet. We then hurriedly withdrew the orders as terror and dread overcame us.[31]

Here Mabini paints a lurid account of Revolution unmoored from Reason and bereft of virtue. No doubt this scenario was based on reports that the Malolos Republic was constantly receiving regarding the abuses of the revolutionary army.[32] The "fever" of revolutionary pride leads them to assume arbitrary power over their prisoners, women, and property. It leads them, that is, to take exception to all consideration of law, natural as well as positive, acting with a kind of violence freed from all restraints. For them sovereignty devolves into sheer destructive power, and it is not until Divine retribution is threatened that they are overcome with the very terror that they themselves had unleashed.

Side by side with the concept of the Revolution as the collective sacrifice and struggle with which to restore a people's natural rights protected by a Republican state there is thus the ongoing danger of the Revolution as the dissolution of such rights, unleashing a state of permanent violence by way of civil war. In such a case society would be reduced to a "corpse," a body without its soul. Mabini writes, "The same happens in all societies. If there is no more than the reunion of men that move with neither direction, nor order nor harmony, society becomes a veritable corpse, because what one does the other will surely undo. It will not be long when this gathering will fight among themselves and dissolve themselves like a corpse that does not take long to decompose. It is thus necessary to have a soul that will move this gathering toward one sense or another, and this soul is authority. How does authority function? It functions like the human soul, inasmuch as society is nothing more than a great individual, comparable to a giant."[33]

By raising the possibility of pure violence, the Revolution turns every man against every form of authority and thus threatens to rob society of its soul. In doing so it converts society into a spectral version of itself. It is in light of this permanent possibility of social death that authority becomes essential as a way of resurrecting social life. Furthermore it is an authority that, as Mabini repeatedly reminds us, resides in the people.[34] The notion of popular sovereignty thus turns on (in all senses of that phrase) the Revolution as much as the Revolution promises to return popular sovereignty. On one hand, popular sovereignty seeks to contain the Revolution from unleashing pure violence that will kill society. On the other, it is precisely the Revolution that creates the people as the locus of sovereign power in the first place. The Revolution, then, constantly disrupts the question of sovereignty. It not only challenges the colonial state's and the Catholic Church's claims of possessing absolute power; it also sabotages popular assertions of such power. Similarly the Revolution dramatizes the innate capacity of a people guided by a law natural to all humans to protect their rights and demand recognition from others. At the same time, it threatens to violate not only positive human laws but putative natural laws—what today we more commonly refer to as "human rights"—giving rise to a spectral society incapable of making or preserving laws as such, and thereby unable to distinguish between just and unjust acts.

In Mabini, then, we get a sense of the Revolution as an event that periodically calls into question various claims of sovereignty, whether based on the reason of force or the force of reason. It undermines imperial hegemony and its political theology, linking the nation with other global movements of progress and democracy. But it also excavates the irrational foundations of rational institutions, exposing the terror-filled excesses of the sacrificial economy of virtue. It is, however, important to stress that the deconstructive effects of the Revolution do not end with the sheer destruction of oppressive social orders, nor does it rest mainly on the propagation of terror and the spread of criminality. Other accounts of the Revolution left behind by Filipino fighters suggest that it was always something more than the practical appropriation and unraveling of the received notions of sovereignty that we have seen in our reading of Mabini. They also reveal how the Revolution occasionally opened up the possibility of another kind of sovereignty, one that did not entail the exercise of power and the delusions of empowerment. Rather it stemmed from a vernacular experience of freedom, or what in Tagalog is called *kalayaan*: not only freedom from the violence of colonial law but also one that arises from a popular conception of solidarity and compassion.

Vernacularizing Freedom

A popular song in the southern Tagalog region about the Revolution during the early years of the twentieth century begins:

Halina, halina mga kababayan
Ating salubungin itong bagong datal
Mga Pilipinong panguloy si Sakay
Silang nagmatuid nitong ating bayan.

. . . .

Come on, come on countrymen
Let us greet the new arrivals
The Filipinos led by Sakay
Who will set this country on the right course.

. . . .

Ang binabanig nila'y malamig na lupa
Ang kinukumot nila'y damong mahahaba
Ayao magpatulog—mga kaawa-awa
Kaya tayong lahat mag-kaisa
Sa pagmamalasakit sa patria.[35]

. . . .

They use the ground for their sleeping mats
They use the long grass for their blankets
Unable to sleep—how pitiful they are
So then let us become one
And have compassion for the motherland.

When Rousseau asks what is "the act by which a people becomes a people" and so sets "the real foundation of society,"[36] the song provides one answer in the Philippine context: the act of welcoming. The song calls out the people (mga kababayan), who are also its singers and listeners. It conjures a "we" that comes about in the process of hailing and being hailed (halina, halina) to greet (salubungin) the Filipino fighters led by General Macario Sakay who are coming to their town. In the song the arrival of the fighters coincides with the coming to be of the singers and listeners through the performance of their song. Both fighters and singers and listeners are joined as part of the emergent bayan (hometown), which can be glossed as "nation," indicated by the Tagalog word for countrymen, kababayan, literally "one who is part of or attached to the same country."[37]

In contrast to the Proclamation of Independence and to Mabini's discourse on popular sovereignty derived from natural law, the song evinces no hierarchical relationship between "we" and "they." Rather it declaims each one to be part of the other, kababayan, that is, to become the people whose gathering and emergence as a people is occasioned by the act of inviting and welcoming revolutionary fighters who are also a part of them. The people come to exist, then, by inviting and welcoming the other, who is also a part of themselves and not merely their representatives. It is not the Word of God, the ruler's decision, or the passing of laws that brings about the existence of a people. It is the people themselves who, in singing, proclaim and so generate their own existence. That they do so in the midst of greeting the fighters means that their identity comes not before but only in the very act of welcoming the other regarded as part of themselves. We can think of the song, then, as revolutionary insofar as it sets forth a singular event: the self-constitution of a people that occurs in the very act of inviting and welcoming their own arrival, but an arrival that is never completed and is always unfolding. In breaking with the norms of colonial hierarchy, this act of self-constitution, open-ended and always yet to come, is, of course, the event of popular sovereignty itself.

There is, however, another dimension to the event of the people's self-becoming. In the other stanza of the song "we"—both the singers and the hearers—are asked to attend to the suffering and deprivation that revolutionary fighters have had to undergo. It portrays them as "pitiful" (kaawa-awa), like the rest of the country. Their suffering in fact is a response to the hardships experienced by the "motherland," which is also "ours," its children. Their pitiful state is thus already a sign of compassion for the motherland's prior suffering that in turn can be interpreted as an invitation to respond in kind. Turning to the image of suffering fighters, "we" are drawn to have compassion for them (*pagmamalasakit*) and, in doing so, become one with them (*tayong lahat mag-kaisa*). Here the words for "pity," *awa*, and "compassion," *pagmamalasakit*, convey the sense of collective sharing in the other's loss. The imperative to come together is spoken of as *mag-kaisa*, formed by the addition of the prefixes *mag* and *ka* to the root word *isa*, "one," that envisions the serial, open-ended addition of other ones. It is realized through an act of mourning whereby one is exposed and so taken up by the loss of the other (in both senses of the genitive). As with the acts of hospitality—of invitation and welcoming—mourning constitutes a "we" who comes to be by sharing and partitioning itself with the other who is also torn apart. Sovereignty as the event of self-constitution constitutes an exception to the norms of colonial rule. But it does so through acts of self-partitioning by way of hospitality, pity, compassion, and mourning—in short, by an ongoing orientation to the coming of the other that one seeks to join rather than master. This joining with the other, or *damayan* (about which I will say more later), in turn comprises the vernacular experience of freedom, *kalayaan*, as I hope to show in two other accounts of the Revolution.[38]

The first comes from Santiago Alvarez (1872–1930), one of the leaders of the Revolution. In his memoirs written in the 1920s Alvarez recalls life in the liberated towns of Cavite, a province south of Manila, during the initial flush of victory against the Spanish forces in September 1896. Reading it we get a sense of the sheer enjoyment that comes not only from being freed from Spanish rule but also from the unexpected experience of coming together through ongoing acts of generosity:

> During those times, the Enemy did not launch any attacks. . . . The people were truly happy [*totoong masaya*]. Free in their enjoyment of different diversions, abundant food, everything was cheap, and there were no criminals, no thieves, or pickpockets. Each loved the other [*lahat ay may pagmamahal sa kapwa*] and from one end of the town to the other, sibling love [*pag-ibig-kapatid*] which is the teaching of the Katipunan, reigned supreme. The terrifying envoys of death, as signaled by the rushing sounds of cannons fired by the Enemy, were regarded with indifference. Every-

one simply ducked and avoided them, and trusting in God, the children, the elders, women and men, did not fear death.[39]

In another passage Alvarez speaks of people "mad" (*nag-uulol*) with happiness: "At the sound of cannon fire, they would laugh as if these were merely the sound of fireworks at a celebration. . . . There was singing, dancing, eating under the shade of trees, gambling and cockfighting everywhere, all of which set aside the anticipation of having to offer blood and life."[40]

Alongside accounts of horrific battles, heroic sacrifices, and unforgivable betrayals, Alvarez's memoirs are peppered with recollections of these moments of "mad" (*ulol*) happiness. To be sure these did not last long. The state of "sibling love" could neither be consolidated nor sustained in the face of Spanish attacks and the factional strife that would eventually tear apart the revolutionary movement. But it is precisely the surprising and exceptional occurrence of "love" (*pagibig*), the joining of one with the other outside the norms of colonial convention and law, that Alvarez and his readers savor. They linger on the memory of moments that could neither be consolidated nor institutionalized. Rather the pleasure of recalling the experience of liberation here comes precisely from their vanishing. What remains are the images of laughter and celebration in a time suspended from the temporality of both Spanish and U.S. colonial rule. Like the revolutionary song, Alvarez's account conveys a sense of the people realizing their sovereignty as an emergent unity enacted through quotidian, ongoing acts of hospitality.

Sovereignty in this context is less a decisive break with the norm than ordinary gestures taking on extraordinary significance. It is perhaps for this reason that rather than exercise a newfound mastery over the Enemy, popular sovereignty assumes a happy indifference to its threats. These moments in Alvarez's account resonate with the memoirs of one of the most prominent revolutionary leaders and president of the First Philippine Republic, Emilio Aguinaldo. Like Alvarez, Aguinaldo wrote in Tagalog rather than Spanish, reflecting his lack of formal education. Both also came from the ranks of the municipal elite and, unlike the wealthy ilustrados who dominated the Republic, were far more in tune with the people who fought in and supported the Revolution from its inception. Writing in the 1960s Aguinaldo relishes the "delicious" memories of the early days of the Revolution: "How delicious [*sarap*] to remember the purest [*dalisay*] and perfect oneness [*pagkakaisa*] during those days when revolutionaries and townspeople were joined in one purpose: to save the Mother Country [Inang Bayan] from its pitiful condition."[41] Aguinaldo refers to this intimate "oneness" between and among fighters and townspeople as *pag-iibigan*, or "love." Such love was "truly impressive." Because of this "one would never hear of robberies, or rapes, or extortions that used to happen night and day. And it was even delightful to see men and women going about all day in complete peace without anyone disturbing them, and that everyone greeted each other brother/sister [*kapatid*]."[42]

This sense of oneness and ease of movement bespoke a freedom from fear and need. Felt as a kind of intense love between revolutionary fighters and townspeople, this freedom arises from what Aguinaldo refers to as *damayan*, from the root word *damay*, "to mourn a loss as well as to sympathize with that of another's." It also means "to participate and share in the other's work," "to bear the other's sorrow and so to answer to his or her need."[43] As an ethic of compassion, *damayan* generates the radical identification of one with the other, implicating each in the other's deeds and sentiments. Revolutionary love consists, then, of continuous acts of *damayan*, as when townspeople enthusiastically greet arriving revolutionaries with great shows of generosity: "They invited all of the troops to come and eat so that all the houses served food without anyone asking them to"; "When those from there [Talisay] saw us . . . they were overcome with joy [*galak*]. . . . All of the houses, even the smallest huts, eagerly fed and welcomed the troops"; "When we arrived in Silang, we were enthusiastically greeted and the food they served the troops was incredible."[44] These and similar accounts of generosity are described by Aguinaldo as examples of *buong pagdamay*, of complete sympathy and reciprocity between the fighters and the people. *Damayan* as the basis of revolutionary sociality brings *galak*, or "joy," and *ginhawa*, "peacefulness, ease, and comfort," to everyone, regardless of their social position. It is for this reason that acts of *damayan* conjure a sense of freedom, or *kalayaan*: "We should not forget the sweetness of our *damayan*," Aguinaldo says at one point to hundreds of followers wishing to follow his troops into the mountains as they retreat from advancing Spanish forces, "that sooner or later we might attain our cherished freedom [*kalayaan*]."[45] *Damayan* is thus not only the substance of revolutionary love; it is also the path to a different kind of sovereign existence.

We can perhaps better appreciate this notion of sovereign experience in the memoirs of Alvarez and Aguinaldo by further inquiring into its vernacular context. Sovereignty that arises from acts of *damayan* is deeply associated with *kalayaan*, the Tagalog word usually translated as "freedom." It is important to note, however, that there is no easy correspondence between these two words, *freedom* and *kalayaan*. As the historian Reynaldo Ileto has pointed out, *kalayaan* has meant both more and less than *freedom*, holding a range of connotations that exceed words such as *independence* and *autonomy* and the political-theological implications of sovereignty. Pointing out the historical link between *katipunan*—the word as well as the name of the secret revolutionary organization—and *kalayaan*, Ileto writes:

> The meaning of "wholeness" or "becoming one" implied by the term *katipunan* is also contained in *kalayaan*. Prior to the rise of the separatist movement, *kalayaan* did not mean "freedom" or "independence." [It is] . . . built upon the [root] word *layaw* which means "satisfaction of one's needs," "pampering treatment by parents," or "freedom from strict parental control." Thus *kalayaan* as a political term is inseparable from its connotations of parent-child relationship reflecting social values like the tendency of mothers in lowland Philippines to pamper their children and develop strong emotional ties with them. Childhood is fondly remembered as a kind of "lost Eden," a time of *kaginhawaan* (contentment) and *kasaganaan* (prosperity). . . . In "*kalayaan*," revolutionists found an ideal term for independence that [signified] . . . the "coming together" of people in the Katipunan. *Katipunan* is *kalayaan* in that it is a recovery of the country's pre-Spanish condition of wholeness, bliss and contentment, a condition experienced as *layaw* by the individual who is thus able to leap from the "familial" to "national." As a revolutionary document put it, the "Katipunan of Man" is none other than the extension of the experience of the unity between mother and child.[46]

Ileto asks us to consider *kalayaan* in its proto-political sense as a return to the state of *layaw*, the pre-Oedipal moment of perfect reciprocity between mother and child. Idealized as a state of bonding without bondage, the condition of *layaw*, similar to that of *damayan*, comes from acts of giving that do not expect a return, of taking without incurring a debt, and so dispense with the formation of hierarchy. Freed from the need to calculate and wait, reciprocity ceases to be reciprocal altogether. Similarly recognition is no longer recognizable, having done away with the protocols of mediation and forms of social hierarchy. Indeed one might even say that the state of *layaw*, so far as it centers on the relationship between mother and child, is one where the father counts for little, if at all. He has yet to make his presence felt, much less assert his authority over the family by establishing the law regulating the relationship between mother and child.

It is not difficult to see how *kalayaan*, or freedom understood as *layaw*, can easily slide into the sense of *damayan*. It too conjures a scene of sovereignty that, as in the revolutionary song and in the accounts of Alvarez and Aguinaldo, engenders constant caring. Outside the violent inequalities and inequities that inhered in the colonial and Republican state, the state of *kalayaan* comes across as a site of unconditional hospitality whereby whoever or whatever comes, whenever it comes, enters without need for permission. For all these reasons sovereignty as the experience of *kalayaan* is not so much the power to decide on the exception, as Schmitt would put it. Relying on the reliance of every one on every other, *kalayaan* is contingent on everyday acts of *damayan*. For this reason the realization of sovereignty as freedom, like that of love and pity, will always be halting, episodic, always to come, and thus always to be welcomed.[47] In both Aguinaldo's and Alvarez's account of Cavite, we can imagine life briefly attaining the state of *kalayaan*. The people momentarily free themselves from the labor of fighting and the struggle for recognition. There is only consumption beyond necessity, sibling love without patriarchal law, and collective joy in the face of terrible threats from the Enemy. In the midst of the Revolution the world appears not simply upside down but wholly new. It is new because its appearance could have been neither anticipated nor calculated, happening suddenly only to vanish, always, it seemed, for the first and for the last time. For this reason we can think of popular sovereignty generated by the coming of *kalayaan* as a state of exception, perhaps akin to a miracle.

Mabini, as we saw, considered popular sovereignty in such terms: as the decisive and therefore miraculous moment when Divine Reason was made manifest in human reason. However, the accounts I have been analyzing also suggest a way of thinking about the miraculous in its atheological sense, which is less about the revelation of Divine Sovereignty than about the surprising occurrence of an event woven into rather than separate from the fabric of everyday life.[48] It is surprising inasmuch as the exact moment and meaning of its arrival surpass whatever horizon of expectation or detailed calculations we might have had. Thus does a miraculous event compel multiple and repeated interpretations, retellings, and rememberings, none of which can ever exhaust much less fully account for what happened, let alone its full significance.

The miraculous, if it exists, furnishes a sign for an open-ended future of interpretive possibilities and the social lives these bring forth. As such it calls for an ongoing response to and responsibility for what or who comes in its wake. In this way the miraculous has the power to awaken the transformative potential of ordinary acts, exposing the contingency of the everyday and the everydayness of contingency. In the context of Filipino revolutionary history, the extraordinary, if temporary, occurrence of *kalayaan* brought about the miracle of popular sovereignty. In this connection we can think of Bataille's notion of the miracle as "sovereign life, beyond the necessity that suffering defines."[49] Sovereignty as the miracle of *kalayaan* entailed, as we have seen, not only the rupturing of daily life but also the intensification of its possibilities. Such possibilities included but were not limited to the contagious spread of mutual pity, the extravagant displays of generosity, alongside the blissful if fleeting feelings of solidarity that came with the act of welcoming the coming of the Revolution.[50]

Coda

The political theology of the Spanish Empire asserted the possibility of the impossible: Divine force as absolute power incarnated in the sovereign's body and expressed in his capacity to take exception. The Filipino Revolution, as I have argued, simultaneously dismantled even as it reappropriated this enduring and terrifying fiction, locating it in the body of the people, at once the agent of and threat to the realization of a postrevolutionary Republic where its leaders were concerned. But from another perspective the Revolution was also capable of bringing about popular sovereignty as the ordinary experience of extraordinary joy, of freedom arising from compassion and generosity, and of the miraculous, if evanescent, opening of an entirely new life whose traces continue to arrive from the future within and beyond the nation-state.

CHAPTER 2

....

Wars of Translation

American English, Colonial Schooling, and Tagalog Slang

Language has always been a key battleground in nationalist attempts at decolonization in many parts of the world. In the case of the Philippines, the legacy of American colonial education included the use of English as a medium of instruction. Learning English, however, required that students suppress their vernacular languages. The classroom thus became the site for a kind of linguistic war or, better yet, a war of translation. The postwar nationalist response has been to denounce the hegemony of English as a morbid symptom of a "colonial mentality" whose continued use would doom national culture and kill the emergent Filipino nation. Yet, as I argue in this chapter, such a critique rested on colonial assumptions about the sheer instrumentality of language. Nationalism, like colonialism, was tied to the ideology that translation was a means for the speaker to assert his or her will to dominate speech, whether one's own or that of the other. This view tended to set aside the historical reality whereby noncolonial and nonnationalist practices of translation flourished. Such practices were predicated on the play rather than on the domination of language. I examine how such possibilities emerged both in the resistant soundings of English on the part of native students in the classrooms and in the emergence of Tagalog slang between the 1960s and the 1970s in the streets. Formed from the grammatical weave and jagged shards of vernacular languages, creole Spanish, and American English, Tagalog slang gives us an alternative understanding of the role of translation in democratizing expression in a postcolonial context.

Education as Counterinsurgency

In the face of a fierce and protracted war between 1899 and 1902, the United States sought to counter Filipino insurgency by establishing a network of public schools all over the archipelago. The military governor, General Arthur MacArthur, hoped that the schools would have a counterinsurgent effect, serving as "adjuncts to military operations" needed to "expedite the restoration of tranquility throughout the archipelago."[1] American soldiers were initially assigned to serve as teachers. They were shortly followed by an army of American civilian teachers known as the "Thomasites" (named after the USS *Thomas*, the army transport that brought them to the country) in 1901. By the 1920s, however, most American teachers had been replaced by Filipinos as part of a larger effort to Filipinize the colonial government en route to granting the colony eventual independence.[2]

The key feature of the colonial public school system was the adoption of English as the sole medium of instruction. From the U.S. perspective conditions in the archipelago made such a policy necessary. The Philippines has always been characterized by a staggering linguistic diversity. At the turn of the twentieth century more than eighty mutually unintelligible languages continued to be spoken throughout the islands, while only about 5 percent of the population claimed to be fluent in Spanish (though more could read it) despite 350 years of Spanish rule. In the face of these realities American policymakers deemed it necessary to use English as the dominant language of rule and education. Within weeks of the occupation of Manila on 13 August 1898, the U.S. military reopened several schools in the city, assigning from among its ranks a teacher of English to each of them. In January 1901 the colonial civilian government passed a law known as Act 74 establishing the Bureau of Education. Among its provisions was the mandatory use of English as the "basis of instruction."[3]

From the start, the decision to use English, like that of colonizing the Philippines, was fraught with contradiction. It had the effect of simultaneously incorporating Filipinos into the emergent colonial regime while keeping them at a distance from the metropolitan center. On the one hand, English was meant to speed up pacification, drawing Filipinos closer to

American interests and thereby putting an end to their resistance. It was to be a key part of what President William McKinley called a project of "benevolent assimilation." Deemed an essential element for their "uplift," English would inject erstwhile "savage" Filipinos with "Anglo-Saxon" values. On the other hand, its teaching coincided with the designation of Filipinos as colonial subjects with limited rights. Segregating the archipelago from the mainland, the U.S. Supreme Court had defined the Philippines an "unincorporated" territory, or, in the words of Justice White, "foreign in a domestic sense." Its people were thus consigned to a racial state of exception. They were subject to U.S. laws but, by virtue of their racial difference, not entitled to the same rights. In a similar vein mass literacy in English was meant to mitigate social inequalities and pave the way for a more democratic society.[4]

Yet the chronic shortage of funds, the failure to extend universal access to schooling, and the difficulty of retaining most of the students beyond the primary grades meant that education in English was bound to create the conditions for intensifying those inequalities. It eventually created new social divisions based on language use. Alongside a Spanish-speaking elite there arose an English-speaking minority who achieved fluency and with it greater economic wealth and social influence. By the 1930s they comprised an impressive 35 percent of the population, making the Philippines the most literate in any Western language in all of colonial Southeast Asia.[5] However, for the majority who had some years of education, familiarity with English did not necessarily mean fluency, while many others with little or no schooling could neither speak nor write in the new language. Barely literate in English, the majority lived in largely vernacular worlds where English (and Spanish) circulated intermittently, emanating as the language of colonial institutions and elites. In other words, the colonial legacy of English, like that of Spanish, included the creation of a linguistic hierarchy that roughly corresponded to a social hierarchy.

In the wake of American rule Filipino nationalists have sought to come to terms in different ways with this colonial linguistic legacy. One of the most influential and widely read critics of American schooling and the use of English was Renato Constantino. Much of his thinking about these matters was laid out in what remains one of his most influential essays, "The Mis-education of the Filipino."[6] Though first published half a century ago, in 1966, its arguments framed much of nationalist thinking in the postwar era and still hold sway among many nationalist intellectuals both in the

Philippines and among some Filipino American scholars today.[7] Given its staying power on both sides of the Pacific, it is a text that demands serious reconsideration.

Miseducation, American English, and National Death

Renato Constantino (1919–99) wrote his classic essay "The Mis-education of the Filipino" in 1959 but could not get it published until 1966. This long time lag is not surprising given the widespread persecution of the Left and the hostile climate for anti-American critiques of any sort throughout the 1950s. The Cold War raged on while the embers of the communist-influenced Huk rebellion were still glowing.[8] It was not until 1966 that the editor at the newsmagazine *Weekly Graphic* finally published the essay. It appeared at a moment when radical changes were unfolding in the Philippines and across the world: the revival of militant nationalism and a left-wing student movement at home; revolution and decolonization in the Third World; civil rights and women's liberation movements in the Americas; workers and student strikes across Europe and in the United States; and counter-cultural currents and new social movements everywhere else. At the cusp of the revolutionary domestic and international developments, "The Mis-education of the Filipino" quickly became a touchstone for addressing what came to be known as the neocolonial condition of the Philippines. "The response was tremendous," Constantino remarked in an interview. It has since been republished numerous times and continues to be widely read to this day in the Philippines and elsewhere.[9] Much of the essay recapitulates a set of ideas that Constantino began formulating as far back as the late 1930s while he was editor of the *Philippine Collegian* at the University of the Philippines and which he continued to elaborate in his postwar articles for various newspapers. Though inflected with a Marxist sensibility, his essay was influenced primarily by the anti-American arguments of his mentor, the Hispanophile nationalist and senator Claro M. Recto, as well as by some aspects of Jose Rizal's romantic nationalism. But, as I hope to show, it also bore a surprising affinity with American colonial discourse, both critical and supportive, of the public educational system from the 1920s and 1930s.[10]

According to Constantino, if the Philippines remained economically underdeveloped, socially divided, politically corrupt, and culturally bankrupt, it was largely because of the fact that it continued to be a colonial appendage of the United States. Two decades after independence the country's dependency on America had intensified. Not only did Filipinos continue to be subservient to their former colonial masters. Worse, they craved their subservience. For this "shameful" condition Constantino places blame squarely on the country's educational system. Run by foreigners, foreign-trained Filipinos, or, worse, an authoritarian clergy, Philippine schools, he claimed, perpetuated the work of colonial education. They fostered un-critical views of the benevolence of the United States, training Filipinos to blindly embrace American models. "Nurtured in this kind of education," he wrote, "the Filipino mind has come to regard centuries of colonial status as a grace from above rather than a scourge" (29). Rather than enlighten students, schools were guilty of furthering their state of tutelage. They thus educated students by miseducating them, leading students to believe that they could be modern by being "little Americans." Students were consigned to the impossible task of seeking what they could never attain by trying to become other than what they were supposed to be. In this way colonial edu-cation foreclosed their future. It kept them ignorant, holding the country in a state of abject backwardness. While other Asian countries were then vigorously promoting their national cultures along with their national econ-omies, the Filipinos continued to disavow their distinctiveness. Deferring to America, they were deluded into thinking of themselves as exceptional Asians: as "Filipino Americans." In short, schools produced subjects inca-pable of knowing themselves, much less understanding the "basic ills" of their country. Barred from the truth of their being, they were deprived of the true knowledge of their past as marked by imperial injustice and anti-colonial struggles. As such, Filipinos could not be redeemed for the future.

The "tragedy" of miseducation thus revolves around the frustration of a nationalist teleology. Colonial conquest is supposed to beget anticolonial resistance, which in turn is supposed to give birth to a sovereign people steeped in the righteousness of their struggle and the knowledge of their destiny. This is the truth of nationalism, the justice of its cause. Miseduca-tion has concealed and distorted such a truth inasmuch as schools collab-orate in carrying out American designs. For Constantino the chief tool for bringing about the tragedy of miseducation is the very language of instruc-tion, English. The hegemony of English—its power to shape thinking and constrain dissent—stems from its historical deployment as a weapon of colonial conquest.

As the "master stroke" of colonial education (24), the use of English as the sole medium of instruction has had the effect of "separat[ing] the Filipinos from their past" while dividing "educated Filipinos from their countrymen." Thanks to English, native students were turned into "carbon copies of [their] conqueror" (24). Rather than unify native societies by providing a common language, English intensified social divisions while promoting historical amnesia. An alien language, it could produce only alienating effects. It turned natives neither into Filipinos nor Americans but into failed copies of the latter.

Sent ontologically adrift by English, Filipinos could grasp only a "distorted" view of their history: "The history of our ancestors was taken up as if they were a strange and foreign people who settled in these shores. . . . We read about them as if we were tourists in a foreign land" (24). English thus completes the task of conquest by imaginatively displacing the Filipinos from his own land. Compelled to speak the master's tongue, they actively identify and collaborate in their own displacement. As "tourists," they confront their own past as if it were someone else's, just as they regard their own land as a transient possession, as if they were renting it from some other owner. So too with their native tongues. Learning English has meant suppressing the vernacular languages. Here it is worth recalling that as late as the 1960s students were routinely fined 5 or 10 centavos by teachers who caught them conversing in the local language in school. Still the fact remains, Constantino argues, that English could never take the place of the vernacular. It has instead remained irreducibly foreign, incapable of finding a proper home among Filipinos. The foreignness of English comes not only from its association with conquest but also through its very agents of transmission. Early on, American teachers taught the language but were eventually replaced by Filipinos for whom English was at best a second and often imperfectly spoken tongue.

For this reason education in English has produced an intolerable linguistic and social situation. On the one hand, students are unable to master the master's speech inasmuch as its sounds, references, and nuances remain outside of their experience. On the other hand, they have lost their capacity to speak their mother tongue, which has been forbidden to them. Bereft of fluency in any language, students are unable to think and express themselves except in the most "mechanical way." This makes for a "deplorable lack of serious thinking" in society: "We half-understand books and periodicals written in English. We find it an ordeal to communicate with each other through a foreign medium, and yet we have so neglected our native language that we find ourselves at a loss in expressing ourselves in this language" (33). The biopolitical consequences of this situation have been nothing short of disastrous. Having failed in its function as a lingua franca, English lets leaders speak only "in general and vague terms," while reducing the masses to a state of inarticulateness, incapable of "expressing [themselves] in any language" (31). Originally envisioned as a medium for democratizing society, English has proven to be a "barrier" to such a project. Hence not only does English produce historical forgetting. By suppressing native speech while remaining foreign to native speakers, English sets the condition for the self-annihilation of the Filipino people.

For Constantino, then, to embrace a foreign language instead of one's own is tantamount to signing the nation's death warrant. Miseducation thus climaxes with the suicide of the native, who abandons herself to the very forces that negate her. Writing in English himself, the nationalist author, without any trace of irony, warns of its fatal consequences. For English can only render the native immune to the very source of her life, which is her mother tongue—the nature of which remains ambiguous in an archipelago of numerous mother tongues—and in so doing can only lead to her self-destruction.

What do we make of Constantino's diagnosis? Does the promise of a foreign, colonial language always invariably turn out to be a curse? Does it always lead to the self-destruction of the miseducated? Or can miseducation itself give rise to something and someone different from the suicidal colonized subject? Are there ways by which the nation can survive, perhaps even transform, its miseducated state? Can the desire, even if it is forever deferred, for a foreign language—the master's speech—bring about not death but another form of life? And could we think of this life as one that, while steeped in the history of the colonial, also escapes it? And in escaping it, also revises the tragic vision and unfinished history of the national?

In a later section of Constantino's essay we get a hint of this other possibility. Rather than the self-inflicted death of a failed national subject, English could also produce "appreciation" from the masses: "Because of their lack of command of English, the masses have gotten used to only half-understanding what is said to them in English. They appreciate the sounds without knowing the sense. This is a barrier to democracy" (31). Confronted with foreign words, the masses fail to grasp their meaning but nonetheless "appreciate" their sonic qualities. They are drawn to the sensuous features of English and see in them a certain attraction. Constantino laments the failure of the masses to fully understand what is said to them. He assumes this means they cannot speak back, thus hindering their political participation. The masses seem more interested in apprehending rather than comprehending English. They are compelled less by its meaning than by its materiality, or perhaps conflate the one with the other. Such a response suggests a stance toward English at variance with nationalist expectations. In privileging sound over sense, the masses, whoever they are, seem to find a way to make room for English alongside rather than on top of the vernacular. In so doing they seem to translate its strangeness from a menace into a resource. How is this possible? Is there another history working within colonial education that might allow us to see this other kind of relationship with English?

Sonic Monstrosities and the Recalcitrance of the Vernaculars

In 1924 the Lebanese American colonial official and scholar Najeeb Saleeby published a series of lectures he delivered in Manila on the problem of English-language education. Constantino quotes approvingly from Saleeby to support his argument about the inherent inability of English to serve as a lingua franca for democratizing the country. But a closer reading of these passages suggests that Saleeby was not just critical of colonial efforts to use English as the sole medium of instruction in schools. He was equally impressed by the power of the vernacular languages to withstand the deployment of English. Just as "three centuries of Spanish rule . . . failed to check the vernacular . . . twenty five years of intensive English education has produced no radical change. More people at present [i.e., 1924] speak English than Spanish, but the great majority hold on to the local dialect."[11] Writing about forty years before Constantino, Saleeby tells a slightly different story. Where Constantino sees only the overwhelming victory of colonial education and the unquestioned hegemony of English, Saleeby sees the inability of English to take hold in schools and regards this as a sign of the failure and hubris of U.S. colonial policy. Even more significant, while Constantino bemoans the neglect of the vernaculars in the face of English, Saleeby remarks on the tenacity of native languages that students hold onto in the face of English. In reading Saleeby we get a sense that the vernacular could not be repressed. Efforts to supplant it with English produced effects other than those intended by colonial educators and denounced by the nationalist intellectual. It is to these other effects that I now want to turn to.

In 1925 the all-Filipino colonial legislature commissioned a study of colonial schooling from a committee headed by Paul Monroe of Columbia University. The result was a massive report, *A Survey of the Educational System of the Philippine Islands*.[12] The *Survey* sought to assess the conditions of public schooling especially in the wake of the Jones Law of 1916 that had mandated the swift Filipinization of the colonial bureaucracy, including that related to public education. The *Survey* was roundly critical of public schooling. It was especially dismayed at the teaching of English. Citing education as "the most critical issue in the Philippine school situation" (115), the *Survey* devotes detailed attention to investigating the "obstacles" that stood in the way of the teaching of English. While the *Survey* was impressed by the enthusiasm of Filipinos for schools where attendance was free and noncompulsory, it was far more disappointed by the inability of Filipino teachers and students to develop a working fluency of American English. In accounting for this failure it mentions a number of reasons, ranging from the acute shortage of American teachers (roughly 1 percent of teaching personnel by 1920) to the inadequate training of Filipino teachers. The small number of American teachers meant that there was little opportunity to correct Filipino teachers who, as nonnative speakers of English, were prone to transmit and consolidate errors of grammar and pronunciation.

But the most significant obstacle to gaining fluency in English according to the *Survey* were the vernacular languages themselves. Over and over again the *Survey* complains about the great disadvantage faced by English forced to compete with the native languages. Children enter school after seven or eight years of speaking their mother tongue. Physically attuned and mentally habituated to its intonations, referents, and rhythm, they are then expected to switch over to an entirely foreign language. Such a sudden transition, according to the *Survey*, has the effect of deterring children from learning. The task of learning English, which entails unlearning the vernacular, takes them away from the task of learning as such. They are thus burdened with the demand to speak otherwise as a prerequisite to being able to speak at all. In this way English creates a kind of disability. It constitutes what the *Survey* calls a "foreign language handicap" (127):

The foreign language handicap . . . is from the start a serious obstacle to success in teaching. From the day a Filipino child enters school he is confronted by the double necessity of mastering a strange tongue and of carrying out schoolwork in it. At no time in his career does he encounter the single task of studying in his mother tongue. He is required to read not in Visayan, not in Tagalog, not in Ilocano, not in Bicol—but in English. He faces the necessity of mastering the intricacies of oral speech in a language almost completely unphonetic and totally removed in accent, rhythm, tonal expression and phonetic organization from the one which he hears on the playground, at home and in the community. During seven years of childhood . . . he has acquired the difficult coordinations [*sic*] of pronunciation of his native dialect. When he enters school he must disregard and attempt to blot these out of his habit system. . . . Not only do the old habits fail to facilitate but they actually inhibit the acquisition of new ones. (127)

Coming to school meant leaving the home, stepping into a foreign space dominated by the other's speech. One left one's mother and mother tongue to stand before a foreign language. One was exposed to the specific, exacting demands of the foreign for several hours a day, forced to conform one's body and voice to its commands and expectations. Submission to the rigors of English, however, was deemed a way of eventually mastering it. Confronting the other's speech, one was trained to conquer it, to possess it and make it an integral part of oneself. The goal of mastery, however, proved elusive. The child was put at a permanent disadvantage by the historical purchase of the vernacular. He or she was handicapped in view of the persistent influence of the mother tongues that established formidable barriers to learning the other's tongue. In school the child was expected to engage in a veritable war of separation. He or she was supposed to "disregard and . . . blot out" the habits of speech from home. To speak English meant repressing the vernacular. This entailed exchanging the body at home with the first language for a new body capable of conquering a second language. Put differently, learning English required the labor of translation. Compelled to substitute the first "premodern" language for a second, "modern" one, the child was expected to perform the work of translation as the essential prelude to learning. The problem, according to the *Survey*, was that for the Filipino student translation never ceased: "If he is to come from the school a well trained thinker, he must be taught to think in a foreign language. The handicap of translation must be overcome" (128).

The "foreign language handicap" turns out to be the handicap of translation. For learning to occur, translation must be overcome. Indeed it was precisely the problems posed by translation that shaped the American decision to use English rather than Spanish or the native languages as the sole medium of instruction. Fred Atkinson, who served as the first superintendent of public instruction from 1901 to 1902, initially considered using the native languages for the primary grades, but quickly changed his mind, saying that such a move would be "impractical . . . [as] it would necessitate the setting of large corps of translators at work, putting not merely school primers but large numbers of books of every sort into all the principal dialects." Neither would Spanish do since "only a small portion of the native population understood much Spanish," and almost no Americans could be found who could teach in that language.[13] English as the "practical" alternative to other languages implied two things. First, it meant that Americans were saved from the necessity of learning Spanish or the native languages. Instead they shifted the burden of translation onto Filipinos. As native speakers of English, Americans were exempt from the taxing demands of having to speak otherwise, remaining comfortably monolingual. Second, Americans thought that by teaching Filipinos English, they were endowing them with a common language. Learning English would enable natives to move out of their first and into a second language with which to reach across linguistic and social divisions. Thus would they come to have something in common not only with one another but also with those who ruled them. English would allow them to communicate directly with anyone in the country without resorting to another language. In this way they would be freed from the need to translate from one language to another. Once fluent in English, Filipinos would become like Americans, relieved from the arduous task of translating. The "practicality" of teaching English therefore had an ideological dimension.

Realizing this goal, however, proved practically impossible thanks to the workings of the vernacular. "During the years in which children are struggling with the new language . . . their efforts are being combated constantly by the pervasive influence of the dialect with which they are surrounded in all their out of school hours."[14] Children who find themselves assailed by English in school can hope to find relief with the vernacular at home.

Back in school, however, they are plunged into an asymmetrical war with English. They are forced to translate in a particular way, by suppressing their first in favor of a second language. Translation as such was meant to allow one to eventually dominate the language that had until then dominated one. Suppressing the vernacular and gaining fluency in English were thus conceived as part of a single movement that would enable the student to think in the other language. Thinking, in turn, meant no longer having to translate. Overcoming the "handicap" of translation meant making the foreign familiar rather than merely fearsome, taming it into an instrument of one's thoughts and a ready servant of one's expression.

Created as a counterinsurgent response to the Filipino-American War, colonial education sought to train colonized subjects in a different sort of war. We might think of this as the war of translation. This war aimed at the conquest and colonization of languages, both the vernaculars and English. As we have seen, mastering the second language required setting aside the first. School was the site for the production and consolidation of this linguistic hierarchy. The student learned to translate by way of putting the mother tongue in its place, under the domination of a foreign one, thereby coming to dominate the foreign language herself. Winning this double victory would then transform the student into a new subject, standing atop and in control of the linguistic hierarchy. Colonizing both languages, holding each to their respective places, the educated subject can now command language itself in the service of her thoughts and expressions. Doing so meant putting an end to the labor of translation, or at least minimizing its visibility, which could only detract from the appearance of thought. The war *of* translation was thus also meant to be a war *on* translation. It would conclude in the unequal peace among languages that would establish the rule of the thinking subject over the means and materials of its production.

The *Survey* makes clear, however, that the aims of colonial education were far from being realized. There seemed to be no end to the war of translation. English remained foreign and external to students, while the vernaculars refused to keep to their place. In fact it seemed to the Americans that the very attempt to teach English simply inflamed the resistance of the native languages. The insurgent energy of the vernaculars was most visible and audible in their insistent claims on the bodies of the Filipino teachers and students. The vernaculars' ability to infiltrate the scene of instruction became particularly palpable to the Americans when they heard the "Filipinized English" recited daily in the classrooms. Again and again the *Survey* remarks on what appeared to the Americans to be errors that came with Filipino attempts to speak English. It begins with the Filipino teacher. Lacking in training, she addresses her students

> in strange words, words clothed, however, in the familiar . . . monotone of the Malayan dialects. Be their native tongue Tagalog, Ilocano, Bicol, Visayan, Pampangan, what not, the teachers of the Islands are passing on to the children partial English pronunciations set in the rhythm and cadence of their own tongues. It is our judgment that this setting of Malay rhythm, accent and syllabication is the chief source of unintelligibility. . . . The Filipino child learns to attach meanings to familiar objects and actions that have been named by his teacher in strange sounding words. He listens to the new sounds; he tries to utter them. He hears these strange English words uttered with the familiar Filipino intonation. (155)

Hearing the teacher's English, the student follows. But doing so, she is misled, perhaps miseducated, taking a different path. She ends up not on the road to phonetically correct American English but to the "strange and "unintelligible" zone of its Filipinized version. Filipinized English here consists of dressing English in the clothes of Malay sound patterns. It is an English that perplexes the authors of the *Survey*. Students addressed in Filipinized English readily recognize the vernacular shaping the materiality of foreign words, and it is this recognition that allows them to follow the teacher's voice. They see in the foreign the recurrence of the vernacular, not its demise. To translate in this case requires not the suppression of the first for the second language but an alertness to the sound of the first retracing itself around the appearance of the second. In this way the classroom is no longer cut off from the home. The mother tongue insinuates itself into the foreign one, blurring the lines between what is inside and what is outside the school. English thus reframed is no longer simply a weapon of colonial conquest. In the hands and in the mouths of Filipino teachers and students, it becomes a language for accommodating, or at least signaling, the insistent presence of what was supposed to be excluded and overcome. Conserving the foreignness of English also meant making room for the recurring traces of the vernacular.[15]

For the Americans, however, the Filipinization of English was a source of acute annoyance. It was a symptom of the dismal limits of colonial policy and evidence of the racial incapacities of Filipinos. Their "Malay dialects," so different from American English, had the effect of converting their own native tongue into a kind of foreign speech. Filipinos had in effect forced English to appear in drag. Particularly egregious from the American perspective were the "sound mutations" that Filipinos performed on English, resulting in veritable sonic monstrosities. Conducting a series of long and detailed tests among thousands of students throughout the archipelago, the Survey categorized and quantified these phonetic mutations. They considered them to be grave errors that had to be "eradicated" if Filipinos were ever to achieve fluency in English: "If American English is to become the language of the school and eventually the Islands, teachers must work hard to correct these errors. . . . They must learn to say: is, was, and has instead of iss, wass, hass; can instead of caan; river instead of reevair; servant instead of serbant; go instead of gu . . . stream instead of strim; of instead of off; put instead of poot; the instead of de; late instead of let; pen instead of pin; tooth instead of tut; progress and perceive instead of frogress and ferceive" (158–59). And so forth.

For other Americans, Filipinized English was more than a source of annoyance. Some experienced it as a violent assault. There is, for example, the case of Jerome Barry, a former American schoolteacher and superintendent in Albay province in 1918. In an essay titled "A Little Brown Language," he describes instances of Filipino teachers' written and spoken English. These amount, he claims, to the "perversion, contortion and mauling [of] our familiar phraseology out of most of its intelligibility." Filipino teachers are guilty of "years of malpractice . . . in mispronunciation so far-fetched that only one trained by experience could recognize he was not speaking a strange and esoteric jargon. . . . For Filipino English as it is spoken needs but a stride or two to become a foreign language. At present an American requires a brief period of training before his ear can interpret these strange utterances as a version of his mother tongue."[16]

Two decades of colonial education in English have thus produced not the hegemony of English but its transformation into a language foreign to the Americans themselves. Vernacularizing the foreign, Filipinos sustain the work of translation, disorienting their American interlocutors. Indeed Barry blames the unending operation of translation for obscuring thought and confusing conversations between Filipinos and Americans: "Naturally much of his thinking . . . must be conceived in the native dialect, and laboriously translated into English." The result is that "in conversation, the necessity of translation and the frequent literal rendition of native locutions result in many misunderstandings" (16).

Expecting the Filipino to speak in his, that is, the American's language, Americans instead get something else: not English as they recognize it but the sense of translation at work. It is not therefore the Filipino subject that emerges, master of a foreign tongue with which to make plain his thoughts to the American. Instead Americans are confronted with the relentless movements of the speaker, moving back and forth between his own and the other's language. What comes across is neither the meaning of words nor the settled identity of the speaker and the hearer but rather the sense of the unstable and shifting relationship of languages to one another and to their users. Translation results not in the emergence of thought but in the spread of misunderstanding. This misunderstanding, however, is not meaningless. It consists of sending out certain messages. It signals to the American interlocutor, for instance, the ongoing labor of translation and the desire for communication on the part of the Filipino. It is a desire that forms around the conjunction rather than the separation of English from the vernacular. Communication tenuously linked to comprehension, connection loosened from linguistic hierarchy: this is the war of translation that the Filipino brings to the American. It is one where the vernacular escapes the physiological control of the native body and the pedagogical supervision of the American teacher, smuggling its way into the spaces of English, transforming its sounds and displacing its referents. In the ongoing war of translation, misunderstanding proliferates. Rather than defer to thought, language indefinitely postpones its arrival, suspending the authority of both the speaker and the interlocutor over the scene of communication.

Faced with this disconcerting onslaught of what Barry deprecatingly refers to as the "little brown language," what is the American teacher to do? Is there a place where he could retreat and escape the "diverse and astounding quackings" of his students who violate English with their "untrainable tongues," where even the most attentive ones are prone to such utterances as "*Oh, seer, weel you geeve me bock my pod of pay-pair?*" (19). There is, according to Barry, one area of English where the native cannot go. It is a region of speech where Americans can converse among themselves confident that they will remain unintelligible and thus free from the assaults of Filipinization. This zone of safety is American slang. Given the "bookishness" of

Filipinos' English vocabulary, they cannot hope to penetrate the "slang and colloquialisms that are current in our everyday speech" (19). It is precisely because of its currency—its swift changes of meaning as these come in and out of fashion, drawing boundaries around some speakers while excluding others—that American slang can remain impervious to Filipinization. As highly contingent, largely anonymous, and temporally transient speech acts, slang retains a singularity that makes it seem untranslatable. Hence Filipino attempts to use American slang are bound to sound absurd, according to Barry. To prove this he cites a letter from a schoolteacher in Capiz complaining to his American supervisor. Wanting to communicate his anger in English, the teacher ends his letter with "For the love of mud, kid, and why do you do me this way? Dog gone! Great scott! Yours very truly, etc." (17–18).

The laughable conjunction of colloquial expressions with rhetorical deference proves to Barry that American slang "is a sealed book to the ordinary native, educated though he may be" (17). Barry, however, cites one exception: the "Manila *cochero*," or coach driver. He has become "a master of the profane." We can imagine the uneducated cochero, plying the streets of the city, picking up passengers, dodging pedestrians and other *calesas*. Overhearing conversations in English, he intercepts profanities, hurling them at others when he has the chance. Out of school he nonetheless learns a kind of English, one that is close to Americans but closed off to most educated Filipinos. It is not hard to imagine the Manila cochero as part of the "masses" that Constantino describes as "inarticulate." Cocheros, *tinderas*, *cargadores*, *criados*, and other workers may have attended a couple of years of school, but more likely none at all. They were supposed to be reduced to passive acquiescence and confused speech by the hegemony of English and the neglect of the vernaculars. And yet, at least in this American account, they seem capable of mastering the most inaccessible aspect of English.

What do we make of this seemingly flippant observation? Where else can we find evidence of what Constantino referred to as the mass "appreciation" of the sound of English, or what Barry calls the mastery of its most profane aspects? In what way do such appreciation and mastery reflect popular practices of translating the foreign beyond the confines of schooling and the condemnations of nationalist criticism?

The Play of Translation and the Friendship among Languages

Let us go back to the figure of the Manila cochero.[17] Traversing the city's streets, he inhabits a space that is betwixt and between the school and the home. He no doubt would have a place to call home and perhaps would have had one or two years of schooling. But his work situates him in between and at the boundaries of these two places. For this reason he moves between the affective hold of the mother tongue and the war of translation waged daily in the school. As a denizen of the streets he has presumably a different perspective from where to grasp the politics of language that is at the heart of both colonial and nationalist discourses. It is a perspective that no doubt grows out of the conditions of his labor: moving to and from various points of the city, picking up and conversing with all sorts of passengers, surviving on small change, dodging and dealing with corrupt cops, competing with and cooperating with fellow cocheros, and so on. Physically mobile, socially marginal, and economically precarious, the cochero is also, by dint of his promiscuous interactions with people on the streets, linguistically versatile. He "appreciates" the sound of words he may not understand, while proving to be adept at mastering invectives and profanities in English, Spanish, and other vernaculars. And because he is outside the authority of the school and the maternal conventions of home, he is free to speak in ways that would be intolerable in either place. That is, he can slip away from the linguistic hierarchy that governs the mother tongue (replete with honorifics and an elaborate rhetoric of deference) and the school (with its never-ending combat between English and the vernacular). The cochero's linguistic freedom opens up certain expressive and historical possibilities. How do we know this? Where could we go, which calesa can we take to get a glimpse of language freed from hierarchy and thus available for other, yet to be determined uses? One such place might be the journalistic writings of Nick Joaquin (1917–2004).

No other Filipino writer since possibly Jose Rizal was better at chronicling the history of everyday life. Widely regarded as the best Anglophone novelist, Joaquin also wrote a series of imaginative reportage and historical essays. Writing under the pseudonym Quijano de Manila, he produced a series of journalistic accounts, always historicizing contemporary political and popular culture. While he comes from the same generation as Constantino and went to colonial public schools, Joaquin never earned an academic degree and never regarded himself as part of a political vanguard or a nationalist intelligentsia. He was born to a wealthy family: his father was a successful lawyer, a veteran of the Revolution who was close to General Emilio Aguinaldo; his mother was a teacher of Spanish and English. But his father lost his wealth through a series of bad business investments when Joaquin was a young boy. After a brief stint at a seminary in Hong Kong, Joaquin quit school and before the war worked as an apprentice for the English-language newspaper the *Tribune*. He also worked a series of odd jobs, from stagehand at a vaudeville company where his brother played the piano, to a proofreader and copyeditor at the *Free Press* after World War II. Beginning in 1943, and especially in the decades after the war, Joaquin's literary career flourished. He won several prestigious prizes, including being named National Artist of the Philippines for literature in 1976.[18]

Notwithstanding his fame, Joaquin never lost an affinity with street life. His biographers describe his daily habit of taking long solitary walks through Manila's streets. He delighted in observing the details of urban life, forgotten monuments, and local gossip. "He absorbed everything he saw," wrote one of his biographers, "drawing in every sound, every tune heard, from Mexican *canciones* to American jazz numbers. . . . He danced the tango and spoke the latest *kanto boy* (i.e., street corner) slang."[19] There was no topic too lowly for him. As a reporter he took on assignments of all sorts, from crime stories to celebrity profiles. He was at home everywhere, from the presidential palace to political rallies, from the boxing ring to receptions for visiting dignitaries. As the editor of various weekly magazines, he spoke with everyone from janitors to typesetters and in 1971 even led a writers' labor union. Joaquin once described himself in the following terms:

> I have no hobbies, no degrees; belong to no party, club or association. I like long walks, any kind of *guinatan* [stew in coconut milk], Dickens and Booth Tarkington, the old Garbo pictures, anything with Fred Astair[e] . . . the *Opus Dei* according to the Dominican rite, Jimmy Durante and Cole Porter tunes . . . the Marx Brothers and the *Brothers Karamazov*; Carmen Miranda; Paul's Epistles and Mark's, Piedmont cigarettes . . . my mother's cooking . . . playing *tres-siete* [a card game], praying the Rosary and the *Officium Parvum* [i.e., Little Office, or prayers to the Virgin Mary].[20]

Joaquin was an omnivorous consumer of cultural and religious goods, as well as a keen observer of the quotidian rhythms and obscure currents of

Figure 2.1 Nick Joaquin as a young man.
Courtesy of Rosario Joaquin Villegas.

city life. He was a kind of flaneur, taking his time and his pleasures wherever he found them. Whether writing about early Spanish colonial history or the political and cultural celebrities of his day, he kept to a notion of history wherein the past was always current, the present always haunted by the future becoming past, and where modernity was not the negation of tradition but its fictive kin, its *compadre*.

In 1963, around the same time that Constantino's essay had been written and was waiting to appear, Joaquin wrote "The Language of the Streets."[21] It was similarly caught up in the postcolonial obsession with language and nationhood. But unlike Constantino's view of miseducation in English as historical tragedy, Joaquin provides a radically different and far more joyful account of linguistic history, one that gives the cochero and others like him their due. It is an essay that has been overlooked perhaps because it slides away from accepted colonial and nationalist views. It is precisely for this reason that it bears close reading.

Joaquin begins not by continuing to wage the Filipino-American War over the legacy of English and colonial education as Constantino does. Instead he invokes the American literary critic and journalist H. L. Mencken on slang to buttress his argument that "slang, once scorned as the bastard of language, has risen to the status of heir of the house and begetter of literature" (3). With Mencken, Joaquin proposes to treat slang or what he calls "the language of the streets" not as a "debased" or inferior version of standard speech but as the very basis of a national literature. He focuses particularly on Tagalog slang, which he claims has long been the "common possession of Filipinos." As a lingua franca it forms the basis of the true national language: "It in fact is the national language, not Filipino, [one that is] a natural growth from below, not a decree from above. This language . . . is the most daring, the most alive, the most used language in the country today. . . . [It] is being created by the masses, out in the open, to express their lives, to express their times, and just for the fun of it. That's why it promises to be a great language: because it's being created for the sheer joy of creating. *Happy-happy lang!*" (4, 18).

That a national language has emerged outside the control of official academies and colonial education suggests the workings of a history missed by nationalist writers. How can Tagalog slang serve as the basis for the national language? It is because slang, according to Joaquin, works like a lingua franca. It travels across linguistic and social boundaries with great speed, thanks to the commercial mass media, enabling speakers of various vernaculars to understand one another. In this way Tagalog slang assumes the historical legacy of Spanish. Herein lies another startling contrast with Constantino: where the nationalist holds onto the notion of languages as mutually discrete and arranged in a hierarchy—Spanish or English historically and oppressively lording it over the vernaculars—Joaquin sees the colonial language of Spanish at the basis of Tagalog slang, indeed of all Tagalog as it is currently spoken. Such a view is consistent with a recurring theme in Joaquin's literary and historical writing: that the colonial is inextricably wed to the national as the nation's condition of possibility. "Spanish," he writes, "is not dead in the Philippines. We unknowingly speak it every moment of our lives" (12). Castilian loan words such as "calle, mesa, tren, pier, vapor, libro, coche, cine, gobierno, Dios" permeate nearly all Philippine languages. Unlike indigenous words that are genetically related but distinct in their spelling and pronunciation, Spanish words are immediately recognizable across vernaculars (4). This great loan of words has accrued enormous interest over time, investing vernacular languages with something in common. What was once the language of imperial authority has come to be parceled and circulated, borrowed and shared to provide "the foundation of a national language" (4).

Thus the paradox of Spanish: its power is felt most acutely when it has become powerless to command. It has been detached and broken up from its original speakers and woven into the fabric of local languages. The foundational significance of Spanish lies not in its ability to dominate the vernaculars from above or to serve as their horizon of their reference. Rather it has to do with its capacity to connect and conjoin them while leaving them distinct. It allows, that is, for the recognition of something held in common among languages without reducing their differences.[22] Through three and a half centuries of Spanish rule many Castilian words have seeped through the vernaculars, becoming indistinguishable parts of their vocabulary. By the late nineteenth century, as Emanuel Luis Romanillos and Benedict Anderson have pointed out, a mix of Spanish, vernacular languages like Tagalog, and Chinese languages like Hokkien had amalgamated into a lingua franca known by many names: *español de Parian*, *chabacano*, and *lengua de tienda*, for example. It had become widespread in Manila and its surroundings as well as in other port cities in the Philippines. This creole language grew around the marketplace, spread through the streets, traveled up and down the social hierarchy, and was quickly picked up by new arrivals from Europe. As Anderson describes it, español de Parian (i.e., the Spanish of the Parian, the Chinese quarter designated by the Spaniards just outside the walls of Manila) was "a real, Hokkien-inflected lingua franca for the streets of Manila, egalitarianly [sic] shared by poor vendors and their elite student customers. A patois . . . but also an instrument of social communication, not an emblem of political shame."[23] It continued to survive and even flourish in many parts of the country in the wake of the American invasion and occupation, especially in the Ermita district, until the end of World War II, and is still spoken in parts of Cavite, Cotabato, and Zamboanga.[24]

Joaquin argues that Tagalog slang (and we can perhaps extrapolate this to cover other, non-Tagalog languages) is the proper heir to what he calls "Spanish" but what historically was español de Parian.[25] It "flows" through all the local languages but acknowledges neither source nor directive. It comes instead from "the anonymous word-coiners on the street" who, through no coordinated or systematic efforts, nonetheless "are doing more to speed the coming of a common tongue than all the schools and the academics put together" (5). If this is the case, then the foundational status of Tagalog—or presumably any other vernacular—slang, like Spanish, will have to be qualified. It cannot be seen to form the firm bedrock on which the national language is built; rather it is a shifting and protean node linking various languages as in a network. Slang as the contingent foundation of a common speech operates in a distributive and decentralized fashion. Hence it can have only variable and unknown authors, obscure and unverifiable origins, indiscriminate interlocutors, along with uncertain and erratic life spans. This "coming of a common tongue" feels like a messianism without a messiah. It has always already happened, but it is always yet to arrive.

In coming, this common tongue shows its power to register particular moments in the nation's historical becoming. Constantino feared that colonial education in English would obliterate the true history of the country's anticolonial struggles. Joaquin sees a possible antidote to this amnesia in slang's capacity to "sum up a whole period." It does so by its rampant theft (for this is one of the purported origins of the word *slang*) of other languages, including other vernaculars. For example, there is *sipsip buto* from Ilocano, popular in the 1930s to denote the political sycophants that surrounded Commonwealth president Manuel L. Quezon; *genoowine* from the English *genuine*, widely used during the Japanese Occupation to refer to anything good and of great value; and the withering *Hanggang pier ka lang*, "He's only taking you as far as the pier," often heard during the American reoccupation of the country after the war, addressed to Filipina women having relations with American servicemen (18). Joaquin excavates other linguistic artifacts that preserve the fleeting images and sensations of other eras: from the 1920s, *stamby* (bum, lumpen), who could easily become a thug or *maton*, *sanggano*, and *butangero* (6). In the 1930s a new social type emerged: the fashionable man about town, cocksure and a touch arrogant, known as *hambug*, *sikat*, *siga-siga* (8), while the new urban experience of going out on the town was referred to as *naggoo-good-time*, that is, "having a good time" (9). Flashforward to the late 1960s and 1970s, when *class* replaced *genoowine*, *jingle* was to urinate, and the formative years of a new gay culture is archived by such words as "T-Y (thanks), *sibai* (call boy), *serbis* (paid sex), and *type* (somebody you're aroused by)" (19), as well as the all-purpose affirmation "*Anong say mo!*" (What do you say!). The history of the drug culture, which accompanied the spread of American youth culture in the Philippines, is embedded in the numerous terms for getting stoned, as in *trip, durog, durog na durog, shotgun, iskor* (i.e., to buy drugs), *bitin* (not high enough), *high na high* (very high), and its synonyms, *banggag, sabog,* and *basag* (19–20). Joaquin sums up the whole era with the word that replaces the 1920s *siga: jeproks,* "which can mean anything from hippie to mod to rebel to flamboyant [youth]" (21).

For Joaquin cataloguing slang terms provides hurried glimpses into a history of emergent social types, novel subcultural formations, and popular practices around fashion, sex, leisure, and consumption. These words are shards that do not necessarily add up to a whole. Instead they remain fragments of larger narratives yet to be written, the traces of social histories that may never be told. Here language does not reveal historical truth that brings self-knowledge and national redemption. The bits and pieces of slang instead suddenly trigger the recollection of the past as fractured, inconclusive moments through a series of linguistic associations. One slides gleefully from *trip* to *durog* to *durog na durog,* to *banggag,* to *basag,* to *jeproks,* and so on, without pausing to think what they all mean, only that they stimulate more associations. These chains of associations are potentially endless and so are likely to be of little use to nationalist historiography. In the drama of nationalism, as explicated by Constantino, language linked to education is a matter of life and death. The very survival of a people is at stake in the future of English and the national language. By contrast Joaquin's linguistic history suggests something else is at play. Tagalog slang, in "summing up an era," converts the past into language: history is apprehended as a series of expressive possibilities over which no one has the first or final word. By reconfiguring the past into an ever-expanding constellation of associations, slang for Joaquin opens up speech and loosens the grip of linguistic hierarchy. Such a development leads, arguably, to the very democratization of society that Constantino had longed for. The basis for a common language emerges through the sudden but recurring appearance of slang, converting the most mundane and abject aspects of life into rich and commonly available sources of the literary.

To see these literary possibilities at work, we can look at the following example. Joaquin explicates the Tagalog term *barkada,* made up of one's closest friends, at times referred to as *ka-rancho* (i.e., from the same ranch) or *chokaran* (the syllabic inversion of *ka-rancho*). Popular since the 1950s, the term comes from the Spanish *barco,* or boat, which brings it in association with the precolonial Tagalog *barangay*, the word for "boat" as well as "village." But Joaquin does not stop at translating *barkada* into English. He deploys it alongside related slang terms. In the process of talking about *barkada*, he begins to tell a story not only about its possible associations but of the network of other words that lead away from these associations:

> When a *barkada* has an *atrazo* that means *trobol*, a *rambol*, a *golpehan*, also described as *balasahan*, or shuffle. In a good *barkada*, every member is *kumakasa* or fighter. . . . A *kumakasa* would rather be *tepok*—that is, killed—than find himself turned into an *under*, or stooge. Such a fate is *diahe*, or *hadya*, slang's coyer version of a major Filipino term: *hiya*, shame.
>
> But a *barkada*'s chief foe is always the law, represented by the policeman who is known as *lespo*, *alat* [i.e., *tala* or star spelled backward, a reference to his badge] or—this is the latest term—*parak*. *Alagad ng batas* [i.e., officers of the law] is, like all formal Filipino phraseology, uttered only with a smile. . . . When the *alat* appears it's best to *batse* or *sebat*, derivations from the Spanish *se va* and *pase*. If you don't *botak* fast enough, you end up in *Munti* [i.e., Muntinglupa, the penitentiary] and your *chokarans* explain you're *na sa loob* [inside] where if you're *guwapo* [i.e., good-looking] you may find yourself forced to become some tougher convict's *señorita*. But if you're ugly—*askdad* is the word for it—you'll still have to pay tribute in the form of *yosi* (cigarettes) or *maman* (liquor) or *atik* (money).
>
> *Atik*, one of the most used expressions today is the Tagalog word for earnings, *kita*, spelled backwards. A guy with a lot of money is *maniac*; to be broke is to *lawang-lawa*. The old term for extortion, *diligencia*, has been joined by *kikil* (to chisel) and *arbor* (an anagram of *robar*). *Nakatipak* is to hit the jackpot; and *tipak na tipak* is to be in the chips. Then you can buy *toga* (shoes) a *polo* (shirt) or even a *cana* (coat). . . . And you can go into a restaurant and [*chicha*] eat without having to do the *one-two-three*, which is to flee or *poga* (from the Spanish *fuga*) after eating without paying the bill.
>
> To eat is *enka*, *chicha*, *hatchit*. . . . To drink is to *toma*, *maman*, and *barik*. . . . If the *erbi*, *cuatro cantos*, *markang demonio*, *birginrum* or *white label* goes to your head, you're *groggy*, *wango*, *enggot*, *senglot* or *pass-out*. (13–15)

I could go on but will resist the temptation to quote many other, similar passages in the essay. Reading this excerpt, or better yet reciting it out loud, one gets an acute sense of what Joaquin says are the characteristics of slang: its speed, its spontaneity, and its remarkable capacity to "absorb without fuss" terms from other languages, including Tagalog itself (3). The speed of slang's transmission, enabled by mass-mediated technologies and the spread of the marketplace, endows even familiar words with a recurring novelty. One senses this in the rhythm of Joaquin's telling. He begins with *barkada* but is quickly off to other words: *atrazo, trobol, rambol, golpehan,* and more. What emerges is a kind of accidental narrative about a *barkada* settling a score, or *atrazo,* then getting into trouble with the law, or *lespu,* being sent to jail, *Munti,* having to pay off guards and other prisoners with *yosi,* cigarettes, or *atik,* money. The last word, *atik,* triggers another chain of associations: earnings, *kita,* extortion, *diligencia,* theft, *arbor,* that in turn opens up another set of linkages: jackpot, *nakatipak,* shoes, *toga,* going out and eating, *chicha,* that leads to several words for drinking, alcoholic drinks, then getting drunk. It is as if in talking about slang one ends up talking in slang. One is contaminated by its metonymic pull and disdain for linguistic conventions. Like the *barkada* that has to *botak* fast enough from the *lespu* after settling an *atrazo,* slang evades the institutional authorities of home and school. It is impatient to move on, jumping, as Joaquin does, from one word to another to string together less a story about the national language than an enactment of its expressive possibilities.

For Constantino miseducation in English impaired thinking by impeding the translation of language into thought. Instead, like American colonial officials, the nationalist bemoaned the failure of translation to work properly, that is, to make language, both English and the vernacular, into transparent and servile instruments for the formation of a self in control of its own thoughts. Miseducation meant that colonial education continued in the postcolonial classroom characterized by the war of translation. In seeking to replace English with a vernacular-based national language as the more effective medium of instruction, Constantino sought to win this war—to stop language from posing obstacles to learning by putting an end to the need for translation. Thus does the nationalist, heir to a certain linguistic legacy, unwittingly collaborate with the colonizer. Like the colonizer, the nationalist provides the same answer to the war of translation: a war on translation.

In Joaquin translation has a different trajectory. In the passages above, Joaquin translates Tagalog slang into English. But the English prose is punctuated and punctured by the speedy and restless appearance of slang to the point where the English sometimes blurs into Tagalog. The power of slang to absorb and displace all languages affects the very language that is seeking to capture and objectify it. English is repeatedly ensnared in slang. Most of the time Joaquin provides approximate English equivalents to the Tagalog. At other times the chains of associations move so rapidly as to carry away the English, as when the writer himself is carried away to the point of dispensing with translation altogether: "There was a time when you could say nothing without having some wise guy flatten you with '*May nothing ba sa cano?*' The ritual retort to this was '*Wala, sa Bombay mayroon, hulugan pa!*' The current whoop is: '*Uy, sa akin yata yan!*' Last year produced '*Sino ang kaaway mo?*' and '*Sabi mo, eh!*' But the prime product of the year is '*Happy-happy lang!*' To make *happy-happy* is to drink together, and the *lang* means: '*No trobol*'" (17).

Here entire English phrases are left untranslated as if there was no need for Joaquin to tell his miseducated readers what these meant. And when he does pause to translate the word *lang* (i.e., only, merely, simply), he does so with another slang word, "No trobol!" Tagalog slang has taken over English not by situating itself above but by *folding* itself into its syntax and spelling. "Happy" becomes "happy-happy lang!" Freed from the conventions of home and the institutional constraints of school, Tagalog slang makes possible a way out of the war of and on translation. In lieu of war, it allows for translation as promiscuous and ongoing play. Veering from the serious responsibilities of an officially mandated national language, Joaquin's translation of the language of the streets is underwritten by an ethos of attentiveness to what is new and what passes for new regardless of its provenance or precise meaning. Such is, perhaps, the basis of its literary promise. Translation, liberated from the task of reproducing hierarchy, is another way of experiencing the nation whether in its colonial or postcolonial state. This indecorous, vulgar, miseducated nation is one where, for example, vaudeville actors, like *cocheros*, *atsays*, *tinderas*, and *kanto boys*, might take their place alongside academics, politicians, and landlords to give their own treatise on the national language. We get a sense of what this other nation might be like when Joaquin performs a shtick he doubtless learned from his time working as a stagehand in vaudeville productions. It consists of asking:

Did the English language spring from Tagalog? Yes, averred the vaudeville professors; and they point out that many English words have an obvious Tagalog origin—for example, pussy from *pusa*, mother hen from *inahen*. There's something to this theory, really. Those English words—tot and toy—don't they clearly come from *totoy*, the Tagalog for child? And another Tagalog word for tot, *bololoy*—usually shortened to *boloy* or *boboy*—is just as clearly the source for boy. Where would the English suit have sprung from but from our word for wear, *suot*? . . . What pronoun came first: the Tagalog *ito* or the English it? . . . The friction of our *kiskis* undoubtedly sparked kiss, as the laceration of *gasgas* grows bigger in gash, and the dangle of *luslus* swings again in loose, and the sibilance of *sipsip* is scissored in sip. . . . But what need we to go on? Even the English word for nurse, nanny, is obviously a derivative of *nanay*. (17–18)

Joaquin carnivalizes the relationship between the imperial and subaltern languages, placing the latter not only on top but at the origin of the former. This reversal, however, is less about nationalist revenge or *ressentiment* than about highlighting what Constantino referred to as the masses' "appreciation" for the sound of English—and, we might add, for the sound of any language. The joke here rests on the fact that the vernacular words are neither the semantic equivalents nor the etymological origins of the English. Rather a series of phonic similarities is made to resonate between the two, loosening the authority of English to delimit the vernacular and vice versa. The two are juxtaposed in the mode of call and response: *kiskis* returns as kiss, *gasgas* calls forth gash, *luslus* yields loose, *sispsip* breaks into sip. In retailing this "venerable theory," Joaquin seizes another opportunity to show the literary potential of slang, that which makes it the basis of a national language.[26] Such potential, as I have argued, consists of mobilizing the practice of translation as play. It means being alert to the materiality of languages, beginning with their sounds. Translating after a fashion Tagalog into English reveals neither their semantic equivalence nor their relative capacities for civilizing bodies or yielding thought. Rather, as Joaquin shows, it demonstrates their fleeting kinship. As if descended from Tagalog, English, like Spanish, gives up its power to command and order native speech. It becomes instead a kind of relative, perhaps a friend, a chokaran, a member of the barkada of Tagalog slang. Together they come to share something in common, forming the basis for a kind of national language. *Happy-happy lang!*

CHAPTER 3

The Cell Phone and the Crowd

Messianic Politics in the EDSA II Uprising

The street . . . the only valid field of experience.
—**ANDRÉ BRETON,** *Nadja*

This chapter explores the question of translation as the communication of messages from one medium to another across social space. Seized by those who receive and relay such messages, translation as telecommunication becomes a social force productive of unexpected effects. I examine the workings of this translative force among early twenty-first-century middle-class Filipinos in the context of a particular historical event: the massive "people power" demonstrations in Manila on 17–20 January 2001 that forced the resignation of President Joseph Estrada. My focus will be on two distinct but related media: the cell phone and the crowd. Various accounts of what has come to be known as "EDSA II" (i.e., Epifanio de los Santos Avenue, the same major highway that had been the epicenter of the civilian-backed coup that overthrew Ferdinand and Imelda Marcos in February 1986) reveal certain pervasive beliefs among the middle classes. They believed, for example, in the power of communication technologies to transmit messages at a distance and in their own ability to possess that power. In the same vein they believed they could master their relationship to the masses of people with whom they regularly shared Manila's crowded streets and utilize the power of crowds to speak to the state. Thus they imagined themselves capable of communicating beyond the crowd, but also with it. They kept faith in their ability to transcend the sheer physical density of the masses through the technology of cell phones, while at the same time ordering the crowd's movements and using its energy to transmit middle-class demands.

At its most utopian, the fetish of communication suggested the possibility of dissolving, however provisionally, existing class divisions. From this perspective, communication held the promise of refashioning the heterogeneous crowd into a people addressing and addressed by the coming of justice. But as we will see, these telecommunicative fantasies were predicated on the putative "voicelessness" of the masses. For once heard, the masses called attention to the fragility of bourgeois claims to shape the translation and transmission of messages about the proper practice of politics in the nation-state. In this context, media politics (understood in both senses of the phrase: as the politics of media systems, but also as the inescapable mediation of the political) reveals the unstable workings of Filipino middle-class sentiments. Unsettled in their relationship to social hierarchy, these sentiments at times redrew class divisions, anticipated their abolition, or called for their reinstatement and consolidation.[1]

Calling

Telephones were introduced in the Philippines as early as 1885, during the last decade and a half of Spanish colonial rule.[2] Like telegraphy before it, telephony provoked fantasies of direct communication among the colonial bourgeoisie. They imagined that these new technologies would afford them access to colonial leaders, enabling them to hear and be heard directly by the state. We can see this telecommunicative ideal, for example, in a satirical piece written by the Filipino national hero Jose Rizal in 1889. Entitled *Por Telefono*, it situates the narrator as an eavesdropper. He listens intently to the sounds and voices that travel between the Spanish friars in Manila—regarded as the real power in the colony—and their superiors in Madrid.[3] The nationalist writer wiretaps his way, as it were, into the walls of the clerical residences, exposing their hypocrisy and excesses. In this sense the telephone shares the capacity of that other telecommunicative technology—print—to reveal what was once hidden, to repeat what was meant to be secret, and to pass on messages intended for a particular circle.[4] It is this history of tapping into and forwarding messages—often in the form of ironic commentaries, jokes, and rumors—that figured in the events of EDSA II.

On 17–20 January 2001, more than one million people assembled at one of Metro Manila's major highways, Epifanio de los Santos Avenue, site of the original People Power revolt in 1986 that overthrew the Marcoses. A large cross-section of Philippine society gathered there to demand the resignation of President Joseph "Erap" Estrada after his impeachment trial was suddenly aborted by the eleven senators widely believed to be under his influence. The senators had refused to include key evidence that purportedly showed Estrada had amassed a fortune from illegal numbers games while in office. The impeachment proceedings were avidly followed on national TV and the radio. Most viewers and listeners were keenly aware of the evidence of corruption on the part of Estrada and his family. Once the pro-Estrada senators put an abrupt end to the hearing, hundreds of thousands of viewers and listeners were moved to protest in the streets.[5] Television and radio had kept them in their homes and offices to follow the court proceedings, but at a critical moment, the media also drew them away from their seats. Relinquishing their position as spectators, they now became part of a crowd that had formed around a common wish: the resignation of the president.

Aside from TV and radio, another communication medium was given credit for spurring the coup: the cell phone. Most of the accounts of EDSA II available to us come from middle-class writers or by way of media controlled by the middle class and with strong nationalist sentiments. Nearly all accounts point to the crucial importance of the cell phone in the rapid mobilization of demonstrators. "The phone is our weapon now," we hear from an office worker quoted in a newspaper article. A college student in Manila was quoted as saying that "the power of our cell phones and computers were among the things that lit the fuse which set off the second uprising, or People Power Revolution II." And a newspaper columnist advised "would-be foot-soldiers in any future revolution that as long as you[r cell phone] is not low on battery, you are in the groove, in a fighting mood."[6] A technological thing was thus idealized as an agent of change, invested with the power to bring forth new forms of sociality.

Introduced in the second half of the 1990s, cell phones in the Philippines had become remarkably popular by 1999.[7] There are a number of reasons for their ubiquity. First, there is the perennial difficulty and expense of acquiring landline phones in the Philippines, and the service provided by the Philippine Long Distance Company is erratic. Cell phones offered the promise of satisfying this need for connectivity. In addition, cell phones cost far less than personal computers, which in 2001 were owned by fewer than 1 percent of the population (though a larger proportion had access through Internet cafés). By contrast, in the same year, there were over 10 million cell phone users in a population of about 77 million during the year of the uprising. It is common practice for the vast majority of users to buy prepaid phone cards that, combined with the relatively low cost of phones (as little as $50 in the open market and half this amount in secondary markets), make wireless communication more accessible and affordable than regular telephones or computers.[8]

More important, cell phones allow users to reach beyond traffic-clogged streets and serve as an alternative to slow, unreliable, and expensive postal service. Like many Third World countries recently opened to more liberal trade policies, the Philippines shares the paradox of being awash with the latest communication technologies, like the cell phone, while being mired in deteriorating infrastructures: roads, postal services, railroads, power generators, and landlines. With the cell phone, one seems able to pass beyond these obstacles. And inasmuch as the broken, state-run infrastructure represents government ineptitude, passing beyond it gives one the sense of overcoming a state long beset by corruption.[9] It is not surprising, then, that cell phones could prove handy in spreading rumors, jokes, and information that steadily eroded whatever legitimacy President Estrada and his congressional supporters still had during the impeachment hearings. Bypassing the broadcast media, cell phone users themselves became broadcasters, receiving and transmitting both news and gossip, and often confounding the two. Indeed, one could imagine each user becoming his or her own broadcasting station: a node in a wider network of communication that the state could not possibly monitor, much less control.[10] Hence once the call was made for people to mass at EDSA, cell phone users readily forwarded messages they received as they followed the messages' instructions.

Cell phones, then, were not only invested with the power to overcome the crowded conditions and congested surroundings brought about by the state's inability to order everyday life. They were also seen to bring about a new kind of crowd that was thoroughly conscious of itself as a movement headed toward a common goal. While telecommunication allows one to escape the crowd, it also opens up the possibility of finding oneself moving in concert with it, filled with its desire and consumed by its energy. In the first case cell phone users define themselves against a mass of anonymous others. In the second they *become* those others, accepting anonymity as a condition of possibility for sociality. To understand how the first is transformed into the second, it is worth examining the way the vast majority of cell phone messages are transmitted in the Philippines: as text messages.

Texting

Text messages, or SMS (Short Message Service), are electronic messages sent over mobile phones that can also be transferred to the Internet. By the 1990s the verb *texting* had emerged to designate the act of sending such messages, indicating its popularity in such places as England, Japan, and Finland (where text messaging was first commercially available). In the Philippines texting has been the preferred mode of cell phone use since the late 1990s, when the two major networks, Globe and Smart, introduced free and, later on, low-cost text messaging as part of their regular service. Unlike voice messages, text messages take up less bandwidth and require far less time to convert into digitized packets available for transmission. It thus makes economic sense for service providers to encourage the use of text messaging in order to reserve greater bandwidth for more expensive—and profitable—voice messages. Calling cards and low-cost texting, as opposed to expensive long-term contracts, give cell phone service providers a way to attract a broad spectrum of users from different income levels. Thus from an economic standpoint, texting offers a rare point of convergence between the interests of users and those of providers.[11]

But it is obviously more than low cost that makes cell phones popular in the Philippines. In an essay sent over the Internet by "an anonymous Filipino," the use of cell phones in Manila is described as a form of "mania." Using Taglish (the urban lingua franca that combines Tagalog, English, and Spanish), this writer, a Filipino *balikbayan* (one who resides or works abroad and periodically visits the motherland), remarks:

> HI! WNA B MY TXT PAL? They're everywhere! In the malls, offices, and schools, the MRT [Manila Railroad Transit], and what-have-you, the cell

phone mania is on the loose! Why, even *Manang* Fishball [Mrs. Fishball, a reference to older working-class women who sell fish balls by the side of the road] is texting! I even asked my sisters how important they think they are that they should have cells? Even my nephew in high school has a cell phone. My mom in fact told me that even in his sleep, my brother's got his cell, and even when they have a [Philippine Long Distance Company landline] phone in the house, they still use the cell phone.[12]

According to the *Oxford English Dictionary, mania* is a kind of madness characterized "by great excitement, extravagant delusions and hallucinations, and, in its acute stage, by great violence." The insistence on having cell phones nearby, the fact that they always seem to be on hand, indicates an attachment to them that surpasses the rational and the utilitarian, as this excerpt indicates. The cell phone gives its owner a sense of being important even if he or she is only a street vendor or a high school student—someone who can reach and be reached and is thus always in touch. The "manic" relationship to the cell phone is just this ready willingness to identify with it, or more precisely with what the machine is thought capable of doing. One not only has access to it; by virtue of its omnipresence and proximity, one becomes like it. That is to say, one becomes an apparatus for sending and receiving messages at all times. An American journalist writing in the *New York Times* observed as much in an article on Manila society from 2000:

"Texting"? Yes, texting—as in exchanging short typed messages over a cell phone. All over the Philippines, a verb has been born, and Filipinos use it whether they are speaking English or Tagalog. The difference [between sending email by computers and texting] is that while chat-room denizens sit in contemplative isolation, glued to computer screens, in the Philippines, "texters" are right out in the throng. Malls are infested with shoppers who appear to be navigating by cellular compass. Groups of diners sit ignoring one another, staring down at their phones as if fumbling with rosaries. Commuters, jaywalkers, even mourners—everyone in the Philippines seems to be texting over the phone. . . . Faye Sytangco, a 23-year-old airline sales representative, was not surprised when at the wake for a friend's father she saw people bowing their heads and gazing toward folded hands. But when their hands started beeping and their thumbs began to move, she realized to her astonishment that they were not in fact praying. "People were actually sitting there and texting," Sytangco said. "Filipinos don't see it as rude anymore."[13]

Unlike computer users, cell phone owners are mobile, immersed in the crowd, yet able to communicate beyond it. Texting provides them with a way out of their surroundings. Thanks to the cell phone, they need not be present to others around them. Even when they are part of a socially defined group—say, commuters or mourners—cell phone users are always somewhere else, receiving and transmitting messages from beyond their physical location. It is in this sense that they become other than their socially delineated identity: not only cell phone users but cell phone "maniacs." Because it rarely leaves their side, the phone becomes part of the hand, the digits an extension of the fingers. In certain cases the hand takes the place of the mouth, the fingers that of the tongue. One Filipino American contributor to Plaridel, an online discussion group dealing with Philippine politics, referred to a Filipino relative's cell phone as "almost a new limb."[14] It is not surprising, then, that the consciousness of users assumes the mobility and receptivity of their gadgets. We can see how this tendency to take on the qualities of the cell phone comes across in the practice of sending and receiving messages:

The craze for sending text messages by phone started [in 1999] when Globe introduced prepaid cards that enabled students, soldiers [and others] too poor for a long-term subscription to start using cellular phones. . . . People quickly figured out how to express themselves on the phone's alphanumeric keypad. . . . "Generation Txt," as the media dubbed it, was born. Sending text messages does not require making a call. People merely type in a message and the recipient's phone number, hit the phone's send key and off it goes to the operator's message center, which forwards it to the recipient. . . . Sending text messages by phone is an irritating skill to master, largely because 26 letters plus punctuation have to be created with only 10 buttons. Typing the letter C, for example, requires pressing the No. 2 button three times; an E is the No. 3 button pressed twice; and so on. After the message is composed it can be sent immediately to the phone number of the recipient, who can respond immediately by the same process. People using phones for text messages have developed a shorthand. "Where are you?" becomes "WRU." And "See you tonight" becomes "CU 2NYT." People have different styles of keying in their messages. Some use their index fingers, some, one thumb, others, both. . . . [Others] tap away with one hand without even looking at [their] phone.[15]

As with email, conventions of grammar, spelling, and punctuation are frequently evaded or rearticulated in texting. The constraints of an alphanumeric keypad require users to type numbers to get letters. As a result counting and writing become closely associated. In the keyboards available in the late 1990s, digital communication required the use of digits, both one's own and those on the phone keypad, as one taps away. But this tapping unfolds not to the rhythm of one's speech or in tempo with one's thoughts but in coordination with the numbers by which one reaches letters: three taps on 2 to get a C or two taps on 3 to get an E. Texting seems to reduce all speech to writing and all writing to a kind of mechanical percussion, a drumming that responds to external constraints rather than an internal source. In addition there are no prescribed styles for texting: one or two fingers or a thumb will do, and skilled typists can text without looking at the screen. Nor are standardized body postures required while texting: one can sit, walk, or drive while sending messages. If handwriting in the conventional sense requires classroom instruction in penmanship and disciplined posture under the supervision of teachers, texting frees the body from these old constraints.

Mimicking the mobility of their phones, texters move about, bound to nothing but the technological forms and limits of the medium. The messages they send and receive condense whatever language—English or Tagalog and, more frequently, Taglish—they are using, and so are proper to none. This hybrid language follows the demands of the medium itself rather than the idiosyncrasies of its users. The service providers' introduction of fees for text messaging has led to the further shortening of words and messages. Instant messaging, along with the mechanical storage and recall of prior messages, requires only highly abbreviated narrative constructions with little semantic deferral or delay. Using the cell phone one began to incorporate its logic and techniques to the point of identifying with what, in the late 1990s, seemed like a novel social category: "Generation Txt."

An obvious pun on Generation X, Generation Txt was first used as an advertising gimmick by cell phone providers to attract young users to their products. Defined by its attachment to and ease with the cell phone, Generation Txt troubled older generations uneasy about the rise of texting. In a newspaper article from 2001, an anthropologist from the University of the Philippines addressed the dangers of texting in terms that were familiar in other countries where the practice had become popular, especially among youth. He cites the cell phone's propensity to stifle literacy by "[wreaking] havoc" on spelling and grammar and its erosion, "in tandem with mindless computer games and Internet chat rooms, [of] young people's ability to communicate in the real world in real time."[16] Rather than promote communication, texting, in this account, obstructs it. Indeed, cell phones are thought to cultivate a kind of stupidity. For the anthropologist, this is evident in young people's gullibility for the marketing ploys of cell phone providers: they end up spending more money sending messages of little or no consequence. He further charges cell phones with leading to "anti-social" behavior: "children retreat to their own cocoons," while parents who give them the cell phones evade responsibility for "interacting" with them in any meaningful way.[17] Other writers reported students' use of texting to cheat on exams and the role of cell phones in spreading slanderous rumors and gossip that may ruin someone's reputation.[18] As one Filipino online writer put it, cell phones are like "loaded weapons," and their use must be tempered with caution. Another contributor wrote, "If the text [I received] felt like a rumor masquerading as news, I didn't forward it." An office worker from Manila added, "Sometimes whenever you receive serious msgs [sic], sometimes you have to think twice if it is true or if perhaps someone is fooling you since there is so much joking [that goes on] in txt."[19]

Part of the anxiety surrounding texting arose from its perceived tendency to disrupt protocols of recognition and accountability. Parents were supposedly disconnected from their children, who in turn defied parental authority. Cheating was seen to be symptomatic of teachers' inability to monitor students' cell phone use. And the spread of rumors and gossip, along with irreverent jokes, was taken to mean that the senders of messages readily give in to the compulsion to forward them without, as the writers above advise, weighing their consequences or veracity. Indeed, it was the power to forward messages almost instantaneously that transformed the cell phone into a "weapon." The urge to retransmit messages is difficult to resist and, under certain conditions, irrepressible, as we learn from the events leading up to People Power II. An actor and writer, Bart Guingona, who organized a demonstration at EDSA on January 18, describes his initial doubts about the effectiveness of cell phones in a posting to the Plaridel listserv: "I was certain [texting] would not be taken seriously unless it was backed up by some kind of authority figure to give it some sort of legitimacy. A priest who was with us suggested that [the church-owned broadcasting station] Radio Veritas should get involved in disseminating the particulars. . . . We [then] formulated a text message . . . and sent it out that night and I turned off my phone. . . . By the time I turned it on in the morning, the message had come back to me three times. . . . I am now a firm believer in the power of the text!"[20]

The writer was initially hesitant to use texting, reasoning that messages sent this way would be perceived as groundless rumors. Anonymously circulated from phone to phone, the text would seem unanchored to any particular author who could be held accountable for its content. Only when the church-owned radio station offered to broadcast the same information did he agree to send a text message. Upon waking up the next day, he saw the effect of his emission. Not only did his message reach distant others; it returned to him threefold. He is converted from a doubter to a believer in the "power of the text." Such power has to do with the capacity to elicit a surplus of replies.

There are two things worth noting, however, in this notion of the power of texting: first, that it requires, at least in the eyes of this writer and those he sends messages to, a higher power to legitimate the text's meaning, in this case the church-run radio station; and second, that such a power comes through the repeated transmissions of the same text. The power of texting has less to do with the capacity to elicit interpretation and stir public debate than it does with compelling others to keep messages in circulation. Receiving a message, one responds by repeating it. The message is forwarded to others, who are expected to do the same. In this way the message returns, mechanically augmented but semantically unaltered. They crowd one's phone mailbox. The multiplication of the same message anticipates the multiplication of the crowd in the streets, drawn there by their reception of and belief in the truth of the call they receive. In this account the formation of crowds answers to the repeated call of texts. One is drawn to the crowd to the extent that one regards it as having the sanction of a greater authority: the electronic voice of the Catholic Church. The voice of the Church in effect domesticates the uncertainty associated with the electronic repetition and promiscuous circulation of texts. Users forward texts and likewise feel forwarded by the expectations these texts give rise to. Finding themselves called by the message and its constant repetition, they become "believers," part of Generation Txt.

Generation Txt thus does not so much designate a new social identity as a desire for seeing in messages a meaning guaranteed by an unimpeachable source residing outside the text itself. In this sense there is nothing very new or different about this technological fantasy. Most of those who gathered at EDSA and marched toward Mendiola—the road leading to the presidential palace—were united by anger at the corrupt regime of President Estrada and by their wish to replace him with a more honest leader. This said, the protesters challenged neither the nature of the state nor its class divisions. Indeed, everything I have read by the participants of EDSA II emphasized the constitutional legality of these protests and their institutional legitimacy vis-à-vis the Supreme Court and the Catholic Church (as opposed to the army or left-wing groups). In the end, Estrada's replacement came from within his own circle of power: Gloria Macapagal-Arroyo was his vice president and the daughter of a previous Philippine president. It would appear, then, that Generation Txt are "believers" in a "technological revolution" that simultaneously set social revolution aside.

Put differently, texting is "revolutionary" in a reformist sense. Its politics seeks to consolidate and render authority transparent, whether this is the authority of the state or of text messages. In an exemplary manifesto titled "Voice of Generation Txt" ("Tinig ng Generation Txt"), which appeared in what was then one of Manila's more widely read tabloids, *Pinoy Times*, Ederic Peñaflor Eder, a twenty-something University of the Philippines graduate, credits the "power" (*lakas*) of "our cellphones and computers" for contributing to the "explosion" of People Power II. Texting, he declares, became the medium through which "we" responded quickly to the "betrayal" (*kataksilan*) of the pro-Estrada senators who had sought to block the impeachment hearings. Elaborating on the "we" designating Generation Txt, Eder writes in Taglish:

> We are Generation Txt. Free, fun-loving, restless, insistent, hard-working, strong and patriotic. We warmly receive and embrace with enthusiasm the revolution in new technology. Isn't it said that the Philippines rules Cyberspace and that the Philippines is the text messaging capital of the world? Our response was rapid to the betrayal of the eleven running dogs [*tuta*] of Jose Velarde (a.k.a. Joseph Estrada).

The information and calls that reached us by way of text and e-mail were what brought together the organized as well as unorganized protests. From our homes, schools, dormitories, factories, churches, we poured into the streets there to continue the trial—the impeachment trial that had lost its meaning. . . .

Our wish is for an honest government, and a step towards this is the resignation of Estrada. We are patriotic and strong and with principles, since our coming together is not merely because we want to hang out with our friends, but rather to attain a truly free and clean society brought by our love for the Philippine nation. . . .

There were those from our generation that have long since before the second uprising chosen to struggle and fight in the hills and take up arms, trekking on the harsh road towards real change. Most of us, before and after the second uprising, can be found in schools, offices, or factories, going about our everyday lives. Dreaming, working hard for a future. Texting, inter-netting, entertaining ourselves in the present. But when the times call, we are ready to respond. Again and again, we will use our youth and our gadgets [*gadyets*] to insure the freedom of our Motherland. . . . After the second uprising, we promise to militantly watch over the administration of Gloria Macapagal-Arroyo while we happily push Asiong Salonga (a.k.a. Joseph Estrada) into the doors of prison.

We are Generation Txt.[21]

This manifesto of sorts does not specify the social identity of the "we" that speaks and is spoken to. Instead "we" here comes across as those who "warmly accept and embrace" the "revolution" in new technology. The "we" is established through an identification not with a social class but with technological novelty that gives to the Philippines the distinction of being the "text messaging capital of the world." This is perhaps why the message reads as if it were meant to be received, then forwarded: it begins and ends with exactly the same lines: *Kami ang Generation Txt* (We are Generation Txt). Instead of ideals or a critique of social relations, Generation Txt is characterized here by attitudes and affects: it is *malaya* (free), *masayahin* (fun-loving), *malikot* (restless), *makulit* (insistent), *masipag* (hardworking), and so forth. Its members pride themselves on having principles and courage, and, unlike the rudderless and Westernized Generation X, they have direction.

They stand for "transparent" government and a "free" and "clean" society. In this sense they do not see themselves as different from their elders: they are patriots (*makabayan*) dedicated to using their "gadgets" for the sake of the motherland (Inang Bayan). Such commitment comes in the form of a "militant" readiness to watch over the workings of the new government in order to ensure "justice" (*katarungan*). Unlike those who have chosen to take up arms and go to the mountains, Generation Txt can be found in schools, offices, and factories, ready to respond to the call of the times. They watch, they wait, and they are always ready to receive and forward messages.

Generation Txt is concerned not with challenging the structures of authority but with making sure they function to serve the country's needs. This reformist impetus is spelled out in their demand for accountability and their intention of holding leaders up to scrutiny. Through their gadgets they keep watch over their leaders rather than taking their place or putting forth other notions of leadership. Thus does Generation Txt conceptualize its historical agency: as speedy (*mabilis*) transmitters of calls (*panawagan*) that come from elsewhere and have the effect of calling out to those in their "homes, schools, dormitories, factories, churches" to flood the streets in protest. Rather than originate such calls, they are able to trace them to their destination, which, in this case, is the nation of middle-class citizens that seeks to renew and supervise its government. Like the first generation of bourgeois nationalists in the nineteenth century, Generation Txt discovers yet again the fetish of technology as the capacity to seek access to and recognition from authority.[22]

Crowding

In the Generation Txt fantasy, texting calls into being a new form of social movement, one that is able to bear, in both senses of the term, the hegemony of middle-class intentions. As we have seen, texting is sometimes used to escape the crowd. But as a political technology it is credited with converting the crowd into the concerted movement of an aggrieved people. In short, the middle class invests the crowd with the power of the cell phone—the power, that is, to transmit their wish for a moral community. Indeed the act of transmission would itself amount to the realization of such a community. This fantasy projects a continuity between the crowd and the middle-class texters. Nevertheless during EDSA II the middle-class interest in ordering the crowd sometimes gave way to its opposite. At times it was possible to see the materialization of another kind of desire, one that had to do with the democratization of society through the dissolution of class hierarchy. How so?

André Breton once said that "the street . . . [is] the only valid field of experience."[23] The streets of contemporary Manila would seem to bear him out. They furnish the necessary backdrop to understanding the contradictory nature of middle-class ideas about crowds. The city has a population of over 10 million, a large number of whom are rural migrants in search of jobs, education, or other opportunities unavailable in the provinces. Congested conditions—packed commuter trains, traffic-clogged roads, crowded sidewalks, teeming shopping malls—characterize everyday life in the city, slowing travel from one place to another at nearly all hours of the day. These conditions affect all social classes. And because there is no way of definitively escaping them, they constitute the most common and widely shared experience of city life.

Just as Manila's roads are clogged with vehicles, its sidewalks seem unable to contain the unending tide of pedestrians who spill out onto the highways, weaving in and out of vehicular traffic. Indeed among the most anomalous sights on city sidewalks are signs for wheelchair access. Given the narrow and uneven surfaces that make for packed conditions on the sidewalks, these signs are no more than the traces of a possibility never realized, a future overlooked and forgotten. It is as if at one point someone had thought of organizing urban space along the lines of a liberal notion of accommodation. Instead, that thought quickly gave way to what everywhere seems like an inexorable surrender of space to the people who use it—and use it up.

In the wake of the city's wholesale destruction in the Battle of Manila in 1945, urban space in Manila was haphazardly planned, given over to corporate developers, property owners, and informal settlers, mostly from the provinces. The overall feeling one gets is the absence of central design. City planning seems piecemeal, as if it there was no rationalizing authority at work in organizing and coordinating the movement of people and the circulation of things.[24] Instead, these movements occur seemingly on their own accord. Pedestrians habitually jaywalk and jump over street barriers. Cars and buses belch smoke, crisscrossing dividing medians—if these exist at all—and inching along to their destinations. Traffic feels like it proceeds at its own pace, as the thousands of drivers, commuters, and pedestrians submit to the simultaneous decisions of every single individual rather than to the overriding authority of traffic cops (who exist, of course, but are easily ignored and rarely give chase to violators of laws). Drivers and passengers find it difficult to see more than a few feet beyond their vehicles. The windshields and windows of most jeepneys, tricycles, and taxis are often cluttered by decals, curtains, detachable sunshades, and other ornaments that make it difficult to get a view of the road, in effect obstructing vision and further heightening the sense of congestion. Indeed, Manila's topographical flatness makes it impossible to find a vantage point from which to get a panoramic view of the city except from commuter trains and the tops of tall buildings. In the West, the "view" is understood as the site for evacuating a sense of internal unease and a resource for relieving oneself of pressure, both social and psychic.[25] Commanding views are privileged assets in real estate properties for the God-like perspective they give to their owners, affording them the illusion of transcendence and control over all that their eyes can see.

This panoramic notion of the view is not possible at the level of Manila's streets. Caught in traffic, one sees only more stalled traffic, so that the inside and the outside of vehicles seem to mirror each other. The overwhelming presence of garbage only adds to the sense of congestion. Garbage disposal has long been a problem in Manila, owing to a shortage of adequate landfills, among other reasons. As a result trash seems to be everywhere, dumped indiscriminately on street corners and around telephone poles, some of which bear signs that impotently forbid littering and public urination. What appear are thus scenes of near ruin and rubble. While certainly not exclusive to Manila, these scenes bespeak a city in some sense abandoned to the pressures of a swelling population. Instead of regulating contact and channeling the efficient movement of people and things, the city's design—such as it is—seems to be under constant construction from the ground up and from so many different directions. The thought of regulation occurs, but the fact that construction never seems to end—stalled by crowded conditions, periodic typhoons, floods, and the accumulation of garbage—makes it seem as if these sites were permanent ruins. The sense is that there is no single, overarching authority. Walking or riding around Manila, then, one is impressed by the power of crowds. Their hold on urban space appears to elude any attempt at centralizing control. This is perhaps why the largest private spaces open to the public in Manila, shopping malls, play what to an outsider might seem like extremely loud background music. A shopping mall manager once told me that turning the volume up was a way of reminding mall-goers they were not in the streets, that someone was in charge and watching their actions.[26]

The anonymity proper to crowds makes it difficult, if not impossible, to differentiate individuals by precise social categories. Clothing sometimes indicates the social origins of people, but with the exception of beggars, it is difficult to identify class on the basis of looks alone. The sense one gets from moving in and through crowds is of a relentless and indeterminable mixing of social groups. This pervasive sense of social mixing in the streets contrasts sharply with the class-based divisions and linguistic hierarchies that govern political structures and social relations in middle-class homes, schools, churches, and other social spaces.[27] One becomes part of the crowd only by having one's social identity obscured. Estranged, one becomes like everyone else. Social hierarchy certainly does not disappear on the streets. But like the police, racketeers, and gangsters who are barely visible, appearing mostly to collect payoffs (*tong* or *lagay*) from jeepney drivers and sidewalk vendors, hierarchy feels more arbitrary, its hold loosened by the anonymous sway of the crowd.

The power of the crowd thus comes across in its capacity to overwhelm the physical constraints of urban planning and to blur social distinctions by provoking a sense of estrangement. Its authority rests on an ability to promote restlessness and movement, thereby undermining pressure from state technocrats, church authorities, and corporate interests to regulate and contain such movements. In this sense, the crowd is a sort of medium, if by that word one means a way of gathering and transforming elements, objects, people, and things, mixing them up and converting them into other than what they were. As such, the crowd is also a site for the articulation of fantasies and the circulation of messages. It is in this sense that we might think of the crowd as not merely an effect of technological devices, but as a kind of technology itself. It calls incessantly, and we find ourselves compelled to respond to it.

As a technology, the crowd represents more than a potential instrument of production or an exploitable surplus for the formation of social order. It also delineates the form and content of a technic of engaging the world. The insistent and recurring proximity of anonymous others creates a current of expectation, of something that might arrive, of events that might happen. As a site of potential happenings, it is a place for the generation of the unknown and the unexpected. Centralized urban planning and technologies of policing seek to routinize the sense of contingency generated by crowding. But in cities where planning chronically fails, the routine sometimes gives way to the epochal. At such moments, the crowd takes on a kind of telecommunicative power, sending messages into the distance while bringing distances up close. Enmeshed in a crowd, one feels the potential for reaching across social, spatial, and temporal divides.[28]

As we saw, middle-class discourses about the cell phone tend to oppose texting to the crowd. Under normal conditions, texting is meant to transcend and overcome the masses of people and mess of things. But during more politically charged moments such as EDSA II, cell phones take on a different function. They were now credited, along with radio, television, and the Internet, for summoning the crowd and channeling its desire, turning it into a resource for the overthrow of the president. Other accounts, however, suggested the crowd's potential for bringing about something else: the transmission of messages, which at times converged with, but at other times diverged from, those emanating from cell phones. For at times, the crowd made possible a different kind of experience. Plunged into the crowd, one felt compelled less to represent them than to become one with them. In so doing the crowd became a medium for the recurrence of another fantasy that emanates from the utopian side of bourgeois nationalist wishfulness: the abolition of social hierarchy.[29] We can see a recurrence of this democratizing fantasy in one of the more lucid accounts of the crowd's power in a posting by "Flor C." on the Internet discussion group Plaridel.[30] The text, written in Taglish, is worth following at some length for what it tells us about this other kind of political experience.

"I just want to share my own way of rallying at the EDSA Shrine," Flor C. begins. She invites others to do the same, adding, "I am also eager [sabik] to see the personal stories of the 'veterans' of Mendiola." The urge to relate her experience of the protests comes with a desire to hear others tell their own stories. What she transmits is a text specific to her life, not one that comes from somewhere else and merely passes through her. Yet by identifying herself only as Flor C., she makes it difficult for us to locate her narrative beyond its signature. Nor can we determine who authorizes its telling. In this way she remains anonymous to her readers, the vast majority of whom likewise remain unknown to her.[31] What is the relationship between anonymity and an eagerness to share experiences, one's own as well as those of others?

Flor C. refers to the "buddy system" used by protest marchers in the 1970s and 1980s to guard against infiltration by fifth columnists and military and police harassment. But, she writes, because "my feet were too itchy so that I could not stay in the place that we agreed to meet," she ends up without a "buddy" at EDSA. Instead, she finds herself swimming in an "undulating river [ilog na dumadaloy] without letup" from EDSA and Ortigas Avenue that formed the "sea at the Shrine." She can't keep still. She feels compelled to keep moving, allowing herself to be carried away from those who recognize her. At EDSA, she knows no one and no one knows her. Yet the absence of recognition causes neither dismay nor a longing for some sort of identity. Instead, she relishes the loss of place brought about by her absorption into the movement of the crowd. She finds herself in a community outside of any community. It fills her with excitement (sabik).

However, rather than reach for a cell phone, she does something else: she takes out her camera (at a time when cell phones were more rudimentary and did not always come with cameras):

> And so I was eager to witness [kaya nga sabik akong masaksihan] everything that was happening and took photographs. Walking, aiming the camera here and there, inserted into the thick waves of people who also kept moving and changing places, walked all day until midnight the interiors of the Galleria [shopping mall], around the stage and the whole length of the EDSA-Ortigas flyover. Sometimes stopping to listen for a while to the program on stage, shouting "Erap resign!" and taking close-ups of the angry, cussing placards, T-shirts, and posters and other scenes; "Good Samaritans" giving away mineral water and candy bars, a poor family where the mother and child were lying on a mat while the father watched over, a group of rich folks on their Harley Davidsons, Honda 500s, and Sym scooters that sparkled. . . . And many other different scenes that were vibrant in their similarities but also in their differences.

Immersed in the crowd, Flor C. begins to take photographs. Here, the camera replaces the cell phone as the medium for registering experience. In this passage she initially refers to herself as ako, the first-person singular pronoun in Tagalog. But once she starts to take photographs, the I disappears. The sentences that follow do not contain any pronouns at all. It is as if her walking, moving, listening, and looking are performed impersonally. While we can certainly imagine a person carrying out these activities, Flor C.'s narrative suggests some other agency at work: an *it* rather than an *I*. That *it* of course is the camera Flor C. takes out and begins to aim (*tinutok*). Led by her desire to join the crowd, she begins to act and see like her camera. She stops, then moves on, taking close-ups of "scenes" (*eksenas*) made up of the juxtaposition of various social classes. She is drawn to the appearance of sharp "contrasts" (*pagkaiba*) that are thrown together, existing side by side as if in a montage. The juxtaposition of contrasts, the proximity of social distances, the desire to close in on all sorts of expressions and signs, to draw them into a common, though always shifting, visual field: these are what interest Flor C.'s camera.

These are also precisely the features of the crowd. It is the crowd that drives Flor C. to take out her camera, and in registering the mixing of differences the camera reiterates its workings. Identifying with a camera that brings distances up close and holds differences in sharp juxtaposition, Flor C. begins to take on the telecommunicative power of the crowd. Yet unlike the cell phone, whose political usefulness requires the legitimation of messages by an outside authority, the crowd in Flor C.'s account seems to derive its power from itself. At least in this instance the crowd is sovereign.[32] It does not look beyond itself precisely because it erodes any boundary between inside and outside.

We can see this blurring of boundaries again in Flor C.'s account of entering the Galleria shopping mall next to the center stage of the EDSA protest: "Many times I entered the Galleria to line up for the restroom and at the juice store. During one of my trips there, I was shocked and thrilled [*kinilabutan ako*] when I heard 'Erap resign!' resonating from the food center, cresting up the escalator, aisles, and stores. The mall became black from the 'advance' of middle-class rallyists wearing the uniform symbolic of the death of justice. But the whole place was happy [*masaya*]. Even the security guards at the entrance simply smiled since they could not individually inspect the bags that came before them." She is thrilled and shocked (*kinilabutan ako*) by a sonic wave making its way up the shopping mall. Middle-class "rallyists" dressed in black surged through the aisles, protesting rather than shopping. Like all modern retail spaces, the shopping mall has been designed to manufacture novelty and surprise only to contain them within the limits of surveillance and commodity consumption. But during EDSA II, it is converted into a site for something unexpected and unforeseen. Ordinarily the mall is meant to keep the streets at bay. Now it suddenly merges with them, creating a kind of uncanny enjoyment that even the security guards cannot resist. Formerly anonymous shoppers, middle-class protestors now come across en masse. As shoppers they consumed the products of others' labor and constituted their identity in relation to the spectacle of commodities. But as demonstrators they now shed what made them distinct: their identity as consuming individuals. They are instead consumed and transformed by the crowd. While they may still be recognizably middle class, they simultaneously appear otherwise, advancing in black shirts and chanting slogans. To Flor C. their unfamiliar familiarity produces powerful effects. In the mall Flor C. finds herself somewhere else. As in the streets, the intensification of her sense of displacement produces the sensation of a fleeting, pleasurable connection with the crowd.

However, this pleasurable sense of connection can, at certain times, also turn into a source of anxiety and fear. What is remarkable about Flor C.'s narrative is the way it embraces rather than evades this fear. The result, as we see in the concluding section of her story, is not her mastery or overcoming of the crowd's disorienting pull. Rather, it is her realization of what she takes to be the *saving power* of the crowd. Back on the streets, she wanders onto a flyover, or on-ramp, at the EDSA highway:

When I first went to the flyover, I was caught in the thick waves of people far from the center of the rally. I could barely breathe from the weight of the bodies pressing on my back and sides. I started to regret going to this place that was [so packed] that not even a needle could have gone through the spaces between the bodies. After what seemed like an eternity of extremely small movements, slowly, slowly, there appeared a clearing before me [lumuwag bigla sa harap ko]. I was grateful not because I survived but because I experienced the discipline and respect of one for the other of the people—there was no pushing, no insulting, everyone even helped each other, and a collective patience and giving way ruled [kolektibong pasensiya at pagbibigayan ang umiral]. The night deepened. Hungry again. Legs and feet hurting. I bought squid balls and sat on the edge of the sidewalk. . . . While resting on the sidewalk, I felt such immense pleasure, safe from danger, free, happy in the middle of thousands and thousands of anonymous buddies.

Finding herself amid a particularly dense gathering of bodies, Flor C. momentarily fears for her life. She can barely breathe, overwhelmed by the weight of bodies pressed up against her. Rather than a medium for movement, the crowd is, in this instance, a kind of aporia, a trap, fixing her in place and offering no way out.[33] Yet ever so slowly the crowd moves as if on its own accord. No one says anything, no directives are issued, and no leader appears to reposition bodies. Instead a kind of "collective patience and giving way ruled." The crowd gives and takes, taking while giving, giving while taking, and so suffers the presence of all those that compose it. It is for this reason "patient," which is to say forbearing and forgiving, while forgetting the identities of those it holds and is held by it. Forbearance, forgiveness, and forgetting are always slow, so slow in coming. They thus share in, if not constitute, the rhythm of the work of mourning that in turn always entails the sharing of work.

After what seemed like an eternity of waiting and very little movement, Flor C. suddenly arrives at a clearing. "Lumuwag bigla sa harap ko" (it suddenly cleared in front of me), she says, which can also be translated as "the clearing came before me." Who or what came before whom or what remains tantalizingly uncertain in the text. Earlier, she regretted being trapped in the crowd. But now, she is thrown into a sudden clearing by a force irresistibly intimate yet radically exterior to her. Flor C. is grateful, even as she remains uncertain about the locus of her gratitude. She survives, but for her this is not the most important thing. Rather, what matters is that she was given the chance to experience the "discipline and respect" of a crowd in which no one was pushing or insulting, and everyone seemed to help one another, a condition that in Tagalog is referred to as *damayan*, or cooperation, the very same word used to connote the work of mourning.[34] It is a peculiar sort of discipline that Flor C. undergoes, one that does not interpolate subjects through hierarchies of recognition.[35] Instead, it is a discipline born of mutual restraint and deference—what we might think of as collective caring—that, inasmuch as it does not consolidate identity, loosens the hold of social distinctions.

Crowding as collective caring gives rise to a sense of forbearance and a general economy of deference. At the same time, it does not precipitate recognizable social identities. Rather, it gives way to a kind of saving that Flor C. refers to as the experience of "freedom" (*kalayaan*). Far from being a mob, the crowd here is an embodiment of freedom and incalculable pleasure. It is where a different sense of collectivity resides, one that does away momentarily with hierarchy and the need for recognition. Constraint gives way to an unexpected clearing, to a giving way that opens the way for the other to be free, the other that now includes the self caught in the crowd. And because it is unexpected, this freeing cannot last—just as it cannot be the last, or final, experience of freedom. Here, emancipation, however transitory—and perhaps because it is felt to be so—does not depend on submission to a higher authority that guarantees the truth of messages. Rather, it relies on the dense gathering of bodies held in patient anticipation of a clearing and release.

Accounts of EDSA II indicate that over a million people gathered in the course of four days. These protestors were not all from the middle class. As Flor C.'s remarks show, many who opposed Estrada drew from the ranks of the working class and the urban and rural poor. This heterogeneous crowd was not entirely constituted by texting, for obviously not everyone owned cell phones. It emerged primarily, we might imagine, in response to a call for and the call of justice. Put another way, the crowd at EDSA was held together by the promise of justice's arrival. Here justice is imagined not simply as a redistributive force acting to avenge past wrongs, its violence producing yet more injustice. The nonviolent nature of EDSA II instead suggests that the crowd formed not to exact revenge but to await justice. In so doing it dwelt in a promise that was always yet to be realized. Like freedom and no doubt inseparable from it, justice is always poised to arrive from the future. And it is the unceasing uncertainty of its arrival that constitutes what we might think of as the active passivity and wakeful waiting of the crowd. It is a gathering that greets those whose arrival is never fully completed and that forbears a coming always deferred. Yet it is precisely because justice experienced as a promise comes by not fully coming, and coming in ways unexpected, that it appears as that which is free from any particular sociotechnical determination.

This promise of justice is what Flor C.'s experience of the crowd conveys. The promissory nature of justice means that it is an event whose eventfulness occurs in advance of and beyond any given political and social order. Evading reification and exceeding institutional consolidation, such an event entails a telecommunication of sorts—what Derrida might call "the messianic without a messiah." It would be "the opening up to the future or to the coming of the other as the advent of justice. . . . It follows no determinable

Figure 3.1 The crowd at EDSA II, 2001. Photo by Flor Caagusan.

revelation. . . . This messianicity stripped of everything, this faith without dogma."[36]

In the midst of messianic transmissions Flor C., along with others around her, imagines the dissolution of class differences and feels, at least momentarily, that it is possible to overcome social inequities. She sees in crowding a power that levels the ordering power of the social as such. Past midnight Flor C. finds herself no longer simply herself. Her body hurting, bearing the traces of the crowd's saving power, she sits on the sidewalk, eating squid balls, happy and safe, free in the midst of countless and anonymous "buddies."

Postscript

Utopias, of course, do not last, even if their occasional and unexpected happenings are never the last. Some three months after EDSA II, the newly installed government of President Gloria Macapagal-Arroyo made good on its promise to arrest Estrada on charges of graft and corruption. On 25 April 2001 he was taken from his residence, fingerprinted, and photographed, his mug shot displayed in the media for all to see. The sight of

Estrada treated as a common criminal infuriated his numerous supporters, many from the ranks of the urban poor who had helped him win the largest majority ever in a presidential election. Spurred on by the middle-class leaders of Estrada's party, Puwersa ng Masa (Force of the Masses), and swelled by the ranks of the pro-Estrada Protestant sect Iglesia ni Cristo and the populist Catholic group El Shaddai, a crowd of perhaps 100,000 formed at EDSA and demanded Estrada's release and reinstatement. Unlike those who had gathered there during EDSA II, the crowd in what came to be billed as "Poor People Power" was trucked in by Estrada's political operatives from the slums and nearby provinces and provided with money, food, and, on at least certain occasions, alcohol. In place of cell phones many reportedly were armed with slingshots, homemade guns, knives, and steel pipes. English-language news reports described this crowd as "unruly and uncivilized." They roundly castigated protestors for strewing garbage on the EDSA Shrine, for harassing reporters, and for publicly urinating near the giant statue of the Virgin Mary of EDSA.[37]

Other accounts qualified these depictions by pointing out that many in the crowd were not merely hired thugs or demented loyalists but poor people who had legitimate complaints. They had been largely ignored by the elite politicians, the Catholic Church hierarchy, the middle-class-dominated reformist groups, and the NGOs. Even though Estrada manipulated them, the protestors saw their ex-president as a patron who had given them hope by way of occasional handouts and who addressed them in Tagalog. The middle-class media treated Estrada's supporters as simpletons deficient in moral and political consciousness but worthy of compassion. The vast majority of middle-class opinion thus shared the view that the pro-Estrada crowd differed profoundly from the one that gathered in January during EDSA II. While the latter was technologically savvy and politically sophisticated, the former was retrograde and reactionary. Generation Txt spoke of democratization, accountability, and civil society; the "tsinelas crowd," so-called because of the cheap rubber slippers many protestors wore, was fixated on its "idol," Estrada. In their mystified state they seemed to the middle class barely articulate and incapable of formulating anything other than a desire for revenge on those they deemed responsible for victimizing their patron. If the crowd of EDSA II responded to the circulation of messages sanctioned by a higher authority and the prospect of justice as the promise of freedom, the masa (masses) of People Power III were merely playing out a tragically mistaken identification with their idol. They sought, or so it was assumed, the crude sort of payback typical of many of the ex-president's movie plots.[38]

Middle-class accounts of this other crowd regularly made mention of the "voicelessness" of the urban poor. At the same time, these accounts showed a relative lack of concern with actually hearing—much less recording—any distinctive voices. By emphasizing this voicelessness, the middle class in effect redoubled the masses' seeming inarticulateness. It was as if the masses, without anything intelligible to say, could only act irrationally and violently. "Voiceless," the masses, it was feared, might riot in the streets. Indeed, in the early morning of May 1, they marched from the EDSA Shrine to the presidential palace. Along the way they destroyed millions of pesos' worth of property and caused several deaths and scores of injuries. They were finally dispersed by the police and palace guards.

It is important to note, however, that the protestors were not, in fact, voiceless. While marching to the palace, the masses chanted slogans. Newspaper reports quoted these slogans and in so doing give us a rare chance to actually hear this other crowd: "*Nandito na kami, malapit na ang tagumpay!* [We're here, our victory is close at hand!]" and "*Patalsikin si Gloria! Ibalik si Erap! Nandyan na kami! Maghanda na kayo!* [Get rid of Gloria! Return Erap! We are coming! Get ready!]"[39]

Here the crowd is fueled by the desire to give back to Macapagal-Arroyo what it thinks she gave to them. In return for her unseating of Estrada, it wants to unseat her. She took his place, and now it wants him to take hers. Through its slogans the crowd expresses this giving back of a prior theft. It says, "We are here, our victory is close at hand! We are coming, you'd better be ready!" The crowd thereby took itself for an apocalyptic power. The "we" referred to here has already arrived, even as it continues to come. Certain of their arrival, the protestors ask those who hear to be ready. Having arrived, they will settle their debts, collect what is owed to them, and thereby put an end to their—the crowd's and its audience's—waiting. While the crowd at EDSA II clung to a sense of the messianic without a messiah, this other crowd came as a messianic specter delivered by resentments whose satisfaction can no longer be deferred. It is perhaps for this reason that middle-class observers repeatedly referred to it (in English) as a "mob," "rabble," or "horde." These words imply more than savage or disordered speech and appearance. As the use of the word *horde* indicates, the masses

Figure 3.2 EDSA in 2015, fourteen years after EDSA II. Photo by Gilbert Daroy.

were also seen to be irreducibly alien: foreign invaders encroaching upon a place they had no right to occupy.[40]

Eschewing a stance of forbearance, this crowd demanded recognition without delay. "Here we are!" it shouted. "Be prepared!" For many among the middle class, to hear this crowd was to realize that they were not quite ready to hear them, indeed, that they would always have been unprepared to do so. The masses suddenly became visible in a country where the poor are often viewed by the middle class as literally unsightly, spoken about and spoken down to because they are deemed incapable of speaking up for themselves. They are acknowledged only to be dismissed. Marching to the palace, however, and chanting their slogans, they assumed an apocalyptic agency. They threatened to bring about a day of reckoning that was simultaneously desired and dreaded by those who saw them. In their uncanny visibility, the masses did not so much gain a "voice" that corresponded to a new social identity. Instead they communicated an excess of communication that could neither be summed up nor fully accounted for by those who heard them. Unprepared to hear the crowd's demand that they be prepared, the middle class could only regard it as monstrous. They instead issued their own calls, addressed to their own class, for the conversion of the masses and their domestication by means of "pity," "compassion," and some combination of social programs and educational reform. These calls, however, also demanded that those who made up the crowd, one that was now totally other, be put back in their place. They were to be removed like so much garbage from the EDSA Shrine and the perimeter of the presidential palace.[41]

By late morning on Labor Day, the military, spooked by the specter of Poor People Power, had violently dispersed the marchers. The crowd's outburst, like their abandoned rubber slippers, was relegated to the memory of injustices left unanswered, fueling the promise of revenge and feeding the anticipation of perhaps more uprisings to come.[42]

PART II *Weaponizing Babel*

Figure P.2 (*overleaf*) Iraqi interpreter masked to hide his
identity, Baghdad, 2007. Photo by Danfung Dennis.

CHAPTER 4

Translation, American English, and the
National Insecurities of Empire

Imperial Dialects

Addressing a gathering of university presidents attending a conference at
the State Department on 5 January 2006, President George W. Bush spoke
of the country's dire need for translators to shore up national security. He
promised to spend $114 million to expand the teaching of so-called criti-
cal languages such as Arabic, Farsi, and Chinese at the university as well
as K–12 levels as part of a new federal program called the National Security Language Initiative. The president then illustrated the importance of
learning such languages in the following way: "In order to convince people we care about them, we've got to understand their culture and show
them we care about their culture. You know, when somebody comes to me
and speaks Texan, I know they appreciate Texas culture. When somebody
takes time to figure out how to speak Arabic, it means they're interested
in somebody else's culture. . . . We need intelligence officers who when
somebody says something in Arabic or Farsi or Urdu, know what they're
talking about."[1]

Bush's view on the learning of foreign languages, however crudely
phrased, reflects certain ideas about translation and empire that have a
long history. Since the Spanish conquest and religious conversion of the
native peoples of the New World and the Pacific, various projects of translation have enabled as much as they have disabled the spread of European

empires. Spanish missionaries, for example, labored to Christianize native peoples in the Americas and the Pacific by preaching in the local languages while retaining Latin and Castilian as languages of ritual and rule. British philologists codified Indian languages to spread and consolidate imperial power, and in a similar vein French and Belgian missionaries and colonial administrators seized upon Swahili as an instrument for establishing knowledge of and control over Central Africa in the late nineteenth and early twentieth centuries.[2]

In this chapter I focus on the United States to show not so much its similarities with or differences from earlier empires—though such comparisons are implicit throughout—as to delineate the historical specificity of a nationalist idea of translation in the making of an American Empire. Can translation provide us with a perspective from which to understand the history of the United States in relation to the spread of its power overseas? In particular what role does American English as the national language of rule and allegiance have in shaping American ideas about the translation and, by extension, assimilation of foreign languages and their speakers? What are the limits of this American notion of translation as assimilation? At what point does such a connection fail? And what are the consequences of such a failure for thinking about America's imperial presence in the world?

To address these questions, let me return briefly to Bush's remarks. In referring to his language as "Texan," Bush in fact indexes the centrality of English in mapping America's place in the world. Though perhaps it was said half in jest, his reference to Texan as his native idiom nonetheless makes it sound like a kind of alien tongue analogous to Arabic, Farsi, and Chinese. Like them, it would call for translation. But if Arabic, Urdu, and Chinese are functionally equivalent to Texan, they could also be construed merely as dialectical variations of the universal lingua franca, which no doubt is imagined by Bush to be English. By placing these languages in a series so that they all appear equally foreign, the president reduces their singularity. Setting aside their incommensurability, he sees them all terminating in English. He thereby evacuates foreign languages of their foreignness. From this perspective learning one language is no different from learning another in that they are all meant to refer to English. In this way all speech comes to be assimilated into a linguistic hierarchy, subsumed within the hegemony of an imperial lingua franca. The strangeness of Arabic, Farsi, and so on, like that of Texan, can be made to yield to a domesticating power that would render these languages wholly comprehensible to English speakers and available for conveying American meanings and intentions. As supplements to English, so-called critical languages are thought to be transparent and transportable instruments for the insinuation and imposition of America's will to power.[3]

The systematic instrumentalization of foreign languages to serve nationalist ends runs far and deep in American thinking. It is evident, for example, in the discourse of the Department of Defense. Recent documents such as the "Defense Language Transformation Roadmap" describe knowledge of foreign languages as "an emerging core competency of our twenty-first century Total Force." The ability to translate is deemed "an essential war fighting skill," part of the "vital force capabilities for mission accomplishment." In this regard critical languages, or what are sometimes referred to as "Global War on Terrorism languages," can exist only as part of a "critical weapons system." As a "war-fighting skill," translation is thus weaponized for the sake of projecting American power abroad while ensuring security at home. Such sentiments circulate as common sense in official circles regardless of political affiliations. Hence it is not surprising that Senator Daniel Akaka, a liberal Democrat and chair of the Oversight Committee on Homeland Security, should state in a congressional hearing, "We know that proficiency in other languages is critical to ensuring our national security. The inability of law enforcement officers [and] intelligence officers . . . to intercept information from [foreign] sources . . . presents a threat to their mission and the well-being of our Nation."[4]

The current preoccupation with foreign-language proficiency has its roots in the cold war. In 1958 Congress passed the National Defense Education Act in response to what it called an "educational emergency." In the midst of widespread anxieties about the threat posed by Soviet scientific advances such as the launching of the satellite *Sputnik 1*, the Act provided funding for the development of what Congress referred to as "those skills essential to national defense." Such skills included knowledge of what even then were referred to as "critical languages." These were to be taught in area studies programs newly established in various universities and colleges. From the point of view of the state, the teaching of foreign languages was not about eroding the primacy of English but rather the reverse. Programs for the study of "critical languages" tended to be limited to graduate students and a smaller number of undergraduates. They were designed to create area studies experts whose knowledge of other cultures would help to shore up "our way of life," where English naturally held unchallenged supremacy.[5] We might paraphrase the logic of the law this way: By fostering the ability to translate, "we" make use of the foreigner's language in order to keep their native speakers in their proper place. In learning their language, therefore, "we" wish not to be any less "American" but in fact to be more so. For "we" do not speak a foreign language in order to be like them, that is, to assimilate into the culture of their native speakers. Instead, we do so because "we" want to protect ourselves from them and to ensure that they remain safely within our reach whether inside or outside our borders.

From this brief historical sketch we can glean the rough outlines of the state's interest in foreign languages—an interest that, I hasten to add, did not always coincide with that of individual area studies scholars. To begin with, it is unsurprising that a nationalist imperative linked to an imperial project has governed the programmatic teaching of foreign languages. Translation can be useful to the extent that it responds to this imperative. It is possible, then, to begin to see an American notion of translation, at least as it is articulated from above and ratified, though unevenly, from below. Such a notion turns on at least four assumptions. The first assumption is that language is merely an instrument of communication subservient to human control. It is thus considered to be no more than a malleable medium for conveying human ideas and intentions, as if ideas and intentions could exist outside their material constitution in writing and speech. The second assumption is that languages are inherently unequal in their ability to communicate and, as such, can be arranged into a hierarchy—for example, "critical" over "less critical" languages—depending on their utility and reach. In the U.S. context, American English, as I mentioned earlier (and will return to later), has been deemed exceptionally suited above all other languages for conveying all things exceptionally American to the citizens of the country and to the rest of the world. The third assumption is that given the exceptional qualities of American English as a kind of universal lingua franca, all other languages ought to be reducible to its terms and thereby assimilable into the national linguistic hierarchy. Finally, the fourth assumption is that this process of reduction is precisely the task of translation. In times of emergency, translation is pressed to mobilize foreign languages as parts of a "complex weapons system" with which to secure America's borders even as it globalizes the nation's influence.

The U.S. state thus sees the relative value of foreign languages in relation to their usefulness in the defense of the nation. Their translation is meant to inoculate U.S. citizens from foreign threats. Through translation, foreign languages furnish the tools with which to understand and domesticate what is alien and unfamiliar. In this way they are charged with the job of keeping America at home in the world. In the official and arguably popular imaginary, the foreign can be recognized only when it is subordinated to the domestic. It follows that the apprehension of alien tongues can only amount to their conversion into appendages of a common national speech: English.

Americanizing English

The relationship between the task of translation and the privileged place of English in the United States has a complex history. From its beginnings, the United States has always been a polyglot country.[6] While the majority of European settlers were English speakers, there have always been sizable communities of non-Anglophones. By the late eighteenth century, over one-fourth of the white population spoke a language other than English. In Pennsylvania alone there were enough German speakers that Benjamin Franklin thought of publishing his first newspaper, the *Philadelphische Zeitung* (1732), in that language, and another founding father, Benjamin Rush, even put forth the idea of establishing German-language colleges. Additionally Dutch and French were spoken in various parts of the early Republic, and so too were hundreds of Native American languages both in and outside the Union.

There is also ample evidence that enslaved Africans, in resisting their abject condition, continued to speak their native languages well into the nineteenth century or, in the case of Muslim Africans, knew Arabic, even as Americanized Africans developed a creolized version of English.[7] Continental expansion by way of purchase and war throughout the nineteenth century incorporated large numbers of non-Anglophone groups into the Union, such as French and Spanish speakers in the Northeast, South, and Southwest, while the Treaty of Guadalupe in 1848 was interpreted to mean that Mexicans who had chosen to stay in the newly annexed areas of the California and New Mexico territories retained the right to use Spanish in the public sphere. In the wake of the wars of 1898, the colonization of Puerto Rico in the Caribbean, of Hawaii and Guam and other islands in the Pacific, and of the Philippines in Southeast Asia, where more than one hundred languages in addition to Spanish are spoken, increased the linguistic complexity of the United States. In addition waves of immigration from East, South, and Southeast Asia; eastern and southern Europe; Scandinavia; Africa; the Caribbean; and the Middle East through the past 250 years have further intensified the nation's linguistic mix. Indeed, today one can wander around large metropolitan areas such as New York, Los Angeles, Chicago, and Seattle without having to hear or speak English. As the Canadian scholar Marc Shell once remarked, "If ever there were a polyglot place on the globe, other than Babel's spire, the U.S. is it."[8]

It is important to note, however, that this history of linguistic diversity has unfolded in the shadow of a history of disavowal, a history that insists that the United States has always been, was meant to be, and must forever remain a monolingual nation. John Jay, for example, writes in *The Federalist*, "Providence has been pleased to give this one connected country to one united people, a people descended from the same ancestors, speaking the same language, professing the same religion."[9] Conceived as Anglophone by divine dispensation, "America" is understood here to be a unitary formation, a place where language, religion, and kinship are seamlessly woven into each other.

Still, in the aftermath of the American Revolution, the fact remained that English was the language of the British colonizer. It could not become the language of the new republic without first being transformed—or, better yet, translated—into a distinctly American idiom. Postcolonial figures such as John Adams, Noah Webster, and Franklin felt that British English bore all the hallmarks of the decadence of its native speakers. Americans believed that British English of the 1780s, unlike the English of Milton, Locke, and Shakespeare, was in a state of serious decline. "Taste is corrupted by luxury," Webster intoned, "utility is a forgotten pleasure; genius is buried in dissipation or prostituted to exalt and to damn contending factions."[10] For Americans, then, there was a pressing need to "improve and perfect" English, to remake it into something wholly American. At stake was nothing less than the very survival and progress of the nation. Adams, for example, wrote optimistically about the prospects of this new American language. It was destined to become, like Latin, "the language of the world," furnishing "universal connection and correspondence with all nations."[11] Once Americanized, English would serve as the medium for imparting the exemplary nature of the nation abroad. It would also serve as the means for cultivating a democratic citizenry. According to Adams, the "refinement" and "improvement" of the English language was essential in a democracy where "eloquence will become the instrument for recommending men to their fellow-men, and the principal means of advancement through various ranks and offices."[12] In a society where aristocratic filiations no longer mattered, "eloquence," or a certain facility with the national language, would be an important way of making and remaking reputations and delineating social distinctions.

Early American concerns with the transformation of English in some ways echoed long-standing European attempts to reform vernacular languages in the wake of the hegemony of Latin. As early as the momentous year of 1492, for example, the Spanish humanist Antonio de Nebrija wrote in the preface of his grammar of the Castilian language that "language is the perfect instrument of empire." Looking back at antiquity, Nebrija concluded that "language was always the companion of empire; therefore, it follows that together they begin, grow, and flourish and together they fall." Securing Castilian hegemony in the Iberian Peninsula and spreading it overseas would thus require the codification of the Castilian language.[13]

In eighteenth-century England political, commercial, and imperial expansion led to calls for linguistic reform with the view of establishing a "systematized doctrine of correctness."[14] Various attempts were made to standardize spelling and punctuation and codify grammar in order to lend English the uniformity necessary for governing all spheres of life. In part this search for linguistic regularity grew out of a widespread anxiety among English writers that their language had been on the decline from the standards of Latin and earlier English writing. Jonathan Swift complained in 1712, "From the civil war to this present time I am apt to doubt whether the corruptions in our language have not at least equaled the refinements to it." And John Dryden remarked that the inadequacies of English in his time forced him to first think in Latin as way of arriving at the proper English expression. In *An Essay Concerning Human Understanding*, Locke warned that one of the dangers of writing contracts was the "doubtful and uncertain use of Words, or (which is the same) indetermined Ideas, which they are made to stand for." Thus the need to "purify" English and guard against its "degeneration" from arbitrary foreign borrowings and idiomatic "barbarisms" was inseparable from securing the social contract on the basis of a commonly understood language of consent. So did Samuel Johnson regard his task in writing his dictionary as one of "refin[ing] our language to grammatical purity [and] clear[ing] it from colloquial barbarisms, licentious idioms, and irregular combinations." The "purification" of English would allow the English themselves to "ascertain" and "perfect" its use. This would lead, Joseph Priestly wrote, to the spread of "their powers and influence abroad, and their arts, sciences and liberty at home."[15]

These projects of linguistic reform tied to the imperatives of both domestic order and imperial expansion clearly influenced early Americans such as Webster in their efforts to, as he saw it, "redeem" English from the "degradations" of empire.[16] For Webster, the revolution that overthrew British imperial authority should continue with the overthrow of its linguistic standards. "As an independent nation," he wrote in 1789, "our honor requires us to have a system of our own, in language as well as in government. Great Britain whose children we are, and whose language we speak, should no longer be our standard, for the taste of her writers is already corrupted and her language on the decline."[17] Ridding "ourselves" of a corrupt state necessitated purifying its "corrupt" speech. Hence while "we" have abandoned the mother, we can retain the mother tongue only if it can be reformed and turned into "our" national language. The emergence of this revitalized American English, Webster speculated, would prove to be momentous. In the face of its inevitable advance "all other languages [spoken in the country] will waste away—and within a century and a half, North America will be peopled with hundreds of millions of men all speaking the same language. . . . The consequence of this uniformity [of language] will be an intimacy of social intercourse hitherto unknown, and a boundless diffusion of knowledge."[18]

Webster thus envisions the national language as poised between overcoming its origins in the "corrupt" language of empire and laying the foundation for a kind of new empire over all other languages in the Republic. Once established, this "common tongue" promised to subsume linguistic differences into what Webster calls a "uniformity." At the same time, and for the same reason, American English would foster an "intimacy of social intercourse hitherto unknown." Its telecommunicative force, that is, its capacity to bring distances up close, would conjure a perfect union. But that union would be one where multilingual realities would have to give way to a monolingual hegemony.

In his attempts to wean English from its British origins, Webster laid great stress on reforming by simplifying spelling in order to standardize a distinctly American pronunciation. His spellers and his dictionary initially met with resistance and ridicule but came to be widely used in schools and by the American public. Addressing the readers of his dictionary as "my fellow citizens," Webster viewed his linguistic work as part of "the common treasure of patriotic exertions." The United States emerges here as the rejection of a certain Europe, one "grown old in folly, corruption and tyranny . . . where literature is declining and human nature debased." By developing a "purity of language," this "infant Empire," as Webster calls it, would come to "promote virtue and patriotism."[19] In a similar vein he was also concerned with correcting what he regarded as the "barbarisms" and "gross violations" that local idioms committed against English, as evident in the "vicious pronunciation that had prevailed extensively among the common people of this country."[20] He urged Americans to "unite in destroying provincial and local distinctions, in resisting the stream of corruptions that is ever flowing from ignorance and pride, and in establishing one uniform standard of elegant pronunciation." It was in the interest of protecting the language from "disfigurement" that Webster put forth his orthographic reforms in what would become his remarkably popular spelling book.[21] "Nothing but the establishment of schools and some uniformity in the use of books can annihilate differences in speaking and preserve the purity of the American tongue," he wrote.[22]

Like Adams's interest in the popular acquisition of eloquence, Webster's fixation on elocution and "a sameness in pronunciation" grew out of a larger political concern: that local variants of English, no matter how small, would inevitably "excite ridicule—[for] a habit of laughing at the singularities of strangers is followed by disrespect; and without respect, friendship is a name, and social intercourse a mere ceremony. . . . Small causes such as a nickname or a vulgar tone in speaking have actually created a dissocial spirit between the inhabitants of a different state." Left to themselves linguistic differences would proliferate and inflame "pride and prejudice," leading Webster to worry that without "uniformity" in speech, "our political harmony" would be at serious risk.[23]

It is possible to see in Webster's linguistic reforms a practice of translation working within the same language, or what some scholars have called intralingual translation.[24] We can think, for example, of such locutions as *in other words, put differently, that is to say, for example,* and so on, as speech acts that indicate the working of translation within the same language. In Webster intralingual translation is twofold. The translation of the more mannered British speech into the more straightforward American idiom occurs alongside the attempt to contain or "annihilate," as Webster puts it, dialectical variants of American English. The national language thus emerges from a kind of double translation. On the one hand, the original language is altered, its spellings "simplified" and "purified." On the other hand, what Webster referred to as the "shameful mutilations" wrought by local idioms are corrected and superseded.[25] American English as the language of "political harmony" and democratic civility requires as its condition of possibility the violent reworking of differences into sameness. The original in all its "corrupt," which is to say stylistic, profusion is to be sublated, while local variants, which is to say all other competing translations, are to be suppressed. Out of this prescribed supersession and suppression a "uniformity" of speech is thought to arise, one that would underwrite the national security of the republic. Translation within the same language thereby brings about the promise of a lingua franca connecting citizens across geographical and social divides, allowing them mobility and advancement. But it also requires the "annihilation" of differences, effecting the systematic annexation of mother tongues and their wayward children into the governing home of a single national speech.

I want to hypothesize that the Americanization of English, which is to say the translation of English into a national language popularized by Webster in his spelling books and dictionary, served as an important model for dealing with foreign languages in the years to come. In the following section, I argue that the early American history of vernacularizing English offered a way to assimilate non-Anglophone languages into a linguistic hierarchy, thereby containing polylingualism within the borders of national monolingualism.

The Babel of Monolingualism

In the wake of Webster's reforms, it is not difficult to detect in both liberal and conservative writers a recurring insistence on the unassailable link between American English and American nationality conceived as synonymous with American democracy. One is seen to be inconceivable without the other. A common language ruling over all others is held to be the prerequisite for achieving a common life steeped in an egalitarian ethos. Non-Anglophones have long been expected by the nation and by the state—at least since the later nineteenth century—to exchange their mother tongue for the national language in order to become full citizens.[26] Equality under the law implied—though it did not legally mandate—the inequality of languages. Non-English speakers marked as foreigners are expected to publicly set aside their first language in acknowledgment of the ever-present demand to speak the lingua franca. The priority of the latter lay in the fact that it is the language of laws and rights. In this regard it is useful to note that American English has never been declared the official language of the United States, though a number of states have written such a provision into their own constitution.[27] Rather, its hegemony is based precisely on the fact that it seemed to arise as a handmaiden of democracy. English is the lingua franca with which to claim equal protection under the law. From the perspective of compulsory monolingualism, English is thus invested with an uncommon power that no other idiom has been able to match.

The systematic privileging of American English not surprisingly sustains a pattern of marginalizing the mother tongues of native peoples and non-Anglophone immigrants alike.[28] At the best of times and places such marginalization might give rise to a liberal tolerance for bilingualism, whereby the first language is seen as a way of bridging the speaker's transition to English. Within the context of this liberal view, the retention of the mother tongue is a means by which to soften the shocks of assimilation. Rather than an alternative, the native language is regarded like any other foreign language: as an instrument for consolidating the dominant place of English.[29] In times of crisis and war, however, the marginalization of non-Anglophone languages tends to give rise to urgent calls for the rapid assimilation or expulsion of their speakers. For instance, the 1887 annual report of the federal commissioner of Indian affairs reveals the great animosity toward native languages that was commonly felt by whites. In the interest of crushing Indians' resistance and producing among them a "sameness of sentiment and thought," the commissioner urged that "their barbarous dialects should be blotted out and the English language substituted." It was only through English that Native Americans, rendered irredeemably foreign in the eyes of white settlers, could be converted into real Americans, "acquir[ing] a knowledge of the Constitution and their rights and duties there under." For unlike Indian languages, which were regarded as "utterly useless," English was seen as "the language of the greatest and most powerful enterprising nationality beneath the sun . . . which approaches nearer than any other nationality to the perfect protection of its people."[30]

In the name of maintaining this "perfect protection," translation would not only substitute the first for a second language but also obliterate the former and presumably the very cultures that it sustained. Theodore Roosevelt wrote in a similar vein in 1917 about the danger of harboring immigrants who, by virtue of speaking a foreign language, were most likely "paying allegiance to a foreign power." Riding the wave of anti-immigrant hysteria (directed particularly at German speakers) that swept the country amid the First World War, Roosevelt explicitly links the question of language to national security: "We have room for but one language here, and that is the English language. . . . It would be not merely a misfortune but a crime to perpetuate differences of language in this country." For Roosevelt the "crime" of allowing linguistic diversity to prosper would result in opening up the country to foreign agents who, in their comings and goings, would transform America into a "huge polyglot boarding-house." Doing so would subvert the very idea of America as a "crucible [that] must melt all who are cast in it . . . into one American mould." As "children of the crucible," Americans were the products of "the melting pot of life in this free land," where "all the men and women of all nations who come hither emerge as Americans and nothing else. . . . Any force which attempts to retard that assimilative process is a force hostile to the highest interest of the country."[31]

English, of course, would be the measure and means of assimilation. Being "American and nothing else" meant speaking English and nothing else. Roosevelt thus situates monolingual citizens on the side of national identity and security. But in doing so he also places them in relation to the menacing presence of their shadowy other: the polyglot foreigner whose uncertain allegiance and rootless existence make him or her a dangerous enemy. In the context of this militant monolingualism, we sense how the work of translation was geared to go in only one direction: toward the transformation of the foreign into an aspect of the domestic, and thus of the plurality of native tongues into the imperious singularity of a national tongue. The imperative of assimilation underlay the substitution of languages so that translation was directed toward not only the subordination of the original but its outright abandonment. But there is something more. Roosevelt and those who follow in his wake—for example, the "100 percent American" nativists of the early twentieth century, the advocates of the Official English constitutional amendment of the 1980s, the proponents of English Only laws in the 1990s, all the way up to a broad range of Americans today who, anxious about "terrorists" and "immigrants" and often conflating the two, indignantly ask why they should have to be told by phone-answering services and ATMs to "press '1' for English" or "oprima dos por español"[32]—all of them in their mania for monolingualism see translation as a kind of labor that only non-Anglophones should have to do. Since it is "they" who must assimilate, it is therefore "they," not "us," who must translate their native tongue into English. The reverse would be unthinkable. For as citizens of this country, aren't we already fully assimilated? Haven't we already successfully forgotten our polylingual origins? As such aren't we entitled to think that we have arrived at a condition of complete monolingualism?

Thus the thinking behind monolingual citizenship: it is assumed to be a kind of achievement rather than a limitation insofar as it comes about through the violence of translation—the work of repressing one's first language in favor of a second.[33] Monolingual citizenship is perhaps related to settler colonialism. In both cases, it is about the conquest of origins as much as original inhabitants. Regarded as a kind of achievement, they confer on monolingual-settler citizens a sense of entitlement: nothing less than emancipation from the labor of translation and the freedom from the foreignness of languages in one case, and from the foreignness of origins— indigenous and immigrant—in the other. It is not surprising, then, that those who consider themselves assimilated (or on their way to being so) experience the recurrence of signs of linguistic difference alongside ethnic difference either as an occasion for racially tinged humor or as a kind of "cultural assault." In either case evidence of an enduring polylingualism appears to English-only speakers as an unsettling return of what should have been repressed. The sight of Chinese or Hindi writing on billboards or the sound of Tagalog or Arabic can only infringe on the their freedom from translation and the enjoyment that accrues to monolingual citizenship.

From this perspective the popular appeal of American English lies precisely in its capacity to grant U.S. citizens the powerful illusion of freedom from their origins. Monolingualism as the successful substitution of one's first language for a second also affords the semblance of release from the demands of repressing one language in favor of another. Only those still dwelling in the nation's "polyglot boarding-houses" are expected to toil in the fields and factories of translation. By contrast, fluency in English as the privileged proof of full citizenship—certainly in a cultural though not necessarily in a legal sense—means simply this: no further translation is necessary. The end of translation—which is to say, assimilation—thus marks an end to translation. It is the cure for the curse of linguistic difference bedeviling humans since Babel's destruction.

Or is it?

The historical wishfulness for and of monolingual citizenship grows in part out of the remarkable tenacity of the myth of America as exceptional and exemplary in its capacity to melt differences into sameness.[34] This exceptionalist faith, with its Christian genealogy, arguably lies at the basis of American nationalism. It is worth noting, however, that the fable of the melting pot is often accompanied by its opposite image: the fragmentation and confusion of Babel. To cite just one example, in response to the post–civil rights emergence of multicultural and multilingual polities, the historian Arthur Schlesinger wrote, "The national ideal had once been e pluribus unum. Are we now to belittle unum and glorify pluribus? Will the center not hold? Or will the melting pot yield to the Tower of Babel?"[35] The linguist and one-time senator from California S. I. Hayakawa used to put it more bluntly in his campaign mailers for a constitutional amendment to make English the official language: "Melting pot, yes. Tower of Babel, no."[36] "Babel" here is another version of Roosevelt's "polyglot boarding-house," a country besieged by Webster's "dissocial spirit." It is the dystopian counterpoint to the monolingual melting pot, a country where the confusion of tongues augurs national collapse.

It is perhaps worth recalling the story of Babel in the book of Genesis. Coming after the Great Flood, it relates the fate of the descendants of yet another Noah who sought to build a tower that would reach up to the heavens. It is instructive to note in this regard that the word babel has two meanings. The more common root, the Hebrew balal, means "to confuse," but the other, seen in the word's Akkadian root, babilu, means "gateway of God." Babel thus harbors two mutually opposed meanings: a state of confusion and a passage to unification. The very word encapsulates the allegory of exile from the state of perfect unity between words and things, between signs and their referents, thereby making translation an unending task. People's attempts to build a tower that would have led to the heavens was a way of saying that they did not need a messiah, or what in the New Testament would be pronounced as the Word of God; rather they themselves could save themselves, since they already spoke one language. Seeking to punish their hubris, God decides to "confound their language" and scatter them about the face of the earth. Folk retellings and pictorial depictions of this story show the tower itself laid waste by God's wrath.[37]

In the American invocations of Babel, its double meaning is usually forgotten. What is recalled is its divine dispersion into a state of linguistic confusion, not its linguistic unity prior to God's punishment. It is the fallen Babel, with its wild profusion of languages, which is made to stand in stark contrast to the idealized linguistic order of the United States. As Babel redeemed, the United States is precisely where *unum* comes to rule over *pluribus*. Yet the structural proximity of Babel to America suggests that the latter does not simply negate the former but in fact retraces its fate. Babel is the specter that haunts American English. It informs, in the strong sense of that word, the hierarchy of languages on which monolingual citizenship rests. For as we saw, the hegemony of English is an effect of translation—both intralingual, within English, and interlingual, between English and other languages. In this way national monolingualism is itself divided, requiring even as it disavows the labor of translation. The universality of the lingua franca is thus radically contingent on the endurance and mutation of regional dialects and creole speech: Spanglish and Taglish, Hawaiian pidgin, black English, and rural and regional dialects of all sorts, to name only a few. Similarly American monolingualism is never quite free from the polylingualism of its non-Anglophone citizenry: native peoples of the continent and the islands, first-generation immigrants from all over the world, Spanish speakers from Puerto Rico and Latin America spread out across the country, and so on. Demanding recognition and participation in the public sphere, some push for bilingual education and others for multilingual ballots. Many continue to inhabit mediascapes, from print to TV to radio, in their native languages and expect to press something other than 1 for English on the phone or at the ATM. We can see, then, how America is less the New World repudiation of Babel than its uncanny double. For Babel is not the catastrophic downfall of the city upon the hill, but in fact its condition of possibility. How so?

Recall that the allegory of Babel connotes the state of unregulated linguistic difference. To dwell in this state requires the constant labor of translation—constant insofar as no single act of translation can ever exhaust, much less reduce, the singularity of any particular language. Babel therefore reveals not only the necessity of translation but also its limits. The persistence of difference means that there is something about languages that resists assimilation and therefore translation into a single linguistic hierarchy, into a single tower, as it were, much less into Twin Towers. It is possible, for example, to translate Tagalog or Spanish poetry into English (or vice versa), but not without losing the rhythmic elements and myriad references of the original. To compensate for this loss the translator must provide explanatory notes, thereby introducing an excess that was not there in the original. Subtracting while adding, translations always come up short even as they exceed the original. Thus the impossibility of definitive translations, given that there is no perfect equivalence of one language with another. Rather there are only the uneven and imperfect approximations. In this way each language remains to a significant degree untranslatable even as it calls out for more translation. It is as if in translating your Arabic into my Texan, and my Texan into your Arabic, we find ourselves mutually mistranslating, then trying again, only to add to our earlier mistranslations. And since my Texan and your Arabic are incommensurable, neither of them can be annexed to a single lingua franca. Instead what we come to understand is that there is something that resists our understanding. What we end up translating is the sense that something in our speech remains untranslatable and yet remains the basis for any future translations.

This Babel of ongoing translation amid what remains untranslatable is the "other" that is set against America. Imagined as an egalitarian community based on a unifying language that, as Webster wrote, "lays to waste" other idioms, America is usually conceived as the overcoming of Babel. As the "melting pot," it is that which was ordained to put an end to translation and the untranslatability of all originals. But this idealized vision of America requires that there be a Babel to vanquish and overcome, again and again. For without the specter of the untamed profusion of tongues, the New World myth of a monolingual America would make no ideological sense. At the same time, the very nature of Babel guarantees that there will never be such a thing as a perfectly monolingual country. To put it another way, Babel simultaneously makes and unmakes America as myth and as the reality that requires such a myth in order to make sense of itself in the world. To translate this further would strain the very limits of translation, but let me try: There is America only if there is Babel. But this also means that there can be no America when there is Babel.

This strange intimacy and impossible possibility of Babel and America became quite apparent during the U.S. invasion and occupation of Iraq, which holds the very site of the biblical Babel (or Babylon, as it is more commonly called), along the Euphrates River near present-day Baghdad. It was here that the U.S. military sought to literalize the allegory of Babel even as it sought to re-erect the metaphorical towers of American exceptionalism. Both projects would end in disaster. For in the havoc and confusion of U.S.-occupied Iraq, as I hope to show, translation became dislodged and dislocated from its subservience to assimilation. Rather than render language suppliant to the will of its speakers, translation in this modern-day American Babel confounded (and still confounds) both the identity and the intentions of its users. Yielding neither a stable social nor linguistic order, translation instead brought about the ongoing suspension of both. In the confused conditions of military occupation, the work of translation, as we shall see, was constantly arriving at its limits, overtaken by the return of that which remains untranslatable. How does this happen?

Traduttore, Traditore

From the beginning of the U.S. invasion and occupation of Iraq, a number of news accounts began to appear about the role, at once indispensable and troubling, of Arabic-speaking translators in the occupation. I want to set aside for the moment the role of American and Arab American translators and instead concentrate on Iraqi nationals who served as translators for the U.S. military, though I suspect that my remarks about the latter will have some implications for understanding the role of the former.[38]

Translators are also called interpreters, which is why among the U.S. soldiers they were popularly referred to as "terps." Unlike the Americans they worked for, interpreters were forced to hide their identity. They often covered their face with a ski mask and sunglasses as they ventured outside the military bases and adopted American pseudonyms such as "Eric" or "Sally" so as to protect themselves from being singled out for insurgent attacks. At the same time, their identity within the U.S. military remained unsettled and unsettling inasmuch as their presence generated both relief and suspicion among soldiers. Some interpreters earned the military's trust and gratitude, and a handful of the Iraqi nationals were granted asylum to move to the United States. The small numbers who managed to acquire visas usually did so through the personal intercession of the particular American soldier they worked for rather than through any systematic U.S. policy to resettle them. Once relocated in the United States, they came to depend on the kindness of the soldier who brought them, while often avoiding other Iraqis for fear of suffering reprisals.[39] Aliens in their new surroundings, they continued to be alienated from their own countrymen. Translators who were killed, especially those among the very few women interpreters, were treated with tender regard, often memorialized by U.S. soldiers as "one of us."[40]

Still, doubts always lingered amid reports of some interpreters sending information to the insurgents. As one U.S. soldier put it, "These guys [i.e., interpreters] have guts to do what they do. And we'd be nowhere without them. We'd be lost. But you always have this fear that they might be leaking op-sec [operational security] stuff. You want to trust them, but you're still reserved."[41] Given that most American soldiers did not speak Arabic, interpreters, as one report put it, provided the "public face of the occupation."[42] Essential in conducting military operations, they nonetheless were thought to threaten them by leaking information. They mediated the vast gulf that separated American soldiers from the Iraqi people, often defusing conflict by being able to decipher, for example, documents that to Americans may look like plans for smuggling weapons but that turned out to be no more than sewing patterns.[43] Without them soldiers "were as good as deaf and dumb on the battlefield," as one marine told a Senate hearing.[44]

Yet despite their essential function in fighting insurgents, they were also feared as potential insurgents themselves. Moving between English and Arabic, translators allowed largely monolingual Americans to communicate with Iraqis and for this reason were integrated into the ranks and given uniforms and salaries. But their loyalty remained suspect. Interpreters were the only ones searched within the base (especially after every meal) and forbidden to carry cell phones and cameras, send email, play video games, and even swim in the pool.[45] They were subjected to incessant racial insults—"raghead," "jihad," and "camel jockey," among others—and at the same time were forced to exit the base with neither weapons nor armor to protect themselves.[46]

Just by being who they were, translators thus found themselves stirring interest and sending out messages beyond what they had originally intended. Without meaning to they generated meanings outside of their control. In this way they came across as alien presences that seemed to defy assimilation even as they were deemed indispensable to the assimilation of aliens. They were "foreign in a domestic sense," as much as they were domestic in a sense that remained enduringly foreign.[47]

It was precisely because they were of such great value to the U.S. forces that translators were often targeted by insurgents and reviled by most Iraqis. They were accused of being mercenaries, collaborating with the United States to kill other Iraqis, and so they faced constant threats of being kidnapped and killed themselves. One Iraqi interpreter with the pseudonym "Roger" said, "If you look at our situation, it's really risky and kind of horrible. Outside the wire, everybody looks at us like we are back-stabbers, like we betrayed our country and our religion, and then inside the wire they look at us like we might be terrorists."[48] Interpreters thus came to literalize that old adage "traduttore—tradditore" (translator—traitor), at times with tragic results. Stranded between languages and societies, translators were also exiled from both. Neither native nor foreign, they were both at the same time. Their uncanny identity triggered a recurring crisis on all sides. It was as if their capacity for mediation endowed them with a power to disturb and destabilize far out of proportion to their socially ascribed and officially sanctioned positions. But it was a power that also constituted their profound vulnerability.

These and many other stories about interpreters give us a sense that within the context of the U.S. occupation of Iraq, translation worked only too well. That is, it produced effects and relations that were difficult if not impossible to curb. Faced with the translator, both Americans and Iraqis were gripped with the radical uncertainty about the interpreter's loyalty and identity. Translators came across as simultaneously faithful and unfaithful or, more precisely, faithful to their task by being unfaithful to their origins. Rather than promote understanding and hospitality, the work of translation seemed to have spawned misgivings and misrecognition. In dealing with an interpreter one was addressed in one's own language—Arabic or English—by an other who also had access to an idiom and culture alien because unavailable to one.

Faced with the need to depend on such an other, one tended to respond with ever intensifying suspicions. Such suspicions were repeatedly manifested in racial insults, often escalating into violence and in some cases into murder, thereby stoking even more suspicions. Iraqis saw in the translator one of their own used against them, a double agent who bore their native language now loaded like a weapon with alien demands. For the majority of U.S. soldiers, those whose English only cut them off from rather than connected them with Iraqis, the interpreters' indispensability was also the source of their duplicity, making them potential insurgents. On all sides terps appeared as enemies disguised as friends whose linguistic virtuosity masked their real selves and their true intentions.

In this and other similar contexts the task of the translator will always be mired in a series of intractable and irresolvable contradictions. It begins with the fact that translation itself is a highly volatile act. As the displacement, replacement, transfer, and transformation of the original into another language, translation is incapable of definitively fixing meanings across languages. Rather, as with the story of Babel, it consists precisely in the proliferation and confusion of possible meanings and therefore in the impossibility of arriving at a single one. For this reason it repeatedly brings into crisis the locus of address, the interpretation of signs, the agency of mediation, and the ethics of speech. Hence it is impossible for imperialists as well as those who oppose them to fully control its workings, much less recuperate them. The treachery and treason inherent in translation in a time of war are the insistent counterpoints to the American notion of translation as monolingual assimilation, with its promise of democratic communication and the just exchange of meanings. In the body of the interpreter, translation reaches its limits. As the uncanny doubles of U.S. soldiers and Iraqi insurgents, terps produced neither meaning nor domination, but instead brought about the circulation of that which remained untranslatable. In the endless war on terror, translation continues to be at permanent war with itself.

Translation at war and as war: How do we understand this?

I want to conclude this chapter with a brief response. If translation is like war, is it possible that war is also like translation? It is possible, I think, if we consider that the time of war is like the movement of translation. There is a sense that both lead not to the privileging of order and meaning but to the emergence of what I have been calling the untranslatable. Wartime spreads what Nietzsche called in the wake of the Franco-Prussian War "an all consuming fever" that creates a crisis in historical thinking.[49] So much of the way we think about history, certainly in the Westernized parts of our planet since the Enlightenment, is predicated on a notion of time as the succession of events leading toward increasingly more progressive ends. Wartime decimates that mode of thinking. Instead it creates mass disorientation at odds with the temporal rhythms of progress and civilization. In this way wartime is what Samuel Weber refers to as "pure movement." It is a "whirlwind . . . that sweeps everything up in its path and yet goes nowhere. As a movement, the whirlwind of war marks time, as it were, inscribing it in a destructive circularity that is both centripetal and centrifugal, wrenching things and people out of their accustomed places, displacing them and with them, all [sense] of place as well. . . . Wartime thus wreaks havoc with traditional conceptions of space and time and with the order they make possible."[50]

It is precisely the disordering effect of war on our notions of space and time that brings it in association with translation, which scatters meaning, displaces origins, and exposes the radical undecidability of references, names, and addresses. Put differently, translation in wartime intensifies the experience of untranslatability and thus defies the demands of imperial assimilation. It is arguably this stark exposure of translation's limits that we see, for example, in the uncanny body of the Iraqi interpreter. Such a body, now ineradicably part of our own national-imperial body politic, generates the sense of severe disorientation, sending back to us a Babel-like scattering of discourses and opinions about the war. Just as civilizational time engenders the permanent possibility of wartime, the time that is out of joint and out of whack, so the time of translation is haunted by untranslatability, the feverish circulation of misrecognition and uncertainty from which we can find neither safety nor security, national or otherwise.

....

CHAPTER 5

Targeting Translation

Counterinsurgency and the Weaponization of Language

Colonizing Lifeworlds

On 2 January 2011, the *Washington Post* reported that the U.S. Air Force had unveiled its "new revolutionary surveillance system," calling it, with no hint of irony, the "Gorgon Stare." It consists of a fleet of drone airplanes remotely piloted from the United States, each mounted with nine video cameras, at a cost of $17.5 million per drone. Flying continuously over much of the border between Afghanistan and Pakistan, the camera-laden drones are designed to stream high-resolution images of every movement on the ground in real time to soldiers armed with computer tablets the size of an iPad. Video data are stored for future viewing on servers kept in shipping containers somewhere in Iowa. The air force has also hired private contractors with a background in televising football games on ESPN and producers of reality TV shows to organize the retrieval and replay of images so that "analysts can study them to determine, for instance, who planted the improvised bomb or what the patterns of life in a village are." Touting this immense visual power, an air force officer exults, "Gorgon Stare will be looking at a whole city, so that there will be no way for the adversary to know what we're looking at, and we can see everything."[1]

As with the figure of Medusa, Gorgon Stare sees but cannot be looked at. It refuses reciprocity, assuming a position that is as transcendent as it is all-knowing of whatever it casts its gaze on. Thanks to aerial surveillance refined and expanded by digital technologies, the air force can claim to monopolize vision itself. It transforms seeing into a weapon targeted at any and all things below.[2] But as the rest of the newspaper article points out, the weaponization of vision is mired in certain complications. The all-seeing Gorgon Stare invariably generates "oceans of information" that cannot be fully processed, overwhelming attempts at mining them for actionable intelligence. Assuming the camera's perspective, soldiers "see everything" and so see too much. Their vision is checked by the deluge of data. Paralyzed, they suffer the effects of staring out of, only to stare into, the Gorgon's eyes.[3]

As it turns out, the very power of this air force Medusa is also its liability. High-tech aerial surveillance, to be effective, requires the supplementation of low-tech means. As another official put it, the video-equipped drones must still rely on "eyewitness reports and boots on the ground." These provide views from below by way of face-to-face contacts with the targeted population and a grasp of "local knowledge." "Watching an entire city," another official concedes, "means nothing unless you can put a context to it."[4] To work effectively the panoptic eye requires the aid of partial vision, fleeting glances, and periodic blindness. These constitute the crucial materials for the weaponization of sight. It is precisely the conversion of the local, the particular, and the everyday formed by the ongoing relationships between occupiers and occupied into weapons of war and pacification that has historically informed the strategic thrust of U.S. counterinsurgency. Where conventional warfare has concentrated on the destruction and unconditional submission of the enemy, counterinsurgency—recognizing the shifting lines between insurgent fighter and civilian population—focuses primarily on "protecting populations."[5] Conventional military doctrine has long regarded combat as the primary role of the soldier, who is trained, as one army officer put it, "to be the wrath of God, able to bring death and destruction anywhere at any time."[6]

By contrast, the doctrine of counterinsurgency recasts war fighting in political terms, as a means not only to "clear" the land of insurgents but to "hold" the population and "build" new institutions to "save" the people from future revolutionary "contaminations." Victory in the context of counterinsurgent warfare is measured not by the number of enemies vanquished but by the increase in trust and sympathy among native peoples that would wean them away from the insurgents' influence. Counterinsurgency theorists thus argue for a kind of "sociological mission" whereby the invasion and occupation of a country would not only lead to the provision of basic needs such as "food, water, shelter, health care, and a means of living" but would also "ensure freedom of worship, access to education, equal rights for women." Indeed, counterinsurgent warfare would bring nothing less than the conversion of the population into such "universal values" as "mercy, restraint, proportional force, and just war," providing a "more holistic form of human security" that would include "economic, social, civil, and political rights."[7] In countering the "barbarism" of insurgents, American counterinsurgency would "not just dominate land operations but . . . change entire societies."[8] Such changes would include the institutionalization of human rights and an "environment where business can thrive" and where "providing security" promises to create a "positive business environment . . . to drive the economy."[9] Thus would counterinsurgency channel popular energies into building a new civil society on the basis of a stable nation-state naturally predisposed out of gratitude and economic and political interests to ally itself with the United States.

Recalling earlier imperial projects, counterinsurgency requires ongoing conversion. Just as Habsburg Spain sought to conquer the Americas and the Pacific through the conversion of native peoples to Catholicism in the wake of the Reformation, so the U.S. Empire has sought to dominate the world by seeking to convert its peoples into neoliberal forms of governance in the wake of the attacks of 9/11. Both conversion and counterinsurgency seek to rid the world of insurgents, religious as well as political, establishing in their wake a new order of civic life ordered around the broad concerns of the empire. And since both entail the daily colonization of the lifeworld of both occupiers and occupied, they have neither temporal limits nor fixed spatial boundaries. Like the project of imperial conversion, counterinsurgency is dedicated to "securing all the 'ungoverned (i.e., unconverted) spaces' around the globe." Led by the United States, regarded by its military and political leaders as "the indispensable nation," such a mission enjoins American allies with the call for planetary policing and permanent war.[10]

Much has been written about the vicissitudes of counterinsurgency as a crucial complement to counterterrorism in the U.S. occupation of Iraq and Afghanistan. In response to the disastrous losses on the ground at the hands of Iraqi and Afghan insurgents in 2005, the U.S. military turned to counterinsurgent strategies from 2006 until about the middle of 2012. While recent events such as the Great Recession of 2008 and the increasing reliance on more cost-effective, but no less deadly, drone aircraft have tended to de-emphasize counterinsurgency, it continues to be a significant supplement to counterterrorist and other war-fighting approaches. In this chapter I do not mean to retrace the history of counterinsurgency or comment on its historiography, as many others already have.[11] Instead I want to focus on something I alluded to earlier: counterinsurgency as both the process and the effect of a certain conversion, which is to say translation of, things into weapons. Given its redemptive ambition of "saving" native peoples, I am particularly interested in counterinsurgency's attempts to "weaponize" and "target" one of the most common things in their lives, indeed the very thing that lends to their lives a sense of commonality: their language.

Attempts to convert languages into tools of conquest are neither new nor limited to the United States. They inhere in colonizing practices found in modern Western empires that, to paraphrase Heidegger, have "set upon" the world in order to "unlock" its potential, so that "what is unlocked is transformed, what is transformed is stored up, what is stored up is, in turn, distributed and what is distributed is switched about ever anew." Conversion in this sense entails the translation of things and humans into a "standing reserve," that is, into parts of larger technosocial assemblages for the disposal of a colonizing power. The militarized conversion of languages into weapons is part of this process. It discloses the powerful drive to monopolize the ordering, deployment, and securing of all communicative possibilities by the agents of empire, a drive that engulfs those agents themselves. But as we shall see, the weaponization of languages, like the colonial Christian conversion of native peoples, can run aground. It can be repeatedly undone by the very means used to unlock, deploy, and secure the communicative power of language: translation.[12]

In what follows I ask how the U.S. military has sought to convert languages—those of others as well as its own—into weapons of war through the strategic deployment of translation practices. I examine a range of approaches used to seize and stockpile languages into a standing reserve. These include efforts to train soldiers in foreign languages, attempts to develop automatic translation systems, and the formalization of protocols for expropriating and regulating the mediating power of native interpreters. I also inquire into the contradictions that inhere in such tactics and their implications for the success or failure of counterinsurgency. Finally,

I ask if there are moments when translation works otherwise, evading the instrumentalizing drive of the military in the face of an insurgent force that resides in language as such, one that thwarts attempts at counterinsurgent conversion. Attending to the recurrence of these moments, I suggest, opens us to the ethicopolitical implications that come with probing the limits of the militarized conversion of speech.

The Language-Enabled Soldier

One of the ways the military has sought to weaponize foreign languages is to teach them to soldiers. Since World War II much of the foreign-language training for military personnel has been conducted at the Defense Language Institute Foreign Language Center in Monterey, California; its motto is "Defending Freedom through Linguistic Readiness."[13] However, with the troop surges demanded by counterinsurgency starting in 2005, there emerged the pressing need to develop more language training programs and quickly equip soldiers with some rudimentary linguistic skills. For example, starting around 2007 the Fort Lewis Foreign Language Training Center near Tacoma, Washington, began conducting ten-month courses in Arabic language and culture for members of the Stryker Brigade combat team deploying, at least until 2009, to Iraq. The aim of the program was to produce so-called language-enabled soldiers among select members of the brigade.[14] The very term suggests that Arabic is regarded as a kind of special equipment. Knowledge of Arabic, however perfunctory, would set apart some soldiers from their largely monolingual colleagues, endowing them with a capacity to do what others could not. The program itself is consistent with the plans laid out by the Department of Defense's "Defense Language Transformation Roadmap" to develop a "surge capability to rapidly expand language capabilities on short notice." Acknowledging that "language skill and regional expertise" are essential "war fighting skills," the Department of Defense has conceptualized translation as part of what it calls a "critical weapons system."[15]

It is within the context of linguistic militarization that we can understand the training that goes into the making of a language-enabled soldier. According to an article written by one of the commanders of the program, the learning of Arabic is set up to be "theater-specific." It involves, for example, practicing Arabic commands in parking lots for regulating traffic through checkpoints, ordering cars to stop, and searching their occupants. Soldiers are also taught to eavesdrop during routine patrols or while standing guard over prisoners. They also familiarize themselves with "Arabic children's games so they can interact with children . . . [since] they have often proven to be sound sources of information. . . . Parents who see soldiers interacting with their children in a benign fashion might be more forthcoming."[16] Armed with rudimentary Arabic, Pashto, or Dari, as the case might be, the language-enabled soldiers are thought to be capable of establishing rapport with children and their parents, turning them into conduits for collecting intelligence. Speaking the language of the native other, American soldiers can thus target anyone. In this way they are seen as ideal substitutes for native interpreters. As one of the commanders of the Stryker Brigade pointedly observed, "We would never contract civilians to man a platoon's machineguns, . . . so why rely on them [i.e., native interpreters] for language and culture skills? If we buy into the idea that our nation is at war with Islamic totalitarian terrorists and that culture and language are a weapons system important to victory, training Soldiers to operate this weapon . . . is as important to defeating today's enemy as anyone trained to handle critical combat equipment. . . . [For this reason] the Language Enabled Soldier is as essential as any other part of the intelligence warfighting function."[17]

There are a number of powerful fantasies at work in these remarks. In a profoundly monolingual military, language as such is never thought about except as a marker of the foreignness of the other targeted for conquest and occupation. Seizing hold of their language is seen as crucial to victory. Translation as the weaponization of language, however, is always in danger of falling into the wrong hands, as in the scenario of civilians operating machine guns. If language is to become a weapon, its use must be closely controlled and ideally limited to those with proper training—in this case the language-enabled soldier. But as Mary Louise Pratt has shown, fantasies about the military mobilization of translation constantly run aground on the realities of language learning.[18] For one thing, learning a foreign language, especially one with the degree of difficulty of Arabic or lesser-taught languages like Dari and Pashto, takes a very long time, far longer than the time of invasions and occupations whose temporal horizons usually contract or shift from one national election to another. Even if the United States were to devote considerable resources to producing Arabic-speaking soldiers—whose language skills would at best be elementary—it would find it impossible to transfer these language skills from one theater of conflict to another. It would also be highly impractical for fighters to simultaneously learn the languages of Afghanistan, Pakistan, Yemen, Sudan, Iran, and other areas the United States may be contemplating invading. Designed to be a weapon, the language-enabled solider thus becomes obsolete even as he or she is being trained. As one of the readers of a military blog noted, "The Intel community is going to be in so much trouble when they find out that Arabic isn't spoken in Afghanistan."[19]

Automating Translation

How, then, does the U.S. military respond to the temporal delay and tactical limits of translation and the targeting of foreign languages? One way has been to turn to computational technologies in order to develop automatic translation systems. Unlike the unavoidably embodied and socially contingent figure of the interpreter, automatic translation devices are thought to be dispassionate and highly manipulable instruments designed to fully comply with the intentions of their users. Imagined by both the military and engineers to have capacities that can outstrip and supersede the cultural difference and divided loyalties of human interpreters, machine translation tends to be idealized as sheer media in the Aristotelian sense of a diaphanous membrane or transparent skin that allows for the frictionless transmission of information vital to victory.[20] They thus come to materialize not so much the perfect weaponization of language as the promise of its future perfectibility.

Compared to the U.S. military's impressive advances in the development of vast surveillance systems and weapons of mass destruction, the deployment of automatic translation systems has been modest in scale though no less ambitious in its goals. Its origins can be traced back to the development of the earliest computer systems after World War II to gather and translate intelligence. American and British success in the field of cryptanalysis—the practice of breaking German and Japanese coded messages during the war—guided the early development of machine translation. Cryptanalysis regards foreign languages as if they were secret codes whose surfaces can be broken to bring forth hidden messages in the form of statistically arranged patterns. Such mathematical patterns are believed to be evidence of "linguistic universals" supposedly buried in all languages. From the perspective of cryptology, Russian and Mandarin are no more than instantiations of a universal language that can be deciphered and then recoded into English. Computers along with surveillance systems ranging from satellites to unmanned planes promised to speed up this process of decipherment by mechanizing translation in ways that would allow for the unlimited accumulation and efficient analysis of information from all corners of the globe. Such promises, however, have never materialized. Mechanical translation projects have developed unevenly since the 1950s, and efforts to arrive at linguistic universals have largely failed, along with attempts to capture and crack, as it were, the underlying "code" of natural languages.[21]

More recently research and development efforts around automatic translation devices have been funded and coordinated by the Defense Advanced Research Projects Agency (DARPA). In 2002 DARPA began a number of projects to deal with the problems of cross-cultural communication in occupied territories. Among these was the Babylon Program. According to the DARPA website, "The goal of the Babylon Program is to develop rapid, two-way, natural language speech translation interfaces and platforms for the war fighter for use in field environments for force protection, refugee processing and medical triage. Babylon will focus on overcoming the many technical and engineering challenges limiting current multilingual translation technology to enable future full-domain, unconstrained dialog translation in multiple environments. . . . The Babylon program will [provide] 'RMS' or Rapid Multilingual Support focus[ing] on low-population, high-terrorist risk languages."[22]

This description has the great virtue of laying out the precise terms for the military mobilization of translation. The weaponization of translation entails its technical refashioning into an "interface" and a "platform" from which to launch English and convert it into languages needed to capture targeted audiences. Language here is imagined to be a kind of software, and translation as an "interface" is understood to work like a computer monitor allowing speakers to see the very structures of intelligibility of other languages reduced to programmable codes. By giving language an algorithmic face, as it were, translation as an interface can thus also function as a "platform" from which to manipulate writing and speech. This mechanical model conceptualizes the surge in language capabilities as the complement to the surge of combat forces. Envisioned to be far more efficient than anything approaching the language-enabled soldier, Rapid Multilingual Sup-

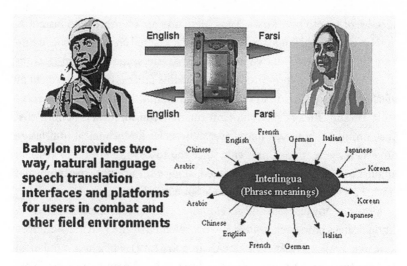

Figure 5.1 The military fantasy of automatic "full-domain, unconstrained dialog translation in multiple environments." From Project Babylon, Defense Advanced Research Project Agency.

port would furnish translations at increased speed with greater accuracy. Not only will translation machines subsume linguistic and cultural differences; they will also close the temporal lag that impedes the surge of the military forces. In so doing translation machines would come to colonize language itself. Putting an end to the material impediments of difference, delay, and deferral, they would render interpreters obsolete and thereby bring an end to the need for translation as such. One speaks directly and plainly, aiming at his or her listener and expecting to be heard and obeyed, much like one holds a gun at the face of someone and expects to win attention and compliance from him or her. In place of the time-consuming, highly contingent, and often volatile practices of negotiation and struggle over meaning and form inherent in acts of translation, this new Babylon sees the triumph of technological systems with which to "enable future full-domain, unconstrained dialog translation in multiple environments."

However, the imperial dream of realizing what the Department of Defense elsewhere refers to as "full-spectrum dominance" where translation is concerned remains largely a science-fiction chimera. [23] The *Star Wars* scenario of intelligent machines having animated conversations with humans and among themselves continues to be perpetually postponed. As of this writing, DARPA has so far only been able to produce through a private contracting firm a handheld device called the Phraselator.[24] About the size of a Palm Pilot, the Phraselator provides "a one-way phrase-based voice-to-voice translation" of American English into a target language, such as Arabic, Farsi, or Pashto. It is designed to accommodate an indefinite number of other languages that can be programmed into its expandable memory. But like a high-tech tourist phrase book, the Phraselator is unable to translate foreign languages back to English. It is thus severely constrained in its ability to engage enemy combatants or occupied populations. The Phraselator works by means of automatic speech recognition (ASR) technology that has been widely available for commercial uses over the past three decades.[25] ASR allows the Phraselator to mechanically recognize the English utterances from a wide variety of speakers, breaking these down into their phonetic elements. These are then converted into an interlingua, which is a kind of third language consisting of a mathematical algorithm that matches the deconstructed bits of English with what it wagers are its corresponding bits in a given target language. Through a voice synthesizer the machine speaks back the resulting words and phrases of its search in that language.

The range of translatable phrases, however, is largely driven by tactical considerations. They tend to be limited to such imperatives as "Show me your identification," "Open your bag," "Stop, or I'll shoot," and the all-purpose declarative "We are the U.S. military. We are here to help you."[26] And since the Phraselator is incapable of translating foreign languages back to English, it can neither interpret responses for their different meanings nor parse descriptions and analysis for their truth content. At best it can issue commands. It can speak, but it cannot listen. For this reason the Phraselator is less than effective at gathering that most precious commodity of counterinsurgency: information.

Meanwhile progress in two-way translation systems has been slow and largely limited to use in medical situations. A device called the Speechalator, for instance, allows doctors to interview non-English-speaking patients with simple questions like "Does your x hurt?" The machine then searches its database to posit the entire range of things that x might be in the language of the patient and matches it with the most likely English equivalent.[27] But like the Phraselator, the Speechalator is far from achieving "full domain unconstrained translation." It is, for example, susceptible to ambient noise that interferes with its ability to identify and correctly match word fragments and phrases between languages. The Speechalator can thus be deployed only in relatively confined conditions when the din of cross-talk and other sounds can be effectively suppressed. This has to do with the fact that the promise of automatic translation relies on the statistical probability that phonetic sounds in English will match up correctly with corresponding phonemes in the target language. It thus rests on a series of high-speed gambles. Underlying the functioning of all ASR technologies is probability theory, characterized by a high degree of mathematical formalism that enables machines to make enormous numbers of wagers and compute possible matches of word fragments at great speeds.[28]

Nonetheless such technologies remain incapable of determining the sociohistorical contexts that shape and inflect the meaning (or nonmeaning) of any given utterance. For this reason they cannot track with the polysemia inherent in speech signaled, for example, by the difference between what is said and how it is said. Like the Gorgon Stare surveillance system, their greatest strength lies in the fact that they do not discriminate and can take in any and all sounds that come their way. Their mode of recognition is quantitative. It cannot be any more different from the drama of Hegelian recognition that entails the struggle unto death between two beings that forces one who is attached to life to submit to the other who risks everything and becomes the former's master. Rather, recognition here is robustly mechanical, entailing neither political distinctions nor historical memory (and its necessary forgetting). We might think of automatic translation technologies, then, as postdialectical. They can recognize potentially limitless quantitative relationships but are unable to sort out their qualitative significance. They cannot process irony, for example, much less respond to humor and laughter. Unable to sort through the ambiguous and unstable use of tropes in idiomatic and literary expressions, automatic translation machines cannot process the poetics, much less politics, that make up all speech acts. For these reasons they are perhaps fated to be rudimentary. They remain blunt weapons easily outmaneuvered by their intended targets.

Thus there seems to be a correlation between the technological sophistication and practical crudeness of automatic translation systems. This Babylon of counterinsurgency has placed the U.S. military in a position of having to increasingly rely on the very figure it had sought to bypass: the native-speaking interpreter. Since its invasions of Afghanistan and Iraq, the Americans have looked to private contractors, many of which are run by former military officials with close ties to Congress and the Pentagon, to fill their acute need for native interpreters. Though regarded as essential, the presence of interpreters is also a source of great unease among the troops. Soldiers see them as Janus-faced: indispensable aides as much as potential spies.[29] They are thus weapons whose effectiveness exists side by side with their danger.

In view of the structurally ambivalent position of native interpreters—whose relationship to their language is less instrumental than it is existential—the U.S. military has issued a series of protocols governing the proper conduct of translation. Designed to systematically exploit the mediating power of the native translator, these protocols are worth reading closely. They tell us a great deal about American attempts to convert language into a "force multiplier," as well as the ways they multiply potential failures inherent in such attempts.

The Protocols of Interpreting

If we turn to *The U.S. Army/Marine Corps Counterinsurgency Field Manual* of 2006 we find an extensive appendix entitled "Linguist Support." It specifically instructs commanders to "protect their interpreters. They should emplace security measures to keep interpreters and their families safe. Insurgents know the value of good interpreters and will often try to intimidate or kill interpreters and their family members."[30] In actual fact these security measures have been minimal to nonexistent. Native interpreters are often compelled to work without protective vests and to venture unarmed with soldiers on patrol. They must hide their identity and assume a pseudonym to protect their anonymity. Many are unable to return safely to their family and often seek asylum in the United States or other countries with little or no help from the U.S. government. As I sought to show in chapter 4, interpreters working for the U.S. military in occupied territories risk permanent exile and estrangement within their own country.

The dangers associated with working for the American forces no doubt contribute to the reluctance of native speakers to serve as interpreters. Indeed one gets a sense from reading American military and journalistic accounts of the acute scarcity of interpreters in the field. It is for this reason that both the United States and insurgents regard them as "valuable resources." The tactical imperative to husband this scarce resource has been the topic of a number of military directives. An army captain who had served as chief of intelligence operations in Afghanistan typifies this regard for what the military refers to as "HNLs," or host nation linguists. "HNLs represent a valuable asset and learning conduit" who deserve "respect . . . that will be noticed, passed on and remembered." So it pays to "listen to their opinion and advice. . . . They've experienced a lot and often can be an important guide to the complex relationships between the various tribes and personalities of your province."[31]

The task of the translator from this perspective is that of a cultural broker and language instructor. She or he is thought to mediate the passage of the American soldier through the uncertain thickets of the occupied territory by giving narrative form to its history and society. Respecting "your interpreters" requires listening to them, treating them as "people," not simply as "tools." Yet the captain also positions native interpreters as "guides" to local culture as much as "teachers" of the local language: native informants whose job is to furnish the military with the medium for gathering intelligence.[32] If native interpreters have value, it is precisely because they never cease to be an asset, which is also a kind of spy, a means or an instrument for accumulating what the occupying forces want: a stockpile of information with which to repel insurgents and stabilize U.S. control.

Giving translators respect and listening to their views does not therefore alter their fundamental relationship with soldiers as part of a standing reserve. They continue to work as tools, albeit valuable ones, for the pursuit of strategic ends. Respect merely refines the process of their conversion into weapons of counterinsurgency. The need to protect interpreters therefore stems from the same imperative to protect complex weapons systems from the risk that they may fall into the wrong hands and be turned against their users. We see this in the same paragraph in the *Counterinsurgency Field Manual* that directs commanders to provide security for their interpreters: "Insurgents may also coerce interpreters to gather information on U.S. operations. Soldiers and Marines must actively protect against subversion and espionage."[33] Put differently, interpreters must be subject to protection as well as policing. They are assets but also threats to occupying forces. Indeed, there have been reported cases of insurgents posing as interpreters to get into U.S. military bases to gather information and set up ambushes. Private contracting firms such as l-3 and Titan have been known to hire translators, many of them poorly vetted in a rush to fill assigned quotas, linked to the abuses and torture of Iraqi and Afghan detainees. Others, through their negligence or sheer incompetence, have failed to properly screen locals hired to work inside the bases.[34] By their actions, these interpreters can be seen as subverting the U.S. military claims of being competent, much less philanthropic, occupiers. Translators are thus doubly positioned. They are valued by the U.S. military because of their scarcity and great utility in the collection of intelligence; at the same time, they are targeted by those seeking to challenge and undo U.S. power.

It is not surprising, then, that U.S. forces should be troubled by the constitutive ambiguity of the interpreter's position. The interpreter's social and ontological instability poses an ongoing problem for counterinsurgency operations that prioritize stability. Weaponized, they can target but also be targeted, fire as well as backfire. To guard against such risks, the military has produced a series of protocols to define and direct the proper conduct of translation governing both speakers and interpreters. Such protocols, however, rest on a series of unexamined assumptions about language and translation. They regard language as a mere vehicle for transmitting a speaker's intentions. If handled properly, like a car or a tank, it can be relied upon to transport one's ideas to their intended destination. Similarly, such protocols view translation as a pliant process for transferring meaning and faithfully reproducing the original into its copies. Just as soldiers are trained to obey orders emanating from the chain of command, so interpreters are expected to be loyal to the speaker whose original words they must convey into their exact copy in another language. As we shall see, these assumptions about the sheer instrumentality of language coupled with a belief in the mimetic capacity of translation give rise to unintended effects. Far from securing the relationship between speaker and interpreter, they further expose its unsecurable basis.

We can see such contradictory effects at work, for example, in the *Counterinsurgency Field Manual*'s criteria for selecting native interpreters. On the one hand, interpreters must be acceptable to the "target audience. . . . Their gender, age, race and ethnicity must be compatible with the target audience," and so too their "mannerisms" and "social reputation" as one who is "least likely to cause suspicion or miscommunication." On the other hand, the translator should act in a way that does not "distract" her or his listeners. The audience "should give no attention to the way interpreters talk, only what they say."[35] Interpreters can thus connect with their audiences only if they first clearly make visible their social identity. Becoming visible to their listeners is a tactic for disarming the latter, as it were, of their suspicions and winning their trust. The effectiveness of native translators begins with their physical bearing, which can be read by others for signs of their social position. Here, the interpreter's appearance matters. It is crucial to establishing the conditions of connectivity with an audience otherwise resistant to being targeted. Seeing the translator, the listener is reassured and thought to become receptive to what the speaker has to say. However, this acknowledgment of the importance of the translator's appearance is negated by another demand: that translators must remain discrete. They are expected to act in ways that obscure their way of acting. They must not "distract" their listeners, for distraction is a kind of noise that draws attention away from the *what* to the *how* of a translated utterance.

Here, the social identity of the interpreter must be so obvious as to go without saying, unremarkable and therefore unmarked by the audience. Hence the visibility of the interpreter is meant to produce his or her invisibility. She or he is seen by the audience only to be ignored. In this way soldiers operating through interpreters are able to effectively hit their targets. As another set of guidelines, this one from the Center for Army Lessons Learned, bluntly puts it, "Ideally, the interpreter should be invisible."[36] This conventional notion of the translator's invisibility takes on an added complexity when fused with the counterinsurgent discourse on linguistic weaponization. What is important to underline here is not only the way invisibility, or what we could think of as stealth, is valued in the conduct of war but also the way it is produced through the tactical deployment of visibility. So too with language: in military terms (which obviously derive from the more common civilian metaphysics of the sign),[37] language works, that is, accomplishes its mission, when its material encumbrances, such as grammar, syntax, spelling, and sounds, can be controlled to the point where they seem to vanish. They matter so that they can cease to matter. Dematerializing language—rendering it transparent—allows for the unfettered emergence of the meaning and will of the speaker. The interpreter in his or her visible invisibility is positioned to be an active collaborator in this task. Just as the interpreter is expected to set the way, then get out of the way for the arrival of the speaker's intentions, so language is seen to furnish the material support for the transfer of ideas and commands, all the while making itself seem immaterial and incidental to such maneuvers.

How does this double operation of appearance and disappearance of the translator and the process of translation happen? In a militarized context, how does it succeed, and at what point does it fail?

"Interpreters," according to the *Counterinsurgency Field Manual*, "should be reliable, loyal, and compatible with military personnel. . . . [They] should be quick and alert, able to respond to changing conditions and situations." Of course they must also "speak English fluently." It is easy to imagine that the qualities expected of good native interpreters would not be too different from those associated with U.S. soldiers. Working closely together, soldier and translator share a common fate, exposed to the hazards of war and the exigencies of occupation. But this relationship is clearly hierarchical. As a subordinate alter ego, the interpreter is meant to be the technical extension of the soldier. The interpreter is assigned the role of serving as the soldier's faithful representative to the occupied population, one whose fidelity consists of mirroring the tone and gesture of the speaker. "The interpreter," the *Counterinsurgency Field Manual* continues, "should watch the speaker carefully. While translating, the interpreter should mimic the speaker's body language as well as interpret verbal meaning." Later on we read that "standards of conduct for interpreters include: being careful not to inject their personality, ideas, or questions; mirroring the speaker's tone and personality; translating the exact meaning without adding or deleting information."[38]

Expected to provide the "exact" equivalents for words, interpreters are also commanded to turn themselves into a mirror image of the speaker, thus becoming who they are not. Like one possessed, interpreters speak not as themselves but as another who arrives by way of English and who insists on being present in the translator's native language. As the copy of the original, the translator takes on that language's foreignness, reproducing sounds and movements that emanate from elsewhere. In doing so the translator becomes the translation, a putatively faithful rendering of unfamiliar elements into familiar terms. Appropriating its distant origins, the interpreter domesticates a foreign power and brings it forth as something intelligible and accessible to the target audience. Put differently, translation as the act of conjuring up equivalents between languages can easily come across as magical. Translators are thus invested with a remarkable capacity for linguistic and ontological transformation: becoming someone other than who one is, taking on and taming the language of a foreign presence, reproducing it in one's own native tongue, and thereby converting it into something other than what it is. By containing, in all senses of that word, the unfamiliar in the familiar and vice versa, the translator thus assumes an uncanny power.

It is precisely this power of translation that the soldier must learn to appropriate and control. The interpreter is a "vital communication link between speaker and target audience,"[39] and it is this vitality that must be seized if it is to be successfully deployed. To this extent soldiers are instructed to "communicate directly to the target audience, using the interpreter only as a mechanism for that communication. One technique is to have the interpreter stand to the side of and just behind the speaker. This position lets the speaker stand face to face with the target audience. The speaker should always look at and talk directly to the target audience, rather than to the interpreter. This method allows the speaker and the target audience to establish a personal relationship."[40] As the mechanical but no less powerful extension of the American soldier's presence, the interpreter has to be put in his or her proper place: behind or to the side of the speaker rather than between the speaker and the listener. The interpreter's vital role as a medium of communication—literally as the middle term that brings distances up close, sounding the foreign in the familiar—is acknowledged at the same time that it is suppressed.

Again we see how the interpreter is seen in order to be ignored. Doing so allows the solider to come forth. Face to face with the target, the soldier appears unarmed, concealing the linguistic power and its embodied agent that makes possible his or her very ability to speak and be heard. With the target disarmed, the soldier can then fire away with confidence. In this *imaginary* scenario, speech gains speed and direction. It reaches its audience swiftly, propelled by the ever-present but largely unseen machine of translation. Weaponizing speech thus entails harnessing the mediating power of translation as it courses through the interpreter while concealing the process of its exploitation and deployment. The soldier thereby overcomes linguistic difference, converting language itself—English as well as the language of the audience—into a transparent window for the smooth passage of meanings and intentions.

Controlling translation, directing and speeding up its trajectory, subordinating the interpreter into a copy at once visible and invisible of the speaking self, and subjugating difference between as well as within languages are thus all of a piece in the work of counterinsurgency. In this sense the

Counterinsurgency Field Manual's protocols for proper translation rehearse the idealized notions of language that we earlier saw in the military's attempts to develop automatic translation systems. From this logocentric perspective the perfect interpreter is a mechanized prosthetic at the command of the speaker's will.

The Insurgency of Language

These extravagant fantasies of perfect communication predicated on the automation of translation and the subjugation of linguistic difference, however, remain largely unrealized. As we shall see, attempts at converting language into weapons for the mastery of the other tend to backfire on their users. What is remarkable is how the frustration of this fantasy always already inhabits the very protocols for translation. Anticipating failure, the military discourse on translation prepares a series of tactical responses. In the *Counterinsurgency Field Manual*, for example, one of the threats most often mentioned to the proper operation of translation is "distraction." In a section entitled "Good and Bad Practices for Speakers," we read how "speakers should not distract the audience while the interpreter is translating. Avoid pacing, writing on the blackboard, teetering on the lectern, drinking beverages, or doing any other distracting activity while the interpreter is translating."[41]

The warning against distraction stems from the fear of disrupting the smooth workings of translation. But as it turns out, it is not only the interpreter who poses such a threat; so does the American speaker. Pulled in different directions, the soldier's body is inhabited by other thoughts jockeying for attention. Exposed to a foreign audience, the soldier restlessly anticipates what to say next, besieged by impulses that he or she struggles to control. Recognizing these surging impulses, the soldier might pace, drink, or write. The body, awash in nervous energy, might begin to move in ways at odds with the mind. At that moment the soldier appears to be one thing while saying another. Instead of coming across as a unified self in full control of itself and its speech, the soldier appears distracted, which is to say divided and thus other than himself or herself. The sight of a divided speaker, one who speaks in a language that is not fully his or her own insofar as he or she is, as it were, not fully himself or herself, brings the soldier in close proximity to the position of the interpreter. Distraction is dangerous precisely because it threatens to blur the distinction between the speaker and the translator and, by extension, between the original and the copy.

To prevent these hierarchical distinctions from being overturned, the *Counterinsurgency Field Manual* advises speakers against "addressing the subject or audience in the third person through the interpreter. For example, avoid saying 'Tell them I'm going to be their instructor.' Instead directly address the subject or audience saying, 'I am glad to be your instructor.' Make continual eye contact with the audience. Watch them, not the interpreter."[42] When addressing the audience, the speaker should always do so as an "I" speaking to a "you."[43] The translator, by contrast, is never to be addressed in the second person but must always assume the position of an occluded third term. In this way the translator is neither a "him" nor a "her" but an "it." It is essential, as the *Manual* emphasizes, for the translator to efface himself or herself so as to give the speaker a face with which to address the subject. The translator's task is literally to give face to the speaker while obscuring his or her own. The danger, however, lies in the constant temptation of the speaker to speak to the interpreter directly. Unsure, perhaps even unnerved by the unfamiliar look of the audience, the soldier would understandably seek out the familiar face of the interpreter. In doing so he or she speaks as an "I" to someone who is supposed to be an "it" but is now addressed as a "you." This inadvertently converts the third term into a second person while placing the listener in the position of the occluded third. The targeted "you" suddenly becomes the vanishing "it."

Complicating this situation is the fact that the interpreter, as we saw, is expected to echo the speaker and so can say "I" only as the simulacrum of another "I." The interpreter therefore is one who is forbidden to say "I" to refer to himself or herself. She or he can do so only to refer to an other, the speaker. It is as a not-"I," and therefore as an "it," that the interpreter seems to vanish from view. This invisibility, which is linguistically produced, endows the interpreter with a kind of disembodied presence. Without a body the interpreter can seem to go through the walls that separate English from other languages. In this sense the position of the interpreter as an "it" whose invisible and disembodied presence allows it to cross linguistic boundaries seems akin to that of a ghost. But in referring to the interpreter in the second person, the speaker confounds the protocols of address. As a "you," the interpreter's spectral presence is revealed to be a conjuring trick.

She or he now comes across as a specifically embodied person, one who can say "I" and actually refer to himself or herself.

This confusion of address has important consequences. The interpreter's recovered visibility threatens to uncover the real nature of the relationship between speaker and interpreter as one of dependency when it is in fact the American soldier who is dependent on the native translator, while both are dependent on the workings of language. Meanwhile the listener, the speaker's target, escapes. It is excluded by having become a third person. By upending the relationship between speaker, interpreter, and listener, the misplaced circulation of pronouns confuses the terms of address and sabotages the proper operation of translation as conceived by the *Counterinsurgency Field Manual*.

Perhaps mindful of the uncanny ways by which language once repressed returns to haunt the work of military occupation, the *Counterinsurgency Field Manual* is replete with advice for speakers on how to conduct not only their behavior but also their mode of address so as not to create distractions. It is also full of recommendations on how to formulate their speech. "An important first step for Soldiers and Marines communicating in a foreign language is to reinforce and polish their English language skills. . . . They should use correct words, without idioms or slang. The more clearly Soldiers and Marines speak English, the easier it is for interpreters to translate exactly. For instance, speakers may want to add words usually left out in colloquial English such as 'air' in 'airplane.' This ensures they are not misrepresented as referring to the Great Plains or a carpenter's plane."[44]

Here the speakers are cautioned not about the ambiguity of another language but about the potential treachery of their own. Even before their speech is translated by the interpreter into another language, speakers must first translate it themselves. By "polishing their English language skills," avoiding colloquialisms and slang, soldiers engage in a sort of intralingual translation. "Before speaking impulsively," the *Counterinsurgency Field Manual* says, "Soldiers and Marines should consider what they wish to say." They should not, in other words, blurt out the first thing that comes to mind but instead convert their thoughts into proper forms of speech. They must follow orders, which is to say, listen to another, higher language issuing from within their own. Doing so entails translating within English, hearing and speaking it as if it were a second language that encapsulates their first.

They thus speak as an "I" in possession of its words only to the extent that they speak in another register, in "polished English," and therefore as some other "I" within a language whose sameness is always already fractured into the colloquial and the officially conventional. To speak properly in "correct English" is to split oneself, moving between one's native tongue and its national official reformulation. In this way self-division and intralingual translation precede any attempt on the soldier's part to engage the native interpreter and the target audience. Such operations are essential, as the *Counterinsurgency Field Manual* points out, "to guard against the risks of mistranslation." One should add *air* to *airplane*, for example, lest *plane* by itself be confused with a geographical region in North America or a carpenter's tool. In doing so the soldier avoids mistranslation that, like distraction, generates noise that detracts from producing exact translations.

Nonetheless, noise never stops running through languages, making mistranslation not only an inevitable event but a constitutive condition of speech. Colloquialisms and slang are impossible to fully expunge. They invariably seep into every conversation for they are precisely what give language its social vitality and historical specificity. There is therefore an element of utter wishfulness that infuses the *Counterinsurgency Field Manual*'s injunction against using

> terms of surprise or reaction such as "gee whiz" or "golly" [since] these are difficult to translate [and] might lose their desired meaning. . . . Speakers should avoid American "folk" and culture specific references. Target audiences may have no idea what is being talked about. Even when interpreters understand the reference, they may find it difficult to quickly identify an appropriate equivalent in the target audience's frame of reference. Transitional phrases and qualifiers may confuse non-native speakers and waste valuable time. Examples include "for example," "in most cases," "maybe," and "perhaps." Speakers should avoid American humor. Humor is culturally specific and does not translate well.[45]

This catalogue of prohibitions points to the difficulties of controlling language in its totality, whether one's own or the other's. The danger lies not only in being misunderstood in the language of the native other but also in failing to make oneself comprehensible in one's own. Rather than face the risk of losing face, of saying something that deters the interpreter, creating distractions and leaving one's interlocutor mystified, the speaker is commanded to repress those aspects of his or her language that defy translation. The speaker must therefore keep in mind what remains untranslatable: "terms of surprise," "folk references," "qualifiers," "humor," and so forth. He or she must labor to keep these out of linguistic exchanges and so accede to the higher language of command that tells him or her what to do. Doing otherwise would jeopardize the work of translation, understood here as the search for exact equivalents that, by fixing the link between English and native words, would also stabilize the relationship between speaker and audience, occupiers and occupied.

Thus does the *Counterinsurgency Field Manual* locate in the national tongue of the American soldier a kind of insurgency fed by the very insistence and intractability of what remains untranslatable. For as the passage above shows, even writers of the *Counterinsurgency Field Manual* fall prey to the insurgency of the untranslatable when they resort to the very features of language that they had targeted for repression. For example, it talks of avoiding "qualifiers," such as "for example," but does so by giving examples, such as "for example." Unable to co-opt linguistic difference, it cannot fully recruit English into the task of weaponizing translation. Instead it calls for the repression of those parts of speech that resist such an operation. That such calls are repeatedly issued along with warnings about distractions and mistranslations suggests the extent to which they fail to be heard and heeded. It is this recurring failure and continued resistance of language to the commands of counterinsurgency that guarantees that translation will misfire and miss its targets, whatever and wherever they may be.

Translating Otherwise

The chronic failure of counterinsurgency to convert language, whether its own, English, or the other's, into a weapon, that is, into a standing reserve that can be switched, secured, and deployed, tends to generate catastrophic effects. Targets are missed or misconstrued, accidents abound, deaths proliferate, while no one is held accountable. As I have been suggesting, the resistance of language to weaponization is not incidental but structurally built into the very discourse and practices of counterinsurgency. That counterinsurgency harbors the very elements of its own undoing can be understood in at least two ways. On the one hand, as military leaders and engineers tend to think of it, the intractability of language may be regarded as a kind of noise that adds to the friction of war, merely a technical problem that can be fixed with greater application of resources, financial and technological, and a strengthening of political will. On the other hand, we could think of the insurgency of language as evidence of the possibility of another kind of translation practice at work. Operating in between the lines of imperial commands, it would be a kind of translation that evades targeting, spurring instead the emergence of forms of life at variance with the biopolitical prescriptions of counterinsurgency. Where might we see this occurring? I conclude with one such instance.

On 1 March 2011, American-led NATO helicopter gunners killed nine Afghan boys between the ages of nine and fifteen as they collected firewood in the remote mountains of Kumar province in eastern Afghanistan, mistaking them for Taliban insurgents who had earlier fired at American troops.[46] The killings followed in the wake of an increase in the number of civilian deaths caused by American-led forces throughout Afghanistan since the troop surge in 2009. "Regrettably there appears to have been an error in the handoff between identifying the location of the insurgents and the attack helicopters that carried out subsequent operations," an official NATO statement explained.[47] General David Petraeus, then commander of NATO forces, issued an apology for this "mistake." Mistaking children for insurgents, the helicopter gunships addressed them accordingly, sending a message whose force could not be denied. The targeted audience of this fully weaponized speech act was not expected to respond. But something else happened: they spoke back, or at least some of them did.

One of them was Hemad, an eleven-year-old who survived the attack. He said to the reporters of the *New York Times* through an interpreter who remains invisible and unnamed, "We were almost done collecting wood when suddenly we saw the helicopters come. There were two of them. The helicopters hovered over us, scanned us and we saw a green flash from the helicopters. Then they flew back high up, and in a second round they hovered over us and started shooting. They fired a rocket that landed on a tree. The tree branches fell over me and shrapnel hit my right hand and my side." Hemad goes on to say that the tree branches hid him and probably saved his life. They also gave him a vantage point from where to witness the helicopters "shoot the boys one after another." Hidden from view Hemad witnesses the helicopter gunship do its work, addressing the boys by turning them into targets. He hears the pilots speak, delivering their message swiftly and directly.[48]

Thanks to the work of translation, the boy's words reach beyond the village and across the globe for others to hear. What comes to us is a story as spare and unadorned as it is vivid and unnerving in its effects. It is a minimalist retelling of counterinsurgency from the point of view of a member of the population it is supposed to protect. Rendered by the translator and the newspaper editor in grammatically correct English, it nonetheless conveys a semantic excess. The English makes legible the boy's Pashto, yet the meaning of its content remains elusive. We recognize the words and can make sense of the form, but we can barely comprehend the implications of what was said. We get instead a number of incommensurable possibilities; we sense, for example, an enormous senselessness, or an unforgivable act, or the monstrous effects of the most precise and controlled use of advanced weaponry. All of these imply that translation does not necessarily bring meaning to the surface for us to see. Instead, as Walter Benjamin once put it in a different context, "meaning plunges from abyss to abyss until it threatens to become lost in the bottomless depths of language."[49] Unable to ground meaning, translation leads to its falling away. Hemad's story is translated not to establish exact equivalents between his Pashto and our English and thereby allow his intentions to come forth. Rather, like an interlinear translation, what reaches us are the inexactness and ambiguity of a message contained in a grammatically correct form.

We sense once more something of this interlinear ambiguity in the translated words of an Afghan shopkeeper, Ashabuddin, reported in the newspaper story: "As soon as we heard about the attack on the village's children, all the village men rushed to the mountains to find out what really happened. Finally, we found the dead bodies. Some of the dead bodies were really badly chopped up by the rockets. The head of a child was missing. Others were missing their limbs. We tried to find the body pieces and put them together. As it was getting late, we brought down the bodies in a rope bed. We buried them in the village's cemetery. The children were all from poor families; otherwise no one would send their sons up to the mountains despite the known threats from both insurgents and Americans."[50]

As with Hemad's story, Ashabuddin's narrative in its English translation arrives dry and bereft of affect. He hears about the attack and connects this with the missing children. Along with other village men, he searches for them and eventually finds them, or rather what remains of their bodies. They see the signature, as it were, of the pilots' language in the boys' "chopped up" limbs. One can only assume that the sight of dismembered bodies would cause anyone to recoil in horror. But Ashabuddin's story continues in the same flat tone as he talks of the men collecting body parts, bringing them down, and burying them. The men in effect reverse the work of targeting. Where the helicopter gunships scattered the bodies of those they addressed, the villagers seek literally to re-collect them, binding them together so that they can be buried and thus rejoined to the living. Mourning their loss, the villagers rearticulate the identity of the pilots' targets into a spare biography: "The children were all from poor families."

Hearing this story translated into English we are once again faced with the workings of a kind of interlinear translation. Just as an interlinear translation seeks to preserve the ambiguity of the original text, safeguarding its mystery and intimating its inexhaustible possibilities for meaning,[51] so Ashabuddin's account comes across as intelligible while simultaneously suggesting something that lies behind or beneath it that can neither be seen nor grasped. It imparts, which is to say divides and shares, a story about the impossibility of restoration and recuperation. Attempting to "find body pieces and put them together," the villagers in Ashabuddin's narrative are left with a sense of something, indeed of many things, missing. He says of Khalid, his fourteen-year-old nephew who was among those killed, "He was studying in the sixth grade of the orphanage school and working because his father had died four years ago due to a long-term illness. His father was a day laborer. He has thirteen sisters and two mothers. He was the sole breadwinner of the family. I don't know what would happen to his family and his sisters and mothers."[52] Gathering the boys and burying them brings no closure but instead intensifies uncertainty about the future and thus about uncertainty itself.

The story and its translation allow us to see that we do not see, conveying a semantic excess that remains impervious to narrative domestication. This imperviousness is perhaps what is indicated by the affectless tone of Ashabuddin's voice rendered in English. Translation in this case is faithful to the original, bringing the story up close, so close as to make it profoundly foreign to us just as it remains irreducibly strange to the Afghan man who tells it. Moving between the lines of Pashto, the English translation conveys a story that remains inassimilable to larger narratives of war just as it proves inhospitable to our attempts to render war familiar and banal. "I don't know what would happen," Ashabuddin says, and neither do we. We apprehend war's violence and its remorseless violation of life even as we are unable to comprehend, much less adequately respond to, its effects.

There is, then, in Ashabuddin's story something else that reveals itself, the nature of which we can never be certain but which nonetheless reaches us. It might be that in the living's attempts to recover the dead and rejoin their missing parts we glimpse at the persistence, even emergence of another kind of life, one that is not reducible to the language of targeting and weaponization. Much less is it likely therefore for this other life to submit to the "saving power" of American counterinsurgency that demands the rational reordering and deployment of all life in the war against terror. Or perhaps it is the voice of those who, speaking in the midst of occupation, find themselves living so intimately with death that they can hardly draw the line that separates them from those they have lost. Barely able to mourn, it comes across as flat and empty of affect.

Yet, this voice is just as likely to call for the other's death. As the newspaper article points out, a few days after the killing of the boys small crowds of people in the village and in the capital, Kabul, gathered to protest, chanting, "Death to America! Death to Obama and his colleagues and his associates! Death to the American government!"[53] Uttered from below, whether in Pashto or its English translation, "death" is less a kind of weapon than a token return, a way of giving back to America what America has left behind in Afghanistan. Rhetorically sounding out a death sentence, such chants understandably call for revenge. As such, they redefine Afghan relations to the United States. We can imagine the chants overturning the discursive hierarchy of counterinsurgency, placing the population in a position of judging their putative protectors. We might even speculate that such calls for revenge bring forth the possibilities of a life that speaks of an afterlife beyond imperial occupation. Or, restraining the reductive force of our own wishfulness, we might pause to consider that they could be merely the traumatized, automatic responses to the inexplicable and unjustifiable loss of life and perhaps even of an afterlife.

We, who are dependent on translation's fidelity to the vagaries of the original, can never be sure. The aporia of translation *detains* us, in all senses of that word. This detaining entails a momentary arrest, compelling us to dwell in that which arrives from somewhere else. In this dwelling we, or at least those of us who are unavoidably implicated in the violence of counterinsurgency by virtue of living in this imperial nation, might be led to see in translation an opening that cannot be closed like the stories of the Afghans, whose words linger, "remaining long in languor and pain,"[54] past the limits of any given reading.

Detained, we might be alerted to the visible invisibilities of the interpreter or the insurgent energy circulating within the very language of command. Alert, we might better sense how translation brings forth the untranslatable, calling us to respond to what cannot be converted and contained, to what, however minor and marginal, evades even as it is constantly menaced by imperial invocations. And it is in tending to the untranslatable that accrues and dissipates in and out of a militarized context that we can, perhaps, begin to assume responsibility for the remains of weaponized speech.

PART III *Translating Lives*

Figure P.3 (*overleaf*) Olga Clemeña Ileto with Reynaldo Ileto.
Courtesy of Reynaldo Ileto.

CHAPTER 6

The Accidents of Area Studies

Benedict Anderson and Arjun Appadurai

The next time I had a chance, I returned to Indonesia. . . . I wanted to become actively confused rather than passively so. There seemed to be numerous invitations. Most of them were, in fact, beyond my expectations. I did not know where they might take me. I decided never to refuse an invitation, even when it led me to places I did not like. In fact, I thought to myself, I should learn to like what I dislike. I could, if not decompose myself, at least in that way put "myself" aside. Here, I thought, was a way to find bewilderment.

—JAMES T. SIEGEL, *Objects and Objections of Ethnography*

In the years following the end of the Cold War it became commonplace to speak of a "crisis" in area studies in the United States, followed by calls to reinvent the institutional infrastructure and intellectual agendas for understanding different regions of the world at century's end.[1] Rather than reiterate those calls, I want for the moment to pick up the notion of crisis and follow it along a somewhat different route.

Crisis connotes emergency, the critical point at which a state of affairs reaches a moment of either turning around or turning into something other than what it had been. We might say that crisis is a time of danger, that is to say, that it is also the time of contingency, when things fall apart and the possibility of something new emerges. If area studies can be said to have a culture that has long been in crisis, it is because it forces us to think about its contingencies and accidents. We might be able to see these if we paused momentarily and considered area studies from the point of view not of its funders, administrators, or metacritics but rather from the particular histories of its practitioners.

Is there something to learn from asking about the experience of area studies prior to its institutionalization—at the point before it requires recognition and validation by someone from above? How does one come to study "others" prior to and beyond having to justify it to a patron, an ad hoc committee, a council, or a corporate foundation? How does a person living in one place come to have an interest in some other, radically different place? What are the conditions necessary for one to invest considerable personal energy and intellectual resources in learning a language, traveling to a village or a city, poring over archival documents and inscriptions, risking one's personal health and safety, in order to pursue a set of questions to which there are potentially no definitive answers? How and why does one return to foreign sites, become attached to them, or conversely come to spurn them? What are the structures of feeling specific to engaging in the study of that which, in order to be studied at all, must remain forever alien however intimate and proximate it may be to one? What are the dynamics of detachment and fixation that come into play when one studies the foreign? And what are the risks and rewards of identification or disidentification with "it" or "them"? Finally what are the politics of these engagements and the ethics of weaving and unweaving such affective bonds with the otherness of the other?

What I am suggesting here is that, alongside institutional histories, we might also ask about the contingent and, for want of a better word, existentially particular and historically specific relationships that area studies practitioners form with their areas of study. In assembling these notes I started by asking colleagues to tell me how they became interested in the region or country they had been working on.

In the Place of the Foreign

For the generation of Euro-American men who became involved in area studies during the Cold War, there were two major routes that led them to their field (and here I will limit myself to Southeast Asian studies): their participation in war, either World War II or Vietnam, or in the Peace Corps. Both entailed travel, extended residence, and sustained contact, hostile as well as friendly, with the peoples of the region; opportunities to learn their languages and histories; and, not uncommonly, love affairs that often enough led to some sort of marriage, family, and, for some, divorce. Both modes of contact also entailed stepping into enormously unequal power relationships. The violence of wars and the authoritarian regimes they install invariably place white men in the position of colonizers vis-à-vis local populations. And the developmentalist altruism of the Peace Corps born in the midst of the Cold War endows the volunteer with considerable privilege backed by the entire apparatus of the American state. Indeed the American state in both cases mediates the conditions that allow for such travel and contact, and the inequalities as well as mutual dependencies that these give rise to. Nonetheless, the state alone cannot determine the origins of such interests, nor can it foreclose their futures. Somewhere along the line there is always an accidental aspect to these contacts, a sense of things unseen and unexpected that results in one becoming drawn to this rather than that country or region or province.

Think, for example, of the path taken by George Kahin, who founded the Southeast Asian Studies Program at Cornell University. Kahin first became interested in Asia during the Pacific War, when he helped campaign on behalf of interned Japanese Americans, urging those who owed them money to honor their debts. Joining the U.S. Army, he was trained in the Indonesian language and was to be part of the Allied forces that would retake the islands. By some quirk of fate he was assigned to Italy at the last moment. After the war he continued to be interested in Indonesia, going there to do his field research in 1948, at the time the revolution against the Dutch was breaking out. He thus had, for a Westerner, unparalleled access to the youthful Indonesian leaders and came to write the landmark study on that country's revolution, notable for its deep sympathy with the nationalist cause. His sympathies with Indonesian revolutionaries led Kahin to become a passionate and committed critic of American imperialism in Southeast Asia, especially the Vietnam War. Thus did his career prove antithetical to the late colonial and Cold War conditions from which it arose.[2]

For American women of this era the route to area studies was equally complex, often linked to generational differences. It was not uncommon for those who went to college and graduate school in the 1950s and mid-1960s to come in contact with Manila or Bangkok primarily through the work of their husbands, who may have been in the Peace Corps or in the diplomatic service or doing graduate research. Marriage and child rearing set limits and so opened up different possibilities for earlier generations of women who, for example, may have started out being students of Western music but, finding themselves without a piano in Mandalay or Solo, may have proceeded to pick up the Burmese harp or play in a Javanese gamelan while their husbands completed their doctoral work in the field. Returning home, children now grown and husband tenure-tracked, they may have decided to enter a PhD program within which to pursue an interest that had developed by a combination of chance and circumstance.[3]

Later generations of women who came of age in the late 1960s through the 1980s and the 1990s undoubtedly had different routes to area studies. Some came through the Peace Corps, others through political activism inspired by social movements such as feminism and civil rights, the opposition to the Vietnam War, the emergence of what we might think of as left-wing Orientalism and its concomitant fascination with things "Eastern" as alternatives to the oppressiveness of the West. Less encumbered by, and even resistant to, received notions of domesticity, they would have been able to travel without the baggage of husband and children, finding themselves both interested in others as well as the object of their intense interest, and turning such gendered predicaments into the texts and contexts of work that could now be more readily pursued (though not without continuing resistance at American universities). In all cases the social facts of race, gender, and domesticity, like the structures of the state, shaped but did not wholly determine the genesis of their interests and the paths that these led to.[4]

Given the specificity of their histories, there exist myriad reasons that led area studies practitioners to arrive at an interest in their particular area. Other colleagues, men as well as women, who were neither in wars nor the Peace Corps tell me that they were drawn to Southeast Asia because they had met by chance someone from there and become intrigued or, by some stroke of luck, had sat in on a class or a lecture on the region being given by a particularly good teacher. Still others recall that hearing the gamelan, seeing the Javanese puppet theater, the *wayang*, or photographs of Angkor Wat had triggered a fascination with Southeast Asia for reasons that remain obscure and indeterminate. In other words, "Southeast Asia" or some aspect of it struck them when they did not expect it, like a stone hitting a windowpane. Surprised, they found themselves responding to this accidental intrusion, following the cracks that were traced around the hole left behind.

An accidental encounter brings with it a force of its own, sending one falling (for, after all, *accident*, like the word *chance*, is formed from the Latin *cadere*, "to fall") into something unexpected and unknown that lies outside yet shapes the limits of what is known. To have an accident is to come in contact with the radically foreign, a kind of otherness that resists assimilation. It is only after the fact of such an encounter that one can look back and see the accident as the first in a series of events that led to the present. Thus do accidents demand recounting even as they evade a full accounting.

Here is an example. As a young boy growing up in upstate New York, one of my colleagues remembers meeting a very well-dressed and dignified-looking man who appeared by chance on his family's doorstep asking to use their telephone. He was on his way to New York City and had been stranded by a winter storm that had blocked all the roads. The stranger turned out to be Filipino and stayed for breakfast until the storm blew over. Intrigued by the stranger, my colleague looked up all the information he could on the Philippines at his local library. Years later he signed up for the Peace Corps and asked to be sent to that country in part because of his memory of this stranger. He realized subsequently that this mysterious man was none other than Carlos P. Romulo (1899–1985), then the Philippine representative to the United Nations and a prominent politician in his home country.[5]

A foreigner appears unexpectedly in one's home, interrupting the flow of one's domestic life, making such an impression that he leaves behind a memory. Picking up that memory, one follows its associations, hearing in it all kinds of other suggestions until finally, or rather retrospectively, one sees oneself being carried physically and imaginatively to the other's home, as if to repay the visit. Drawn to the other, one finds oneself an "other" in turn. It is as if in meeting the foreigner, one hears a call whose message is discovered only after the fact of its transmission. Further, it is discovered to lie elsewhere, outside the limits of the familiar. This discovery of deferred meaning shares in the structuring of a vocation. Years later, making sense of one's professional identity and the pressures that come with it, one reconstructs one's interest in a region as the response to a call whose significance at the time of its issuance had not yet been disclosed. Rather than approach the Philippines in the mode of an explorer seeking to conquer new territories or expand one's power, one instead imagines oneself being summoned by the area itself, crystallized in the memory of a stranger and the sense of something lying behind or beyond that figure. That one doesn't know what the message might mean brings with it the risk of misinterpretation and adds all the more to the urge of responding to that call. To think of area studies as a kind of vocation (from the Latin *vocatio*, derived from *vocare*, "to call") is thus to imagine oneself elsewhere, in the place of the foreigner, as a foreigner oneself, and therefore as capable of the same power of transmitting messages whose meanings are deferred, lying at some other place in some other time.

It is not difficult to read an element of romanticism in the notion of area studies as a vocation. In the most banal terms we say that one is drawn to study Japan or Thailand because one is in love with "it," whatever that "it" might be at different moments in one's life. And it is here, in the realm of the romantic, that sentiment and mystification become difficult to tell apart. Having fallen in love with the foreign, learning its language and reconstructing its history, one might then begin with some justification to consider oneself to be an authority who can speak for the place and its people to those at home. At the same time, one begins to feel a sense of responsibility, even missionizing zeal, about the beloved country's fate, so that one begins to act like an authority among the foreigners themselves, diagnosing their problems, devising solutions, and even demanding adherence through force or persuasion, especially when one thinks that one has the backing of the state and other powerful interests at home. The romance of area studies can thus just as easily, or better yet uneasily, bring with it a kind of sentimental imperialism that the United States is only too famous for.[6]

There is, then, a risk in construing the accidental encounter with the foreign retrospectively as a narrative of vocation, of thinking that falling into the zone of alienation was the first moment of hearing, then responding to an alien call. Edward Said warned us precisely about such risks when he referred to Orientalism as a "battery of desires and dreams" as much as it was a tendentious storehouse of knowledge about the Orient that allowed for the "non-metaphorical advance" and positional superiority of the Occident.[7] In a post-Orientalist and postcolonial world—or at least in a world permeated with the desire for post-Orientalism and postcolonialism—there are good reasons to be wary of such traps.

Thus might we understand the institutionalization of area studies as an attempt, always partial and uneven, to ensure against such Orientalizing risks. It does so in at least two ways. First, institutionalization tends to repress and marginalize the element of the accidental, tending to see the contingency of foreign encounters as historically and structurally determined, and therefore as not contingent at all. From the standpoint of an area studies program, the accidental is merely so, an irregularity of no real consequence. Second, institutionalizing area studies means setting aside its vocational aspect, stressing instead the professional rationality, detached approaches, and practical effects of studying the other. Professionalizing area studies entails, among other things, placing the question of affect and imagination on hold. We see this in the stress on disciplinarity in the university that segregates forms of knowledge and their practitioners from one another. For example, the study of language and literature as a single pursuit has been systematically sundered in area studies programs, just as the study of theory and philosophy once joined to history, anthropology, and sociology is now routinely held apart. As a result real interdisciplinarity, which, in my opinion, requires a relentless skepticism toward disciplinary divisions, becomes a difficult if not suspect activity. Domesticating and regularizing the risks of foreign encounters, the institutionalization of area studies runs the risk of turning area studies into perennial servants of the disciplines and vulnerable clients of powerful corporate and government patrons. One result is that their usefulness will always come under interrogation in a way less likely (though not impossible) for disciplinary departments. Attempting to secure the place of area studies, programs ironically enough invite continued scrutiny and thus live on with a deep sense of insecurity as an irregular, supplementary, and therefore accidental formation in the university.

And yet it is precisely the accidental nature of area studies, or more precisely the accidental ways by which their practitioners stumble into studying specific areas, that makes them worthwhile as sites for encountering regions of otherness the disciplines tend to discount. In this sense we can think of the putative weakness of area studies programs as their actual strength. They serve as terminals for the unlikeliest meetings among the most diverse groups and individuals, who because of some unforeseen occurrence or chance meeting at some point in the past were drawn to go "there," wherever that might have been. What they, or better yet we, have in common is the fact that we not only study "otherness" but often find ourselves through our travels and our readings in foreign languages to be an "other." Thus do practitioners of area studies feel themselves doubled: there is the "I" who comes home and writes about alien places, and another "I," the alien who appears knocking on doors, asking to use a telephone in the middle of a storm, provoking curiosity, irritation, and suspicion at times, and commanding authority at other times from those he or she encounters.

This doubled identity whereby two "I's" exist without one ever fully knowing, much less controlling, the other is present not only among American practitioners, whether male or female, of area studies. It applies with even greater force to immigrant scholars as well. For my last set of examples, I want to look briefly at two of the most respected practitioners of area studies—who are also two of its most imaginative critics—who happen to be immigrants to the United States: Benedict Anderson and Arjun Appadurai.

The Agency of Accident

In the autobiographical introduction to his collection of essays, *Language and Power: Exploring Political Cultures in Indonesia*, Anderson relates how he came to be involved with Southeast Asian studies.[8] It started with a blow to his face. While studying classical languages at Cambridge in 1956, he found himself wandering into a political demonstration held by a small group of South Asians. A fight suddenly broke out, initiated by a group of English students hurling racial epithets at the South Asians. Anderson found himself in the middle, trying to stop the fight. "My spectacles were smacked off my face," he recounts, "and so, by chance, I joined the column of the assaulted."[9] The rest of Anderson's account consists of tracing the cracks created by such a chance encounter, cracks that lead to more fortuitous meetings and unexpected events.

His interest in "Asia" stoked by the violent encounter, he decides to learn about Indonesia, which had been in the news. He had heard that there were only two places where Indonesia was being seriously studied: Yale and Cornell. Thanks to an "old friend," he finds a teaching assistantship at Cornell and there meets three of his most important mentors: George Kahin, John Echols, and Claire Holt. Aside from Kahin, it is Holt, an art historian, who has a profound effect on Anderson, in part because she mirrored his own predicament as an exile many times displaced and yet seeming to be at home everywhere. Anderson describes himself as "someone born in China, raised in three countries, speaking with an obsolete English accent, carrying an Irish passport, living in America, and devoted to Southeast Asia," the author of an "odd book" on nationalism, *Imagined Communities*, "that could only be written from various exiles and with divided loyalties." Holt was the daughter in a wealthy Jewish family from Riga, a dancer in Paris and New York, then the lover of the Dutch scholar William Stutterheim. She had lived in colonial Java in the 1930s, had translated for the U.S. military during the war, and fled the McCarthyism of Washington to Ithaca on the invitation of Kahin to teach courses in Indonesian culture. And it was precisely her lack of formal academic training that made her so valued by her students, particularly Anderson.[10] Her interest in Javanese mythology, arrived at unintentionally through her wanderings and love affairs, encouraged Anderson to think about Indonesian politics differently through the lens of its cultural logics. The result, as many of those in Southeast Asian studies know, has been a series of theoretically rich and highly influential essays on the politics and culture of the Indonesian Revolution and its counterrevolutionary aftermath.[11]

While Anderson was doing fieldwork in postrevolutionary Indonesia during the early 1960s, his interests were again guided by unexpected happenings. Jakarta then was adrift with possibilities, rumors, and contradictions, yet also awash in what appeared to be a genuinely egalitarian ethos. While there, he writes, he "was lucky enough to have two remarkable elderly Javanese teachers who were also brothers" to teach him about "traditional" Javanese culture while remaining "wholly sharp-eyed" about its delusions.[12] "Luck" in this case also foreshadowed catastrophe. The coup and subsequent massacres of 1965–66, which were totally unexpected both in their extent and viciousness, led to Suharto's dictatorship and the subsequent banning of Anderson from Indonesia for having coauthored a report implicating the regime for its role in the coup and the killings that followed.

But again as luck would have it, Anderson's exile from Indonesia coincided with the overthrow of the military dictatorship in Thailand in 1973 and the return to a more open society. Having cultivated close friendships with a number of Thai dissident intellectuals, Anderson was given another chance to pursue his interests in Southeast Asian revolutionary movements. And in an even more fortuitous spin of the wheel, his brother Perry Anderson had been editing the *New Left Review* and had authored important comparative works on the history of nation-state formation in Europe. Thanks to the accident of birth, Anderson found his intellectual and political horizons shifting again, toward more comparative directions. In the midst of repeated displacements and exiles, he finds himself "haunted" by unsettling questions about solidarity, difference, and imagination, while accompanied by a recurring object of love, the "imagined community." The latter is alternately figured as the nation, the family in its most extended forms, mentors, colleagues, students, and friends from various parts of the world linked by the generosity and affection of their regard.[13] The imagined community, born out of a series of violent mishaps and exiles, contingent meetings and ghostly questions, is also a community of sentiment.

It is this very notion of sentiment at the basis of community that Arjun Appadurai theorizes in his book of essays, *Modernity at Large: Cultural Dimensions of Globalization*.[14] Like Anderson, Appadurai is also an immigrant intellectual who writes, among other things, about his "own" country, India. But unlike nationalist scholars, indeed in sharp and self-conscious distinction from them, Appadurai is quick to tell us that his India is "not a reified social fact nor a crude nationalist reflex" but an "optic" from which to gauge the uneven effects of what has been termed "globalization."[15] Appadurai in this sense finds himself in the situation of many immigrant scholars from the so-called Third World working in area studies in the United States. On the one hand, there is the expectation that, unlike European immigrants, they can study only their "own" culture because that is what they are "naturally" interested in. On the other, there is the pervasive assumption that their work, like their country, will be parochial and of little consequence to the "serious" work of theory building and policymaking.

However, Appadurai converts this dilemma into an advantage. He deflects suspicions of parochialism by turning to the question of the "local" and argues that it is really there that one sees the incarnation of the social science abstraction "modernity." What interests me, though, is how this theoretical turn is initiated by an autobiographical note. Whereas Anderson's account tells of how he came to be interested in the nationalisms of Southeast Asia, Appadurai writes of how India, specifically Mumbai, drew him out of the nation and into the world. Mumbai is the setting of his earliest encounters with modernity, and there the modern is experienced in what he calls its "pre-theoretical form": as sensuous immediacy and seductive materiality. He writes of his desire for the modern in the following way: "I saw and smelled modernity reading *Life* [magazine] and American college catalogues at the United States Information Service Library, seeing B-grade movies (and some A-grade ones too) from Hollywood and Eros theaters five hundred yards from my apartment building. I begged my brother at Stanford (in the early 1960s) to bring me back blue jeans and smelled America in his Right Guard when he returned."[16]

In place of England, Appadurai discovers "America" as the site of the modern, or at least the most modern of the modern. "I did not know then that I was drifting from one sort of postcolonial subjectivity (Anglophone diction, fantasies of debates in the Oxford Union, borrowed peeks at En-counter . . .) to another: the harsher, sexier, more addictive New World of Humphrey Bogart reruns, Harold Robbins, *Time*, and social science, American style."[17]

"I did not know then," which is to say he had no idea where he was going, only that he was moving, thanks to coming into contact with the obscure shapes and smells of the "modern." It is not surprising that the modern should also have a foreign, specifically imperial origin: England, then later the United States. Through sudden and inexplicably pleasurable encounters with the objects of modernity, Appadurai comes to know that there is something he does not yet know. To come in contact with the modern in all its lush and sensuous materiality was to come into a fantasy about another "I" speaking a different language and in different accents, choosing among exotic items that seem to appear fortuitously in Mumbai. Confronted by the foreignness that is the very stuff of modernity, both in its colonial and what he terms postcolonial versions, Appadurai becomes an agent of desire whose satisfaction is forever strung out into a potentially endless series of objects: books, movies, blue jeans, deodorants, American social science. Drawn to these objects, he heads out, going from his neighborhood cinemas to the USIS library, to Brandeis University, and finally to the University of Chicago in the 1970s. Whereas Anderson begins with an unintended identification with South Asian students that leads him from England to the United States, then to the revolutions in Indonesia, Thailand, and lately the Philippines, Appadurai begins with an avid identification with commodities and their mysterious allure that leads him to follow their circuitous routes, first around Mumbai, then to the "first world," looping back to India and then back again to the American Midwest, while zigging and zagging to other areas of the physical and virtual world.

Clearly their projects have important differences. While Anderson sees in the nation the utopian possibilities of a post-Enlightenment community subsequently compromised if not violated by the state, Appadurai sees the nation-state as an exhausted form that can no longer respond to the demands of emergent communities. Anderson's interest in modernity is tied to his concern with the possibilities of nationalist revolutions and the tragic loss of such possibilities in Asia, and he has spent considerable time examining the moral, historical, and political consequences of such a loss. Appadurai is far less interested in revolution as a medium of change and far more concerned with the technologies of migrations and mediations chained to capital flows that give rise to a variety of vernacular responses and strategies of local adaptations. Hence while Anderson thematizes the historical possibilities in nationalism and its promises that have yet to be met, Appadurai has signed off (at times too hastily, in my opinion) on the nation-state, bidding it good riddance while keenly anticipating other forms of association that will take its place.

However, despite the differences in the trajectory of their projects, they are also joined by their recurring fascination with the foreign. For both, the "foreign" is memorable, if not the point from which memories arise. Surprised by the foreign, they were provoked to follow its call, drawn into its communicative power. Because it appears accidentally, as their accounts show, the foreign insinuates a gap in their lives that they are compelled to cross imaginatively and physically. Contact thus leads to communication or, more precisely, the fantasy of communication. Such a fantasy is enacted in the process of translation, or what Appadurai theorizes as "vernaculariza-tion," which entails substituting the foreign for the familiar and vice versa.

But such translations, as they point out, are never complete. They are always lacking and are bound to be full of errors and mistakes, thereby making more translations necessary. They thus lead you out: to texts you did not think existed, to places you did not expect to go to, to encounters you did not foresee. Responding, as the epigraph from Siegel says, to the incitement of all sorts of invitations, one finds new ways of becoming bewildered.[18] In this way one becomes a kind of exile, transformed into someone who is, we might say, periodically beside oneself. To the extent that encounters with alien presences compel Anderson and Appadurai to travel and translate, the alien becomes the source of the language with which to fashion their own identities as agents exiled from any fixed identity. Hence when they speak of themselves, it is always in terms of two "I's," one that belongs to them and their disparate histories and the other that belongs to someone else who eludes them but to whom they are nonetheless attached.[19]

The irresolvable doubleness of their identity is, I suspect, prototypical of all other practitioners of area studies. A stranger to itself, it is an identity that is not only in motion but is always in translation. Such translations, which form the stuff of their, and perhaps I should say our lives, are never complete because they are never exact. Working with foreign language sources, we know how words in one language never have their exact equivalent in another. What we have are always approximations. Part of us hopes that somehow these will be heard by others in ways we intended them to. But the other part of us, the other that is our double who resides in language, whether native or foreign, makes sure that this is never quite the case. Meanings remain elusive, and something always escapes only to emerge elsewhere in one guise or another. At times we find them, or more often they find us, confronting us in forms we did not anticipate. And when they do, and we are surprised, or we mistake them for something else but feel compelled to live through that error and follow the traces they leave behind, then we may be certain that our work, the work of area studies, will have begun again.

CHAPTER 7

Contracting Nostalgia

On Renato Rosaldo

Before he even begins his first book, *Ilongot Headhunting, 1883–1974*, Renato Rosaldo offers a gesture at once utterly conventional and endlessly suggestive. He writes in the acknowledgments, "I am most indebted to my Ilongot friends and companions whose names (pseudonyms, for obvious reasons) appear in this book. It has been a pleasure to recollect our conversations and days of walking together along the trails."[1] He says in effect: The Ilongots, who are the subject of my book, are also my friends. They have given me so much, enough to sustain a life of scholarship, we might add, devoted to probing the elementary aspects of social analysis, indeed, the very relationship between culture and truth, which, of course, is the title of his second book. In announcing his friendship with the Ilongots, however, he also renames them, "for obvious reasons." He tells of their lives and relishes his time with them but gives them fictitious names. In keeping with ethnographic convention, he keeps their identities hidden. This hiding is understood as a sign of respect and a form of protection. In revealing Ilongot lives, Renato also keeps something out of view. He guards a secret and in so doing makes a return gift to his friends.

We might ask: what is the nature of this return gift? How is it a response to the gift of friendship he receives from his Ilongot companions? How is it possible for one to befriend the other? Indeed, how do friendship and otherness necessarily go together, along with indebtedness and secrecy?

How do these, in turn, allow for feelings of pleasure in the recollection of "days walking together along the trails"?

Even before he begins, then, Renato has already begun to broach some of the most enduring topics in anthropology: the exchange of gifts, the politics of friendship, the question of otherness, the significance of affect, the work of memory, identity, and secrecy, among others. In the course of rereading his first two books—of walking, as it were, along the trails he had cleared for many of us to follow—I found myself drawn to a particular topic that kept resurfacing, one that seemed to encapsulate many of those questions. I refer to the topic of nostalgia.

Throughout Renato's early writings, nostalgia takes on a number of distinct but overlapping registers. In chapter 3 of *Culture and Truth,* he speaks of it in relation to imperialism. The nostalgic recollection of colonial societies as benign oases of civilization amid so much savagery propped up by racial hierarchies understood as the benevolent ordering of social differences results in the mystification of power relations. As Renato points out, imperialist nostalgia occludes the culpability of the colonizers and their elite collaborators in the oppression of colonized subjects. Rather than "moral indignation," it creates an "elegiac mode of perception" that not only covers over the crimes of empire but also lends an aura of innocence to its agents. Those agents revisit the scene of the crime and are told that they were not to blame but instead to be congratulated. Small wonder that imperialist nostalgia generates a yearning for "the very forms of life they (i.e., the agents of empire) intentionally altered or destroyed." Hence its fundamental contradiction: "A person kills somebody, and then mourns the victim . . . [or he] deliberately alters a form of life and then regrets that things have not remained as they were prior to the intervention."[2] Nostalgia in the service of imperialism memorializes the death of the other's culture while sanctifying the perpetrators of the latter's demise.

In Renato's view, nostalgia appears not merely as an ideology. More important, it is understood as a way of restructuring memory along a cluster of sentiments with which to pass judgment on historical events. Nostalgia in this case promises to purify colonialism's agents, draining their memory of any guilt. The redemptive promise of nostalgia perhaps explains its persistence. It can migrate from its imperialist associations and travel to—or, as Renato puts it, "infect"—postcolonial ethnographers. It is in this sense like a disease that can be contracted by anyone who comes into contact with its carriers. And given the global spread of empire, imperialist nostalgia is bound to contaminate those who come in the wake of colonial rule.

It seems, then, that no one is safe from contracting nostalgia, imperialist or otherwise. Exposing its workings, Renato had hoped to inoculate his readers from its mystifying effects. To do so, he tells stories about his own bouts with nostalgia during his fieldwork among the Ilongots. In foregrounding another register for nostalgia—that of the ethnographic—he shows how its effects can also be transformed. Here's an example:

> In late December 1968, a group of Ilongots and I walked to the nearest lowland municipal center where we witnessed the mayor's inauguration. . . . During that walk, my Ilongot companions appeared in my imagination as if they were Hollywood Apaches (at other times, incidentally, I imagined them as pirates) and the towns we visited appeared (to me) to be straight out of the Wild West. . . . My field journal . . . contains only the laconic phrase "all very frontier town," referring no doubt to my vivid fantasies of cowboys and Indians. In my ethnography, this nostalgia enters, but by then in an ironic mode: "Like William Jones (i.e., the American anthropologist who had written about the Ilongots in the period of US colonial rule), I felt I was bearing witness to the end of an era." Yet no one would have been more surprised than Jones to learn that nearly 60 years after his death I would be meeting Ilongot young men who still walked about in G-strings and red hornbill earrings (a sign of having taken a human head!). . . . I recast nostalgia for the "vanishing savage" in the ironic mode rather than as sincere romance.[3]

Later on, Renato quotes from the field journal of Michelle Rosaldo to further illustrate the ironic shift from imperialist to ethnographic nostalgia: "I was pained to find myself in quest of something everyone said was dying: where are the priests? . . . Which hamlets have most betel chewers, G-strings?" The sense of the Ilongot world on the verge of vanishing while surviving in some other form is reflected in the last, elegiac paragraph of *Ilongot Headhunting*: "If the past is any guide, Ilongot society has followed not a straight line of progression, but an uneven motion, now starting, now stopping, then shifting direction. . . . The present period of transformation— however it turns out in the end—makes especially clear the wisdom and pain in the recognition by Ilongot parents that their children will walk different paths as they grow up into worlds unlike their own."[4]

In these passages, ethnographic nostalgia comes across as an inheritance—a gift that is also a curse—from the imperial past. Renato acknowledges even as he displaces the legacy of the colonial anthropologist William Jones and those of U.S. popular culture. Where imperialist nostalgia disavows responsibility for destroying the very forms of native life it misses, postcolonial ethnographers signal their unavoidable complicity. They take on their predecessors' guilt. Here nostalgia allows for something else to take place: for "witnessing," as Renato puts it, the death not just of cultures but of modes of cultural survival that entail the anticipation of a future yet to come, which is to say, of a future beyond anticipation. Between and betwixt past and present, the ethnographer recalls the possibility of an afterlife for culture. In responding to the traces of colonial history, he takes responsibility for what he sees, knowing that he cannot fully live up to its demands, much less predict the consequences of his intervention. In this way, the ethnographer redoubles his ironic position. He becomes responsible only by being irresponsible, taking on the risk of failing to live up to the ethical demands set loose by the gift of nostalgia.

In a postcolonial context, then, ethnographic nostalgia becomes a practice of witnessing at the same time that it spawns the proliferation of ethical dilemmas. We can see further evidence of this witnessing in the remarkable series of photographs taken by Renato that appear in Ilongot Headhunting. The captions name some of the people, albeit fictitiously, while in others they remain anonymous. At times, the images recall the photographic styles of earlier colonial officials, such as Dean C. Worcester, Charles Martin, and William Jones.[5] Such photographs would seem in danger of repeating the imperial aim of converting natives into a series of visible abstractions, reifying native life into a series of types for illustrating the general category of "savagery." Yet it is possible to read Renato's photographs of the Ilongot as critical displacements of these inherited styles. How so?

Take the portraits of the unnamed Ilongot men that appear on pages 115, 116, and 147.

In these photos, one senses the force of nostalgia at work. The heads of these men remain attached to their necks and shoulders, while the rest of their bodies are left outside of the frame. These are not exactly decapitated

Figures 7.1, 7.2, and 7.3 Ilongot men.
Courtesy of Renato Rosaldo.

heads, the throwing of which Ilongots regarded as crucial for addressing their "anger" and for allowing boys to become men. But neither are they generic renderings of "utter savages" for scientific study. There is instead a startling individuation of their features. This is achieved by the camera's lens as it focuses on the men's faces, foregrounding their features while blurring the background. The heads appear as if surrounded by something invisible or, more precisely, by a visible invisibility. As portraits rather than mere specimens, it is tempting to see their heads suffused in a halo of dignity. They stimulate in us a wish to assimilate them as another version of ourselves, readily translatable into Western humanist ideas of the person. However, looking more closely, there is something else that we see. Face to face with the photographs, we expect to see ourselves mirrored in their eyes. But this does not happen since the men do not look directly into the camera. They do not gaze at the viewer and solicit his or her recognition as conventions of portraiture might lead us to expect.[6] Rather, they look away at some unseen object as if in deep thought. They thus see outside the frame, beyond what the camera is able to show. The camera holds them up close for us to look at. But what we see is that they see something else, beyond the conditions of their technological capture. Their eyes seem to outstrip the mechanical eye of the camera and by extension that of the viewer of these photographs. The effect is one of proximity to a fugitive figure that bespeaks of a persistent difference. Appearing familiar and close, they nonetheless remain irreducibly foreign and distant.

Anonymous *and* intimate, Renato's photographs of Ilongots disclose something that is always yet to be disclosed. They stir our imagination in that they depict figures that are bearers of a certain secret. Here the identity of the other is offered up at the very moment it is withdrawn. As the traces of ethnographic nostalgia, these photographs prompt the apprehension of that which eludes comprehension, inviting us to welcome the coming of those who are never fully present and thus never cease coming. Such images posit something inexhaustible so that the men appear up close even as they remain unapproachable and unconquerable. For this reason, we can begin to imagine them as Renato must have and undoubtedly still does: as friends and companions. With them, he shares a certain singularity, which is to say an irreducible otherness that is the basis of their commonality. Like his camera, he comes to know them and becomes intimate with them, but only to the extent that he can neither see nor know them fully, much less predict and prescribe their future. Between them, there persists a huge divide in power and privilege, in language and life worlds. The photographs do not so much suture this gap as bring such differences up close.

In these textual and photographic examples, we see how nostalgia refers to a state of excitation. In its ethnographic register, it compels us to consider a series of impossibilities: of guilt without absolution; of responsibility that is always already turned toward irresponsibility; of innocence irrevocably contaminated by criminality; of modes of revealing that are also acts of concealing; of intimacy and friendship predicated upon secrecy and estrangement. Whoever contracts the disease of nostalgia and inherits its legacy is provoked into recalling more than can ever be memorialized, much less accounted for. We have seen how this provocation gripped colonial agents and contemporary U.S. ethnographers alike, though in different ways and with different effects. It remains to be seen, presuming that there is still some remainder left to be seen, if nostalgia similarly contaminates native life.

We learn from Renato's accounts that nostalgia among the Ilongots is in fact a recent development. Grief over loss, anger and envy, passion and desires—at least in their masculinized forms—found expression in the practice of headhunting among the Ilongots. Such a practice existed right up to the late 1960s, during Renato and Michelle Rosaldo's first extended stay in the field. But by the 1970s the practice had stopped. A combination of events, such as the conversion of the Ilongots to Christianity by American evangelicals, the opening up of Ilongot territory by airplane, the rush of lowland influences, and, most important, the ban on headhunting enforced by the Martial Law regime of Ferdinand Marcos all conspired to put an end to this highly valued practice. With the end of headhunting, Ilongots were plunged into a profound sense of uncertainty about their future. They were yet to find new ways of escaping from the grip of this anxiety and grief, although some did so by converting to Christianity and abandoning Ilongot ways. It was in the midst of these drastic cultural changes that Ilongots found themselves infected with nostalgia, or at least "something like" it. The carrier of that infection was another machine: the tape recorder brought by Renato and Michelle on their return trip. Renato writes of this event in *Culture and Truth*:

On one occasion, Michelle Rosaldo and I were urged by Ilongot friends to play the tape of a headhunting celebration we had witnessed some five years before. No sooner had we turned on the tape and heard the boast of a man who had died in the intervening years than did people abruptly tell us to shut off the recorder. Michelle Rosaldo reported the tense conversation that ensued:

"Tukbaw, Renato's 'brother,' told us that it hurt to listen to a head-hunting celebration when people knew that there would never be an-other. As he put it: 'The song pulls at us, drags our hearts, it makes us think of our dead uncle.' And again: 'It would be better if I had accepted God, but I still am an Ilongot at heart; and when I hear that song, my heart aches as it does when I must look upon unfinished bachelors whom I know I will never lead to take a head.'"[7]

Renato's reproduction of the notes of the dead—for Michelle had fallen to her death in a hiking accident in 1981—about the effects of listening to the recorded voice of the dead is uncanny, to say the least. Thanks to the me-chanical agency of print and tape recorder, the dead return and commune with the living. This communing, however, cannot but generate unsettling effects. Renato says only that the sound of the dead man's voice emanating from the recorder "evoked powerful feelings of bereavement, particularly rage and the impulse to headhunt."[8] Michelle Rosaldo is more specific in her account of the same incident as it appears in her own book, *Knowledge and Passion: Ilongot Notions of Self and Social Life*:

It was not simply grief, not the old man's voice on the tape, that had disturbed them. It was, they said, the song itself that made their breath twist and turn inside them; it pained them because it made them want to kill. Tukbaw, Insan added, had stepped outside when the tape was play-ing so that the young boys who had never taken heads would not know of the intensity of his reaction; he had wanted to cry and felt ashamed. . . . [The song] could not help but stir them. . . . Surely the recent past had given my friends cause for something like nostalgia.[9]

"Something like," but perhaps not quite nostalgia. The hesitation on Mi-chelle's part is echoed as well in Renato's account, suggesting their, and our, chronic failure to delimit the shape and determine the reach of nostalgia. What is clear is that in the Ilongot case, and no doubt in Renato's quotation of Michelle's retelling of the incident, "something like nostalgia" comes up whenever we are assailed by the material remains of the dead. Exposed to the voices of those who are both radically other yet radically intimate, we find ourselves caught up in a train of involuntary memories. We cannot stop thinking of what we have lost—the companionship of a partner, the exhilarating experience of taking heads—and all that is associated with it.

As far as I can tell, there is no Ilongot word for *nostalgia*. Yet to feel one's breath "twist and turn," to experience pain and suffer shame as Ilongots did at the approach of a dead man's voice singing about a dying culture is surely to come under the spell of some sort of sickness. The *Oxford English Dictionary* tells us that *nostalgia* is synonymous with *homesickness*: "a depressed state of mind and body caused by a longing for home during one's absence from it." Listening to the tape recorder, the Ilongots are overtaken by what they recall. Succumbing to the compulsive aspect of remembering, they feel adrift, cut off from their ability to cut off heads and thus from all that had seemed familiar to this point. For this reason, they no longer felt at home. Their world now seemed inhabited by forces as mysterious as they were alienating. Once the site of hospitality and refuge, "home" had become a place of exile, where shame arose over the incapacity to discharge desire. For the Ilongots the ethnographer's tape recorder brought home the keen realization that they were no longer at home. Thanks to the workings of the tape's mechanical memory, they discovered the impossibility of returning to a memory that nonetheless kept returning to them.

From being a site for the reproduction of life, "home" here becomes a place of unaccountable loss. Indeed, the OED informs us again, one of the meanings of *home* is that of a trope for "referring to the grave, or future state," as in the "last home." Nostalgia or homesickness reminds us of what we often struggle to forget: the irreducible doubleness of home as a site of surviving, but a surviving that takes place always in view of deaths past and yet to come. The ethnographic description of Ilongot homesickness thus allows us to see something of the historical spread of nostalgia made possible by the uncanny and unjust transformation of the experience of being "at home" in the postcolonial world. It allows us to see who "we" are, whoever that "we" might be, in terms of what that "we" will have been.

I want to end with a memory that, like all genuine memories, threatens to carry me elsewhere, far from where I would have wanted to end. I first heard of Renato Rosaldo before I ever met him, by way of the tragic news of

Figure 7.4 Renato Rosaldo at Stanford, 2006.
Photograph by the author.

Michelle Rosaldo's death in 1981. I was then in my second year of graduate school at Cornell in upstate New York, far away from Manila, which was the only home I had known until then. I was sharing a house with three anthropologists, and it was from one of them that I heard the news. At that time, I did not know how to feel about Michelle's death, much less Renato's sorrow. Not knowing Renato personally, hearing of Michelle's death was a little bit like reading about the passing of some public figure in the obituary columns: one took notice of the person's accomplishments but remained immune to any sense of grief.

Five years later, in 1986, I met Renato face to face for the first time while I was a fellow at the Stanford Humanities Center. We had adjoining offices, and I have keen memories of visiting each other's rooms and standing in the hallway before lunch swapping stories and jokes. We laughed at anything and sometimes at nothing. The memory of Renato's laughter revised my earlier memory of Michelle's death. It was hard to imagine Renato angry and grieving. It was not until I read "Grief and the Headhunter's Rage" that I began to appreciate even more the sound of his laughter. Looking back, it now occurs to me that it was the response not only to jokes long forgotten but also to the call of something at once near and far. The wide smile followed by the involuntary convulsions was not simply a kind of release, a recurring catharsis from the insistent claims of death and its ghostly envoys. It was also, like his time with the Ilongots, an opening up to the moment in all its contingency, filled with the living otherness of others. It now makes me think of something like nostalgia, or perhaps nostalgia's estranged cousin, compassion. The philosopher Jean-Luc Nancy writes about "com-passion" as a kind of contagion too: "It is the contact of being with one another in this turmoil. Compassion not as altruism (or pity) nor is it identification; it is the disturbance of violent relatedness."[10]

Nostalgic for those days at Stanford with Renato, I find myself "twisting and turning in pain" at the thought of their loss. At the same time, it also makes me think about the unbridgeable gap between the ethnographer and the natives, one that, as Renato has shown, allows for no definitive suturing and assimilation. Their loss and mourning resists translation into ours. The Ilongots no doubt continue to face an uncertain and precarious future, like all other indigenous peoples in the Philippines. Renato's work brings us and other readers to come into a "violent relatedness" with their lives at a particular moment in history. It is this act of "com-passion" that I am grateful for and for the survivals it has made possible, including these words, here, on this page, that even now is coming to an end.

....

CHAPTER 8

Language, History, and Autobiography

Becoming Reynaldo Ileto

English at the Limit of Tagalog

Reynaldo Ileto is fond of telling a story about the genesis of his book *Pasyon and Revolution: Popular Movements in the Philippines, 1840–1910*. While it is the revised version of his 1973 Cornell dissertation, "Pasyon and the Interpretation of Change in Tagalog Society," the seeds for the book were actually planted in the course of his first overseas trip, in 1965. His Chinese mestiza grandmother, who had lived through the revolution against Spain and the American and Japanese occupations, took him to Hong Kong and Japan for a ten-day tour. Though unremarkable, the trip "made me question what I was studying at the Ateneo." It eventually led him to shift from engineering and science to the humanities. He even took a course in elementary Nippongo. Along with classes in philosophy, the "mélange of humanities subjects . . . formed the core of my thinking for *Pasyon and Revolution*."[1] What is widely acknowledged to be one of the most important works in Philippine history—and perhaps in Philippines studies for over a generation—thus had its origin in foreign sources: first in Japan, then in the United States. Furthermore its beginnings had nothing to do with Philippine history as such, but rather lay outside of it, in the humanities, Western philosophy, even the Japanese language.

Thus the striking irony of *Pasyon and Revolution*: that its meticulous concern for illuminating indigenous ideas of power, structures of consciousness, and notions of futurity comes through only from a position and perspective outside of the native and the national. Similarly, the vernacular specificity of Tagalog ideas such as *awa* (pity), *liwanag* (light), *damay* (mourning or compassion),[2] and so forth, become understandable only through its explication in English. Indeed, Ileto admits that, because he grew up like most middle- and upper-class Filipinos of his generation, speaking English at home and in school, his grasp of Tagalog was weak. In his Batangueño wife, Loolee Carandang, he found a kind of translator, a "living dictionary" of Tagalog.[3] Her knowledge of the language helped Ileto understand the documents he read. Spending a year living with Loolee's family in Tanuan, Batangas, while doing research for his dissertation, further sharpened Ileto's grasp of Tagalog. For Ileto, then, the mother tongue, Tagalog, is actually an other tongue, while the alien language, English, is far more familiar and intimate. While *Pasyon* privileges the semantic power of the vernacular, it is the second tongue, English, that makes the first legible.

Yet while *Pasyon* was conceptualized and written outside of the Philippines, Ileto makes very clear who its intended audience is: "we Filipinos," meaning English-literate, Westernized and, in Renato Constantino's terms, "mis-educated and neo-colonized" members of a small but vastly influential upper and middle class.[4] It is to "modern Filipinos" that Ileto directs his study of putatively premodern peasant movements in an attempt, perhaps, to disabuse them of their "mis-education." His project is predicated on recuperating vernacular sources from colonial archives, examining the obscure history of popular rebellions, recalcitrant nationalisms, and errant communities led by "fanatics" driven by "superstition," and to do so while shedding light on the understanding of those "from below." In doing so, he highlights the language of peasants by resituating key Tagalog words. Standing amid the flow of English discourse, Tagalog terms like *loob* (inside), *lakaran* (pilgrimage), *anting-anting* (amulet), *liwanag at dilim* (light and dark) appear throughout the text in their original form. Further intensifying their visibility are the lengthy passages from the *Pasyon* text as well as other accounts by peasant leaders such as Felipe Salvador that are reproduced beside their English equivalents. The recurring appearance of the original Tagalog words has the effect of interrupting the smooth flow of the English text. They arrest our reading by calling attention to the gap between the two languages. In this way Tagalog words seem to resist reduction and assimilation into English equivalents and, by implication, into colonial and elite categories.

In reading *Pasyon*, one has the sensation of moving between two languages and the worlds they contain. But one is also conscious of a persistent and unbridgeable rift between the two. This is because the Tagalog terms, although given English approximations, nonetheless remain visible and unchanged. They seem, then, like proper names, as they traverse but do not morph into different languages.[5] In their original form Tagalog words seem to insist on their singularity, giving them a certain agency apart from the claims of English. However, the agency of the vernacular—its capacity to withstand and exceed translation into another tongue—is discernible to "us" only as long as it remains suspended in English. For it is through English that Ileto is able to see in Tagalog words a kind of uncanny power to mobilize a mass of interests and commitments at odds with those of the educated and the wealthy ruling classes. In other words, English provides the discursive grid within which to see the textual power of Tagalog. At the same time, Tagalog's power to resist reduction into English is reliant upon the latter's explication. Throughout the book English and Tagalog are thus less opposed than juxtaposed to one another. As the language of American colonial rule and postwar elite nationalism, English furnishes the scaffolding with which to support and make visible the power of Tagalog. Bristling in practically every paragraph of the book, Tagalog emerges as the semantic lodestar that forces "us, modern Filipinos" to rethink the limits *and* necessity of English in conveying a "Filipino" past.

For Ileto, the stakes of this translation project could not be higher. By deciphering the masses' terms for understanding and acting upon their given conditions, "we" can better decide on the direction of "social reform": "We can either further accelerate the demise of the 'backward ways of thinking' . . . in order to pave the way for the new, or we can graft modern ideas onto traditional modes of thought. Whatever our strategy may be, it is necessary that we first understand how the traditional mind operates, particularly in relation to questions of change. This book aims to help bring about this understanding."[6] Here we arrive at a curious contradiction. The implicit political aim of the book—to contribute to "social reform" in a time of growing unrest and recurring class warfare in the Philippines—assumes that "we," the readers and author of the book, are obliged to understand "them," the masses whose words and acts make up the objects of the book's study. And in comprehending the deep structure of their seemingly fanatical actions, we are led to see them as rational actors, every bit as human as "we" are. Thanks to the work of translation, we can come to recognize the other as an aspect of ourselves. Rather than accursed others, we can see them as *kapatid*, or siblings, with whom we share a common national bond and to whom we bear a moral obligation. Hearing their words "we" take on the duty to "reform" and "rescue" them from historical forgetting and social injustice.

It is worth noting, however, that though we might sense the other as akin to ourselves, it is much less certain that the reverse is ever true, that is, that we see ourselves to be like them. This political project of reform invariably places "us" necessarily in a hierarchical relationship with "them." It is "we" who come to understand the "traditional mind" from below (rather than the other way around) from our position above. The social construction of the book's readership is thus at odds with its linguistic features. "We" readers attend to those from below in order to comprehend them and better intervene in their lives without necessarily altering their positions. But the politics of translation moves in a different direction. In the book English highlights Tagalog in order to give way to it. It defers to Tagalog, acknowledging its capacity to organize experience and actualize a world steeped in the ethos of *utang na loob* (debt of the inside), *kalayaan* (freedom), and *damayan* (mourning). From the perspective of language, then, the great accomplishment of *Pasyon* is to chronicle those historical moments when social hierarchy was periodically challenged and also when linguistic hierarchy was loosened. In fact it enacts this very linguistic movement. It shows how the translation of Tagalog into English leads not to the substitution of one for the other but to the decisive displacement of the latter's hegemony to speak for and about the former. In contrast, from the perspective of readers, translation also becomes a way of consolidating social hierarchy, reinforcing "our" position as English-literate Filipinos to represent and intervene into the lives of those other Filipinos inhabiting largely vernacular worlds. Put differently, whereas English posits the power of Tagalog to make the world, the English-literate author and readers posit their power to understand and remake the world of Tagalog speakers.

Translation therefore produces discrepant effects, leveling linguistic hierarchy at one moment, only to shore up class inequality in the next. This tendency, at once contradictory *and* productive of certain possibilities, is perhaps inherent in translation, especially in the case of the Philippines, as I have already suggested elsewhere.[7] It is also manifested in other aspects of Ileto's work. We see this, for example, in his autobiographical writings.

Authorship and Authority

In the course of Ileto's post-*Pasyon* career we can discern an intriguing turn to the autobiographical. Consciously inserting himself into his texts, Ileto has sought to evoke his milieu as a way of accounting for his particular approach to and understanding of such topics as popular movements, contemporary politics, and comparative imperial legacies in Spain, the United States, and Japan. By objectifying the social conditions of his work, Ileto has sought to establish his own life as the context against which a series of historical topics are read and interpreted. Whether it is writing about the postwar development of Southeast Asian studies, the preface to the Japanese translation of *Pasyon*, or, more recently, the U.S. Empire from the perspective of his father's experience in the 1930s to the 1950s compared with the son's travels through the 1960s and 1970s, Ileto's use of autobiography seems to mark a departure from the linguistic concerns of his earlier work. Only rarely does he bring up questions of language and translation, and only then as an adjunct to the more pressing questions of self-discovery and self-transformation amid changing geopolitical and material conditions. In the earlier work the fetish quality of the vernacular to produce and not simply represent the world in which it figured was a major motif. In later writings Ileto seems to sidestep the vernacular world in favor of tracing the self's movement outside and around it. Yet there is, I think, a way to see in the later texts a retracing and working through of the unresolved tensions between the linguistic and the social that remains characteristic of *Pasyon*.

How, then, do we think about autobiography in the context of Ileto's work? Before proceeding any further I should make it clear that the remarks that follow do not make up a historically accurate (if there is such a thing) account of Reynaldo Ileto in all his worldly complexity. It is rather a close reading of Ileto's construction of Ileto—the self-textualization of his life, as it were—which, after all, is what constitutes an autobiography. At no point is my reading meant to refer to the "real" Ileto, whose singularity doubtless exceeds even his own textualization, but only to the figurative "Ileto" who emerges from his own writings. Selective, partial, and retrospectively re-garded from shifting perspectives and interests, autobiographical writing tends to share some of the elements of fiction, if by "fiction" we mean the imaginative (re-)creation of a world related to but always at a tangent from the real one we inhabit. We can think of Ileto's autobiography, then, in this way: as the documentation of a life that, seen from the vanishing point of the present, necessarily entails the work of imaginative recuperation. As with confession, it will contain lapses and errors as much as insights and revelations. Autobiography as the self-conscious reckoning with one's own past thus stands midway between the genres of history and literature. In the writing of the self (in both senses of the genitive) the empirical and the fictional are inextricably bound.

So how does autobiography work in Ileto's writings? It does so in two related ways: as anti-imperialist critique and as nationalist affirmation. In this sense we can think of Ileto as part of a long line of Filipino thinkers, from Jose Rizal to Apolinario Mabini, from Emilio Aguinaldo to Claro M. Recto, from Renato Constantino to Horacio de la Costa. Indeed, these writers serve as the ethicopolitical points of reference in Ileto's work, even as his historiographic and theoretical orientation owes more to his British and American teachers at Cornell and the European philosophers he read at the Ateneo de Manila. We can see Ileto's affiliation with this nationalist generation in one of his most oft-repeated stories about Cornell. He tells of his initial encounter with Professor Oliver Wolters (1915–2000), who was perhaps the most important authority on early Southeast Asian history at the time.[8] Ileto recalls how this former British colonial official, who had been involved in suppressing the communist insurgency in Malaya during the Emergency, sternly warned the young Filipino student in 1967 against writing nationalist history:

> Seated behind his desk, [Wolters] reached back and pulled out of the bookcase behind him a book titled A Short History of the Filipino People,[9] au-thored by a certain Teodoro Agoncillo[, who] was at that time one of the Philippines' most prominent historians, based in the University of the Philippines' History Department. Born in 1912, he was just three years older than Wolters. I didn't know much about this Filipino historian in 1967, because I had attended the Jesuit-run Ateneo de Manila, a rival of the University of the Philippines. . . . I couldn't grasp the full implica-

tions, then, of Wolters' warning about this Agoncillo textbook: *Mr Ileto, you are not going to write history like this!*[10]

Here the professor tells the student what *not* to write. Learning begins with a negative injunction. Forbidden to write like Agoncillo, Ileto nonetheless comes to develop a deep, albeit critical appreciation of his work. He is especially captivated by Agoncillo's book on the Katipunan, *The Revolt of the Masses*.[11] The figure of Andres Bonifacio as it emerged in the book gives Ileto a glimmer of what his dissertation will be about. The professor's *no* thus lays the groundwork for a *yes*. It stirs the student's interest precisely toward what he was barred from. When he sets aside this prohibition, his disobedience proves to be productive. He discovers a thesis topic and writes what would become an astonishingly significant book that, years later, would place his professor in the position of deferring to him in admiration. In this scene of transgression, the lowly brown student initially accedes to, but eventually dispenses with, the order of the white professor. Autobiography allows Ileto to imagine himself divided into two: a younger, naïve "I" who does not know what he is not even supposed to know, and an older, more knowledgeable "I" who looks back in amusement and pride at how the former overcomes his own ignorance and insecurity. He does so by engaging in a dialectical struggle with his professor and eventually prevails, even as he conserves the authority of the younger "I," making it into an aspect of his own self. The young Ileto becomes a professor himself, much admired and cited like the older Wolters.[12] Relaying this story to us allows the older Ileto of the future to recuperate and safeguard the memory of the younger Ileto for a readership in the present. As readers and listeners of the story, we come to register and validate the unification and consolidation of this divided self into a self-authorizing figure, who signs his name in books and articles as "Reynaldo Ileto" across space and time.

In discovering Agoncillo's *Revolt*, Ileto, like Bonifacio before him, engages in a series of other revolts against a number of authority figures. Once at Cornell he rebels not only against Wolters but also against the Jesuit fathers. They "had hidden from" Ileto knowledge of the student movements at the University of the Philippines, as well as Agoncillo's nationalist history. Intrigued by the idea of the "unfinished revolution" in the book, Ileto remarks, "As a student at the Ateneo, I don't think I ever became aware of [this] notion." In reading Agoncillo, Ileto not only finds "inspiration" for his dissertation; he also "wakes up" from the ideological slumber induced by the Jesuit fathers.[13] Finally, in chapter 1 of his book, Ileto manages to take aim even at Agoncillo himself. While acknowledging the importance of *Revolt* in the writing of *Pasyon*, Ileto nonetheless remarks that something is missing in Agoncillo's book: "Although I found the story of the Katipunan and its *supremo*, Bonifacio, vividly reconstructed by Agoncillo, I remained intrigued by the relationship of the title of the book to its body. The physical involvement of the masses in the revolution is pretty clear, but how did they actually perceive, in terms of their own experience, the ideas of nationalism and revolution brought from the West by the *ilustrados*? Agoncillo assumes that to all those who engaged in the revolution, the meaning of independence was the same: separation from Spain and the building of a sovereign Filipino nation."[14] The title of the book, which is to say its head, seems to be at odds with its body. It names one thing but refers to another. Ileto regards this gap as a shortcoming on Agoncillo's part, one that he shares with other *ilustrado* thinkers. For while Agoncillo seeks to speak of the masses, he in fact fails to hear them and, like his predecessors, imposes his interpretation of events on them instead. The masses—avowed agents of the revolution—end up unheard. *Pasyon*, insofar as it seeks to "simply let Bonifacio and the Katipunan speak to us,"[15] corrects the shortcomings of this other father figure. Ileto acknowledges his debt to Agoncillo's book, simultaneously negating and subsuming it as something that his own book will one day come to surpass.

Translating the Father's Name

Containing "Agoncillo"—the name as well as the work—within the boundaries of his work leads Ileto to engage in yet another dramatic struggle, this time with his own biological father. Aside from setting him apart from Wolters and the Jesuits, Ileto writes that Agoncillo also opened up an ideological rift between him and his father, Rafael Ileto (1920–2003). In his essay "Father and Son in the Embrace of Uncle Sam," the son writes about his father in great detail. He tracks the different ways he and his father encountered the U.S. Empire as they traveled from the Philippines to study in the United States. Throughout the essay Ileto contrasts his father's response with his. Where the father enthusiastically participated in the defense of U.S. Empire against its enemies in the 1940s through the 1980s, the son, arriving in the midst of the turbulent 1960s, was deeply skeptical of imperial claims that America was a benevolent and civilizing force. Reflecting the generational divide between Filipinos who grew up under U.S. and Japanese Occupation and those who came of age in the postcolonial era, Ileto's account of his life is a stark contrast to his father's. It is a stance that is perhaps not atypical of many Filipino postcolonials (indeed, of entire generations of postcolonials in many other places in the world) growing up in an era of decolonization and dissent. In what follows I want to trace the dynamics of their relationship for what it might say about the varying constructions of nationhood, on one hand, and the unresolved issues between language and social hierarchy in *Pasyon and Revolution*, on the other.

Educated at West Point, Rafael Ileto was lauded for his wartime heroics against the Japanese as part of the combined Filipino-American liberation forces led by General Douglas MacArthur.[16] He would go on to play important roles in the making of postwar Philippines. He was one of the leaders of the counterinsurgency war against the Huks in the 1950s, after which he served in the administrations of several presidents.[17] Steeped in the ideology of anticommunism, General Ileto was deeply suspicious of anything remotely associated with the Left. Agoncillo, as Ileto points out, had been sympathetic to the Huks, a communist-aligned, peasant movement that began as an anti-Japanese guerrilla resistance movement during World War II and escalated into an anti-Republic rebellion mostly focused in central Luzon until the early 1950s.[18] This was one reason why the publication of *Revolt* was initially blocked by the Committee on Un-Filipino Activities. "To my father, who was working for the Philippine intelligence in the 1960s, *The Revolt of the Masses* was just another subversive book that helped spread communist ideas in school."[19]

Aggravating Ileto's alienation from his father was the son's decision to teach at the University of the Philippines, which his father "considered a hotbed of communism." Worse, in 1978 Ileto traveled to Red China with a group of Filipino historians, "which was a bit too much for my father." Beginning with the proper name "Agoncillo," the son finds a way to challenge and eventually exceed his father as he did with his Cornell and Ateneo professors. He escapes their influence and overcomes their authority after waking up to certain truths that had been kept from him. Banking on Agoncillo's name and work, he writes his dissertation and produces a book that establishes his name for posterity, distinguishing it from his better-known father's. In the battle of proper names "Reynaldo Ileto," the product of split selves that come to be united through the mediation of another proper name, "Teodoro Agoncillo," survives "Rafael Ileto" into the future.

Let us take a closer look at the father's name to better understand the difference between father and son. Rey calls attention to the shifts in Rafael's name as he moved from humble provincial beginnings in Nueva Ecija to positions of metropolitan prominence as a graduate of the Philippine Military Academy in 1939, then as a graduate of West Point in 1943. This journey from the periphery to the center of the U.S. Empire brought about a radical transformation in his father's identity. The change was most palpably registered in his father's name. Rafael was known as "Apeng" in the Philippines, but his efforts to "belong to America culminated in a name change" while he was at West Point. At first "they started calling him 'Ralph' but since Ralph was already the name of a roommate, they settled for a nickname that he would carry for the rest of his life: 'Rocky.'" As Rocky, Rafael sought to assimilate into the "American Dream" at a time of intense racial wars both within Jim Crow America and beyond, in the Pacific War against Japan. He played lacrosse and learned how to box, often defeating much larger white opponents. He worked hard to improve his English and "dreamed of escorting white girls to dances." He even became an honorary citizen of the small Missouri town he visited regularly as a guest of his roommate and with whose sister he exchanged numerous letters.[20]

By contrast Reynaldo Ileto was always known as Reynaldo Ileto, or Rey for short. While his father came to the United States as a bachelor desiring white girls, Rey arrived in Ithaca accompanied by his Filipina bride of two months, Loolee. Rocky moved in a world that was overwhelmingly white and segregated, where he struggled with his English and sought to establish himself as the physical and intellectual equal of any man. As a graduate student in upstate New York, Rey became ever more tied to the Philippines. Coming to America meant learning, or rather relearning, Tagalog, given his ready fluency in English. He counted among his friends many Asian and Filipino students, while his white friends were invariably fellow students involved in the antiwar movement and largely sympathetic to Asian aspirations, as opposed to American ambitions. Where Rocky was anxious to assimilate into the American Dream, Rey, already steeped in the Americanized culture of postwar Philippines, found himself awakening to an American nightmare of imperialist warfare and racial strife. Rarely ven-

Figure 8.1 Rafael Ileto with his son, Reynaldo Ileto.
Courtesy of Reynaldo Ileto.

turing beyond the confines of Ithaca to make friends with other Americans the way his father had done, Rey, as if prefiguring the language of *Pasyon*, recoiled from the "glitter of empire, the false promises and the contradictions between myths and realities. I felt no desire to belong to the America outside Cornell."[21]

On the one hand, the father moved from Tagalog to English to the point of speaking only English to his children in their home. He took on a succession of names, from Apeng to Ralph to Rocky, as he traveled from Nueva Ecija to America. The son, on the other hand, found himself imaginatively returning to the Philippines as he physically moved to America, steadfastly remaining foreign in this foreign setting. He embraced the anti-imperialism of his campus milieu and affirmed what retrospectively he came to reckon as his obscured nationalist roots. Rocky's nationalism consisted of serving the empire in the belief that he was furthering the interests of his people.

Contrast this with Rey's nationalism, which begins with the experience of "awakening," of coming to see the real "light," or *liwanag*, of truth behind the deceiving "glitter" represented by the very promises that his own father had subscribed to. Recalling Constantino's analysis of postwar Philippine society, Rocky and Rey were exemplars of colonial "mis-education." But there were important differences. The father's rite of passage to America transformed him into a "model soldier in the Empire's Army," whereas the son's journey to Ithaca not only turned him against the empire but also turned him toward the Philippines and, even more important, toward Tagalog.

It is in this process of becoming something other than what they were that we can see the connection between translation and autobiography. As we have seen, autobiography splits the self into two "I's" along a temporal axis: a future "I" encapsulating and speaking for a past "I," translating both into a narrative available to a third term, the addressee, who is the present reader or listener. We saw this in Rey's story of his encounter with Wolters at Cornell. But autobiography also depends on the biography of an other who is perhaps less enlightened, more gullible, and not quite modern, against which the self establishes itself to be better educated, more attuned to the world, and more in touch with the truth. This is what we have seen in Rey's use of his father's biography as the backdrop to his own life's story. Key to the difference between father and son was the matter of proper names. Rafael, known as Apeng, is translated into Rocky, who is then enfolded into the designs of empire. Rey, however, remains Rey. His proper name continues to be what it had always been. Unlike the father's, the son's name remains unchanged: it transfers from one country to another, from one language to another, but it does not translate. It crosses boundaries while remaining outside of and distinct from the languages and cultures that lay on either side of the divide. Like the untranslated Tagalog words that pulsate within the fabric of *Pasyon and Revolution*, "Rey" remains resistant to the seductions of empire, escaping the totality of its embrace. The autobiographical vignettes establish a precedent for the resistance of proper names. In Rey's case, the invocation of "Agoncillo," and later on "Bonifacio," serve as talismanic weapons with which to ward off attempts to translate and reduce their lives and works into oblivion. In contrast, the history of his father's name indicates how contingent and fragile such resistance can be, as the name ceases to be "proper" altogether and becomes a common marker of another power alien to the self.

Rey writes about his father, he later says, as a way of simultaneously criticizing and paying tribute to him. He wants to "show his love and gratitude . . . without being colonized by his values."[22] The son emerges as one who distinguishes himself from his origin, yet remains faithful to it. He excavates "Apeng" underneath "Rocky" in the desire to redefine the life of Rafael en route to taking stock of his own. That is, he retranslates his father's name into its putatively proper, native context. Just as in *Pasyon*, where Rey uncovers the obscured history and hidden powers of the vernacular amid layers of English, so too does he rescue, as it were, the vernacular substrate underneath the Americanized surface of his father's name. The irony, of course, is that the significance of the Tagalog "Apeng" as the hidden meaning of the Spanish "Rafael" resonates only to the extent that it can be read—translated, if you will—from the American "Rocky."

There is, however, one final twist in this battle of proper names. The task of translating his father's life in relation to his own turns out to be something carried out for the sake of his mother. Rey writes at the end of his essay, "In the latter part of their marriage, my mother herself adopted a softly critical stance towards her husband. She would agree with much of what I've said here; I have only merely given voice to her unarticulated sentiments. She is the absent presence throughout this narrative of father and son in the embrace of empire."[23] This sudden invocation of the mother brings us back to the problem of address that I mentioned earlier in relation to *Pasyon and Revolution*. Just as the author addresses "us" about "them"—the peasants from below whose history must be heard and understood if they are to become part of "our" nation—so in his autobiography he writes of himself and his father to "give voice" to his mother. It is her "absent presence" that, like the Holy Ghost, hovers over the story of the father and the son. By subsuming the father's history the son makes the mother heard, or at least makes known her "unarticulated sentiments." The son speaks of and for the mother, just as the author speaks of and for the "inarticulate masses," translating their language into something comprehensible to us. The mother, like the peasants, is not so much voiceless or mute as blocked from speaking. Unblocking their speech, the author-son reveals them to be the secret authors of history, as well as his own narratives. She stands as the repressed origin of the two men's lives, just as peasant movements exist as the "underside" of Philippine history, that is to say, as the permanent possibility of class warfare and revolutionary upheaval itself.

However, there is also an important difference between the peasants and the mother. While the peasants are made strikingly visible and readily comprehensible within the context of nationalist history, the mother remains radically other in relation to the stories of father and son. The mother is a heterogeneous element in the son's story, one whose centrality is belatedly acknowledged only to be withdrawn. She occupies two positions: as the absent "you" who receives and registers Rey's stories beyond the grave, and as the object of the story whose presence is assumed but remains repressed. Silent witness and voiceless interlocutor, she remains untouched and yet seems to be in touch with everything. While various father figures are challenged and subsumed in Rey's account, the mother, Olga Clemeña, remains between languages and proper names, circulating between men and their histories, yet barely visible in their autobiographies. She is analogous to the historical described by Deleuze as that which "amounts only to a set of preconditions, however recent, that one leaves behind in order to 'become,' that is, to create something new."[24] Becoming a man like Rey Ileto, or Rocky Ileto, required leaving behind the very history that made it possible for something new to emerge. But it also meant refiguring that history as a mother, for example, or as Inang Bayan, the motherland to whom one returns and on whose behalf one speaks, and in no less than in one's mother tongue, at once lost and found.

In the name of the father and of the son, women emerge as ghostly presences analogous to that "other" nation imagined by "us" as the mass of peasants excluded from nationalist historiography. Whether it is the mother silently agreeing with the son's critique of the father or the wife whose fluency in the vernacular makes her an essential supplement to the work of the author, women come to occupy an ambiguous place in both the historical and the autobiographical text. Like the "masses" they are both central and peripheral. As in Pasyon, so in the autobiographical writings: the author and those he addresses become who they are by virtue of having subsumed and incorporated the Other whom they are not. Seeking to broaden the basis of nationhood and deepen the personal stakes in its imagining, both the book and the autobiography also convert nationalism into a series of stories about self-alienation and its overcoming. That process of overcoming entails the rescue of those below, of those whose names are barely heard, who have been silenced and set aside. Positioned as the privileged agents for granting agency to those below, the son, author, and readers form the upper reaches of a national hierarchy that, as a matter of course, are heirs to a highly gendered colonial history.

By contrast, the linguistic play evinced in *Pasyon and Revolution* between Tagalog and English, as I have suggested, speaks to the possibility of leveling hierarchy. Rey gives a compelling explication in English of peasant movements as political projects intimately tied to ethical norms sustained by a messianic sense of history.[25] But in doing so he also makes clear that the specificity of their thoughts and actions can be grasped only in and through Tagalog. The juxtaposition of the two languages, English and Tagalog, thus allows for the opening of worlds hitherto invisible to "us." The autobiography, however, moves in a different direction. Recounting life as a series of struggles against authority figures, the autobiography betrays an investment in hierarchy whether by way of a self commemorating an absent presence—the young "I," the silent mother—or a self overcoming the other that comes before it, in all senses of that word, whether it be a professor, another author, or one's own father. There is, then, the sense that autobiography forecloses the possibilities raised in *Pasyon*. The book speaks of a kind of unfinished social revolution evinced on the level of language and translation. The autobiography, however, deploys a gendered optic that conventionalizes the process of transformation, substituting social revolution with a narrative of generational masculine succession.

Coda

Let me end with an autobiographical note of my own that might modulate and qualify my observations. It was around 1976 when I first encountered Reynaldo Ileto's work as an undergraduate student majoring in history at the Ateneo de Manila. It was in the Philippine history class of Fr. John Schumacher that I first heard of Rey's thesis. I remember becoming so excited at what seemed to be an entirely novel approach to studying the Revolution, which is to say of studying the newness of what was new, that I borrowed the thesis from the library and paid a typist to make me a facsimile copy, which at that time was actually cheaper than getting it Xeroxed. I had the facsimile bound just like a thesis. On the cover was the title, "Pasyon and the Interpretation of Change in Tagalog Society," and underneath it appeared my name, "Vicente Rafael," inadvertently placed by the typist. It was as if, in having Rey's thesis copied, his name had been erased to make way for mine.

This desire to appropriate *Pasyon* and bring it up close, so close as to blur the identity between the author and reader, has been the ongoing experience I've had with Rey's book. In fact, much of what I have since written has, to some extent, leaned on Rey's ideas, at times peeling away from them, at others displacing and disfiguring them for other uses. I always return to Rey's work whenever I am not sure how to think about the vernacular analogues for *power* and *pity*, *reciprocity* and *revenge*, *shame* and *sovereignty*, and so forth.[26] *Pasyon and Revolution* is like a country I grew up in. One could travel abroad, read other books, and dwell in the shade of other ideas. But so long as I thought about the Philippines, I found myself meandering back sooner or later to the passages of Rey's work. It was *Pasyon* that first gave me a sense of the imaginative possibilities and political salience of the vernacular, especially when deployed beside rather than merely subsumed by English-language historiography. By delineating the power of the vernacular, Rey complicates and detains every attempt to translate Tagalog ideas into English. At the same time, he questions the adequacy of English terms to substitute for the complexity of Tagalog. Reading as the experience of translation; translation as the experience of being detained and stranded between languages; and detention not simply as imprisonment but as the experience of attending patiently to the play of meanings and the expectation of something to come: these are the enduring lessons I've learned—and continue to learn—from Rey's work.

....

CHAPTER 9

Interview

Translation *Speaks with Vicente Rafael*

The following is an edited transcript of a video interview conducted by Professor Siri Nergaard, editor of *Translation: A Transdisciplinary Journal*, at the Nida School of Translation Studies, San Pellegrino University, Misano Adriatico, Italy, on 15 May 2013. The video can be accessed at http://translation .fusp.it/interviews/interview-with-vicente-rafael.

....

SIRI NERGAARD: Hello, Vicente.

VICENTE RAFAEL: Good morning.

NERGAARD: Since our journal *Translation* has the subtitle *A Transdisciplinary Journal*, you are really the perfect person for us to talk to. You are not a traditional scholar of translation studies, but you work deeply on translation from your perspective as a historian. Translation offers a unique perspective on or a new way to analyze colonialism, power, and language, especially in the Philippines, and even today in the United States. I would like you to tell the story of how translation became such a central theme for you.

RAFAEL: Like many things in life, it happened quite accidentally. By "accident" I mean that when I was in graduate school, I was looking for a topic to do and I got interested in the early modern period, the sixteenth century, looking at the Spanish colonization of the Philippines, among other things. I noticed that there were very few sources written by colonized natives themselves. Most of the history was written by Spanish missionaries. I was also quite surprised to see that a lot of the writings of Spanish missionaries had to do with problems of translating the Gospel because they had to preach in native languages in order to be understood, which, from the Spanish point of view, was more practical than translating the native languages into Spanish. It was much more convenient for the missionaries to learn the local languages than for them to teach the natives Spanish. And this was, of course, a practice consistent with what they had been doing in Latin America. So I got very interested in this topic and asked myself what would happen if one were to take a look at native languages as historical agents, because we often think of historical agents as human beings. But there is a certain way in which you can also think of language as a historical agent that is somehow free of human control or, better yet, that exceeds human control, and that's exactly the path I tried to pursue. The result is that I wrote my dissertation, which then became a book, *Contracting Colonialism*, where I talked about the centrality not just of translation but of the relationship between translation and Christian conversion. And it turns out that in the missionary tradition, the two are in fact almost synonymous. To translate, *traducir*, and to convert, *convertir*, are very closely related. And these in turn were absolutely essential for carrying out the imperial projects of conquest and colonization. So from the perspective of translation, conversion and colonization seemed to resonate with each other as part of a continuum, and that has been a recurring concern on my part, and in all of my subsequent work. In my later work, I started looking at the American Empire and American colonization of the Philippines. Along these lines, I have become quite interested in the emergence of English as a kind of hegemonic language. So those are the things that have led to my becoming very interested in translation. Originally the interest in translation grew out of my interest in larger historical issues relating to empire and colonialism.

NERGAARD: As a historian, this attention to language and translation in relation to history became a kind of obsession, as you said. How did the institutions, the universities react to this? The departments of history have not paid so much attention to language—the role of language and translation. So how was your work accepted, how was it received in the universities?

RAFAEL: Yes, I think you are right. Not just history but in many other social sciences, even in the humanities, translation tends to be ignored.

NERGAARD: Even comparative literature has ignored translation for many years . . .

RAFAEL: Among historians and many other social scientists, there is a tendency to see language in purely instrumental terms, as a means to an end, as if thought were possible without language and as if action could be separated from speech. I was truly lucky when I began my work that I found myself at the confluence of many things. I started my graduate training at the end of the 1970s at Cornell, and at that time the United States was just opening up to a fresh wave of Continental theory, mostly from France and Germany. It was the start of the Reagan and Thatcher era, and everyone was trying to think about new languages of opposition. Theory was helpful, and many of us plunged into theories, ranging from hermeneutics to deconstruction, psychoanalysis to feminism, Marxism coupled with the beginnings of postcolonial theory and cultural studies, all of which paid close attention to the workings of language. It was a time that was very hospitable to what they used to call the "linguistic turn," and so it allowed me space and resources to do my own work. But it is still a struggle. In other words, the question of language is not something that is easily thought about in the historical profession. In that sense, my work is still sort of idiosyncratic, but that is okay because then I always feel like I have something different to say than what most other historians have to say. I am not doing what you might think of as conventional historicism. I think I have something different to contribute. There are certain advantages to being on the margins. One just has to know how to take advantage of that position.

NERGAARD: You are speaking about a period in which the so-called linguistic turn took place in philosophy, but it also ignored translation.

RAFAEL: There was another thing that I was doing that made translation absolutely essential: I was involved in what, in the United States, is called area studies, which was something that had been going for a while but which came to be institutionalized with that name during the post–Cold War period. The United States was very interested in competing with and containing the Soviet Union, and one of the things that they did was try to extend not just their military influence, but also their cultural influence around the world. Part of that effort was the funding of universities to put up what they called area studies programs so they would study different regions of the world and develop a kind of scholarly expertise in these areas. These programs were analogous with, though also quite distinct from, departments of Oriental studies that had long existed in Britain, France, Holland, and many other European countries. Area studies programs, not surprisingly, emphasized language training, and of course that brought out the question of translation. There was a whole generation of area studies experts that emerged from these centers who developed fluency in these languages, and some of them became interested in the problem of translation. This included two of my advisors at Cornell, James Siegel and Benedict Anderson, and they had written particularly on problems of translation and vernacularization around the emergence of things like nationalism and authoritarianism in various parts of Southeast Asia. I was also lucky to have as one of my advisors the intellectual historian Dominick LaCapra, who was at that time very interested in Continental philosophy and writing about the historical importance of language. So I was very fortunate to be working with people who already assumed the importance of translation. In my case, as I said, translation emerged organically from the very nature of the problems I was looking at, beginning with religious conversion and then later on with the problem of counterinsurgency and militarization and so forth, where once again the force of language and the attempts to tame this force through translation were absolutely crucial.

NERGAARD: In the last works you mentioned, you introduced new terms and a new vocabulary with which to discuss translation studies: "war of translation," "translation in wartime," "weaponization of translation," "targeting translation in counterinsurgency." This is really a new vocabulary and it is quite strong.

RAFAEL: It's not so much that it is new. The other day I was rereading *The Translation Studies Reader* by Lawrence Venuti. It is very interesting to read his historical introduction to translation studies, in which he talks about, for example, Roman antiquity and the practice of translation as it was understood by the late Roman writers Cicero, Horace, and others. I am not very familiar with that history, but it was interesting to read about competing notions of translation during this era. For example, Roman attempts at translating Greek authors into Latin in great part had to do with the late

Roman desire to rival and surpass the legacy of Greece. Not only were the Romans appropriating Greek literature, writing, and thought, as Nietzsche had pointed out. They also wanted to conquer and subsume these into what we might think of as their empire of letters. It made me think how the idea of translation, at least in the West, has long been implicated in the modes of rivalry and competition—that is to say, war. Additionally, there has always been a contest between rhetorical and grammatical approaches to translation—word for word versus sense for sense—and that tension has animated, for example, translations of the Bible from St. Jerome to Luther. And, of course, it has figured in the history of missionary translations of the Gospel all the way up to today. At the Nida School of Translation Studies, we talk about this frequently.

In this connection, I was reminded by one of my colleagues who is a classicist about the interesting etymology of the word *translation*. It is, of course, from the Latin *translatus*, from *transferre*, which in turn is from *transfero*. When I looked it up in the dictionary, it meant "to transfer, convey over, to bear." It is formed by coupling *trans*, "across, through," and so on, with *fero*, which can also mean "to carry off, take away by force, to plunder, spoil, ravage." This tells us that, at least in the Western context, there is a sense that translation brings with it a history of violation, the forcible removal and transfer of words and things from one language or culture to another.

So it is not surprising that translation should figure in imperial projects of all sorts, including the latest one, which is the U.S. project to maintain its dominant position in the world. All I am doing is simply reminding people of a feature of translation that tends to get lost or submerged. It is that translation turns not just on the transfer of meaning but also on the struggle to control the processes of transferring meaning. It relates to all sorts of tensions around procedures, around the limits of what can be translated, as well as prescriptions for what must remain untranslated. In that sense, translation is always fraught, so it is always at war, as it were. And finally, something I was trying to talk about yesterday: there is what Derrida calls the logocentric tradition in Western thinking, which tends to privilege thought over speech and then, of course, speech over writing, Western scripts over non-Western scripts, and so there emerges a hierarchical chain of signs. And translation figures very prominently in formulating and maintaining this hierarchy, often by force exercised by those whose interests are best served by such a hierarchy: priests, colonial officials, oligarchs, state and media institutions of all sorts and those who identify with them or are invested in their power. Translation practices that emerge from and sustain this logocentric tradition are rampant and very powerful, as they regard languages as mere means to get at specific ends. Often enough that end, at least in the Western context, is to put an end to translation. So you can say that the danger of logocentrism is the way it positions translation to bring about the literal end of translation—the point where people will feel like everything is so transparent that there is no need to translate. That itself is part of this war of domination—over language, over expression and interpretation, over meaning—that is always going on.

NERGAARD: And it is almost always as if there were a ghost, as if that transparency were the ideal, where translation is not necessary any more.

RAFAEL: Yes, exactly.

NERGAARD: With that transparency—the end of translation—we would lose everything. We would lose plurality. We would lose meaning. We would lose everything. Nevertheless, that's the kind of ideal ghost staying there.

RAFAEL: Right.

NERGAARD: As if we could avoid difference.

RAFAEL: It is not so much really to avoid difference or to avoid plurality. It is to be able to exercise total control over linguistic pluralism and to make this control as automatic as possible. This is the dream, for example, of automatic translation systems. Now the attempt to develop automatic translation systems, which I have also written about, is precisely to make everything perfectly equivalent to everything else, which, of course, is the dream of capitalism.[1] This would be a perfectly capitalized world where everything could be exchanged for a single medium that would also act as the general measure of value and the standard means of exchange. Today, that medium and measure of exchange is increasingly English. English is now becoming the equivalent of money, the capitalist sign par excellence. So again it is not so much the disappearance of difference but rather the ability to control the production and circulation of differences that this imperial ideology of translation, in my opinion, has set out to do. It has sought to translate difference into exchange value, and thereby make it available for circulation and expropriation. Languages in this case become resources for producing profits, and translation is often seen as the means to extract the use value of languages and convert it into surplus value. This, I think, is what it means to talk about conscripting translation to produce communication that is deemed to be transparent, and to do so by way of English.

It's important to stress, however, that there are all kinds of resistances to this project, and that is part of the story that I am very interested in: to try and plot not only the ways in which this war on translation is progressing—that is, the war *of* as well *on* translation—but also the way this war is being resisted and evaded, the ways it is being displaced, the different responses to this war in such a way as to make a kind of final victory impossible. In the midst of this war, what you get is the emergence of what I call the ongoing insurgency of language. As you know, there are linguistic insurgencies of all sorts: puns, jokes, the creation of slang, pidgin and creolisms, not to mention slips of the tongue, and of course tropes, those twists and turns of speech that make necessary more speech, more writing, more interpretation—what Roman Jakobson once called "metalanguage."[2] And there is, of course, the most important arena for linguistic insurgency, which I believe to be literature. So long as you have literature you have hope. Because so long as you have literature, you have the need for translation. It works both ways: to the extent that you have translation, literature becomes possible, and to the extent you have literature, translation becomes essential.

NERGAARD: Necessary and essential.

RAFAEL: Right, to that extent you cannot have a single ideology of translation controlling the production of difference, because difference will always proliferate beyond the control of any particular translation ideology, thanks to literature.

NERGAARD: Thanks to literature . . .

RAFAEL: Yes, so literature is a principle of hope as far as I am concerned, or I should say a resource for hope in a world where translation tends to get reduced into merely instrumental terms, as, for example, when the U.S. Department of State calls translation a "complex weapons system."[3]

NERGAARD: Very interesting. And the connections to other areas in translation studies become clear. But I still suggest that you introduce a new vocabulary. With the postcolonial criticism we are familiar with concepts like power and conflict, but you use *war*. You use other concepts, too, such as weaponization . . .

RAFAEL: In part this grows out of the pressure of the events of the past thirteen years or so, including the "global wars on terror," which is a kind of brazen attempt at colonial occupation on the part of the United States in Afghanistan and Iraq as well as interventions in places like Syria, Yemen, Libya, and so forth. Not to mention of course the occupation of the Palestinian territories by Israel, which would not have been possible without the aid of the United States. All these have placed the question of war, I think, in a lot of people's minds, and my attempt to talk about translation in terms of war grows out of my concern with more recent events. There is also another aspect to this concern: that there is a way in which war has always played a central part in the formation of the modern state and society. When you think about how modern nation-states have arisen, almost every one arose precisely in the wake or in the process of engaging in war both against other nation-states, as well as against certain peoples within that particular nation-state. After all, as sociologists have told us, what would a state be, where would it derive its authority if it could not establish a monopoly on violence? So I would think that to the extent that war is constitutive of the nation-state, war also shapes social relations that take place within the state. It follows that this kind of violence would contaminate practices of translation. Indeed, one can see this by looking at the history of translation practices, showing how it is always fraught and involved in all sorts of conflict. Just as there is, as Derrida wrote many years ago, a violence that inheres in writing, so, too, I think, there is a violence that is intrinsic to every act of translation. I think, in certain cases, it helps to think about translation in those terms. I do not, of course, assume it is an appropriate way to think about translation in every possible context, but especially in contexts I have been looking at, the connection between translation and war is very useful.

NERGAARD: You probably could relate this to what Antoine Berman says,[4] that all translation is naturally ethnocentric, so you sense this violence again, because you want to change what is foreign and make it look more like what you are familiar with.

RAFAEL: I agree with that to a certain extent, in that translation might begin in a sort of ethnocentric vein, but to the extent that translation also signals a kind of ineluctable opening to the other, it also initiates a kind of ongoing alterity. Its war-making powers, as it were, invariably become attenuated. There is an alternative to thinking about translation as war, and that is translation as play.[5] The question of play turns conflict and violence in a different direction. Play is about the deferral and deflection of conflict. It is not the banishment of conflict but its reformulation into a kind of indeterminate, ceaseless displacement and dislocation that prevents any particular power relations from congealing. Play is something I would like to explore further. I have only just begun to think about this question of play, and of course there is an enormous literature on this. Play as that which attenuates the particular kind of dialectical conflict that is at the heart of war, and by so doing opens up to other possibilities, the possibilities of the literary, for example, was something I was trying to suggest yesterday. To say that play opens up the possibility of the literary presumes that the literary, as against the institution of literature, entails the practice of saying anything and everything. Play in this way is thus something that is connected to the question of freedom. Why do we play? We play because in some sense play offers a kind of escape. It offers a kind of release. It opens up an other world and an other life where nothing is stable, where no one is permanently on top, no one is permanently at the bottom, where there is a certain kind of joy not so much in controlling the other as in allowing oneself to open up, to become other. So there is a kind of delight, as much as anxiety, in the loss of identity, or the fluidity of identity.

NERGAARD: But you have to be empowered by language before you can allow yourself to play in such a fashion.

RAFAEL: Well, you have to know the rules, of course, before you can play the game, so it also brings in a certain kind of discipline, but a discipline that is not about surveillance, or at least not only about surveillance. It is a discipline that is not about submitting to a particular power but one that enables you precisely to participate in the loss of power, if you will, to loose yourself and the illusion of an undivided, unified self in control of its speech. So much of play is predicated upon this loss of the delusions of power and, as I said, a kind of opening up to a certain kind of freedom. It is to think about translation as that which is connected to an emancipatory project. That is the other side of translation as war. So, on the one hand, translation is war, which is to think of translation as ineluctably implicated in power relations. But, on the other hand, to think of translation as play, which is to regard translation as that which also has the potential to undo and reconfigure power relations, even momentarily, in the name of a more just and free world.

NERGAARD: Yesterday, during your talk at the Nida School in Misano Adriatico, you were discussing the school system back in the Philippines. Can you tell a bit more about that situation in which local languages are prohibited and the use of a foreign language is imposed?

RAFAEL: What I was talking about yesterday was American colonial education and the role it played in regulating language in the creation of what I have been calling a linguistic hierarchy.[6] I think this is typical not just in a colonial context. I think this is typical of all schools, or a majority of schools, where the idea of going to school, among other things, is the idea of learning how to behave in a certain socially acceptable way. And intrinsic to that mode of behavior is learning the ability to speak in a certain acceptable way. So one is educated in a particular way, one becomes recognizably "grown up," one becomes developed. There is this whole developmentalist philosophy that is, I think, intrinsic to all modern educational systems, colonial and postcolonial. And that has to do with being able to speak in a way that is considered "civilized" or "cultured," as they say, in order to become a subject who can claim recognition. This is not anything new. We can think of this notion of education as a set of disciplinary techniques designed to "uplift" students as a feature of modernity.

However, this idea of appearing to be, or sounding, educated means being able to speak a language in a kind of standardized, conventional way. This, in turn, often entails repressing the more idiomatic, more colloquial, more dialectical versions of that language. So one speaks Italian correctly, which means not speaking the local dialects. The local language is seen to be beneath the standard one. There is in education the creation of a linguistic ideology: that there should exist a hierarchy between the second, correct way of speaking, mandated by the modern state insofar as it sees itself to be an agent of modernity, and a first language, what we usually think of as the mother tongue, associated with the local, the provincial, the backward, literally the "vulgar." The second takes priority, becomes the first, while the first becomes second by virtue of being designated as not quite modern. And even in those cases when one of the native tongues is conscripted to become the national language, the state usually submits it to a process of recodification, orthographic regulation, grammatical policing—in short, to a process of translation. It becomes "modernized," as it were, and thus other than what it had been. This is intensified and amplified in the colonial situation. The colonial context I was talking about yesterday had to do with Filipino students who were expected to speak English, but in the process of speaking English were also expected to repress the numerous vernaculars.

And then, of course, the question becomes, to what extent is this repression successful? Or does the repressed always return? And obviously, in the case of the Philippines, this is what happens. The vernaculars cannot be kept in their place, below English and outside of the school. They return to haunt, as it were, various attempts to speak in a standardized and conventional fashion. How do we know this? Very simply, we know this because of the persistence of accents. To the extent that people still speak with accents is the extent to which their speech is always marked by the very thing they were supposed to suppress. And what is that very thing they were supposed to suppress? They were supposed to suppress their native or mother tongue, which is their origin, right? So the origin always comes back in displaced fashion: in the form of an accent. The accent is the trace of an operation— you might think of it as a kind of insurgency—of the first language within the second. And I think this is true every time people speak. They always speak with accents, and those accents always betray where they came from. Their accents always reveal another speech and so intimate another world. Deleuze has this wonderful short essay called "He Stuttered," where what he says about stuttering we can say about accents.[7] Stuttering, he says, reveals the existence of another language within language. And he goes on to talk about this when he talks about style. He says style is the foreign language that dwells within speech. And to the extent that we are enfolded in a certain style of speaking that we cannot avoid because we all speak with an accent, one that we did not necessarily invent but more likely inherited and will pass down, that is the extent to which we are always speaking in another language within the language that is socially acceptable.

So that means we are always translating whenever we speak, whether our own or another's language. We are always speaking in tongues. And it is only by repressing one tongue in favor of another that we can actually make ourselves understood. Nonetheless, there are always those other languages that continuously ebb and flow on the shores of our speech. Indeed, they form those very shores. Accents are but some of the most palpable but all too often repressed manifestation of this other, multiply mothered tongue.

NERGAARD: Can I use the accent because I want to keep my identity too? It is not that I am not able to speak proper English, but I keep my accent because that is part of my origin.

RAFAEL: Yes, perhaps. As you know, the sound of accents is always the sign of translation at work, so another way of thinking about accents is that they are the switch points where translation occurs. With accents, gaps open up and other voices emerge, however furtively. And where there are gaps, there is always the danger of failing to get across, right? This is perhaps why we get so anxious about accents when they stand out too much. Accents are precisely those sites of great danger where we run a real risk of being misunderstood and therefore being mistaken for someone other than who we thought we were. Failing to translate, to speak in the right way, we can't be recognized or end up being misrecognized, and that lack of recognition can have considerable social and political consequences. Now I don't know how you do this, but, in my case, I speak English with what would be considered a standard American accent, but when I go to the Philippines, I cannot speak like this. If I spoke like this, some people would have difficulty understanding me, or they would think that I was putting on airs, that I was trying to be better than they, because I spoke a different, more American-ized English, and so they would expect me to speak in one of the local registers. I would have to change accents, and usually within a day or two I am speaking entirely, as it were, "native." I have to "go native," right? Perhaps this happens to you too when you go to Norway? This usually is the case. So we are always translating back and forth, not only between languages but between accents, because accents are ways of marking our identity, which is to say: difference, right?

NERGAARD: Exactly. I was thinking about the history of Norway when the Danish dominated Norway and the official language was Danish. Our written language was Danish, but the accent persisted: no Norwegian speaker used the Danish pronunciation. These languages are very close, so you have the language, the nonlanguage, the in-between, and the Norwegians were still always in between. They wrote in Danish, but the pronunciation was Norwegian.

RAFAEL: Fantastic. And there is a question of whether or not it is a matter of intention. We like to think so, that our accents are simply a matter of choice. We like to think we are in control of our accents, but, in fact, to the extent that we always speak with an accent is the extent to which we cannot help but speak with one. And even when it seems as if we sound like everyone else, and so seem to have no accent at all, we are merely speaking the way everyone else is and fail to hear the sound of difference in our voices. The persistence of accents or, put another way, the impossibility of speaking in an accentless voice is perhaps due to the fact that speech in unavoidably physiological, so that it is beyond intentionality. Which is to suggest, if you take it one step further, that there is something about translation that arises every time we speak, which is also beyond our intention. There are different ways to think about this. One can think: maybe translation is hardwired into our body. We must translate, we have no choice but to translate within language, across languages, and across accents. It is precisely something that we are compelled to do. Translation is a compulsion, not simply a choice. It is like blinking or stuttering as much as it is a skill and an art. That is the other interesting thing, too, about accents: we find it is not just the sign of translation at work; it is also the sign of a certain kind of resistance to intentionality and thus a kind of resistance to the self seeking to master and dominate its words.

NERGAARD: That's very interesting. That's another area that has not been explored in translation studies at all. The physiological aspect of it also deserves study, so I will look forward to your next book, Vicente.

RAFAEL: It will be on accents.

NERGAARD: Of course. Thank you very much.

RAFAEL: You are very welcome. It has been a pleasure.

NERGAARD: Thank you.

NOTES

....

Introduction

1 See chapter 2 of this book for a discussion of colonial language policies.

2 See chapter 2 for a further elaboration of this point.

3 For the history of Taglish in creolized varieties of late nineteenth-century Spanish, see Anderson, *Why Counting Counts*. See also Rafael, "Taglish, or the Phantom Power of the Lingua Franca," in *White Love and Other Events in Filipino History*, 162–88. Also useful are the recent collections of essays in Bautista and Bolton, *Philippine English*; and Mabanglo and Galang, *Essays on Philippine Language and Literature*. An important study from a sociolinguistic perspective is Gonzalez, *Language and Nationalism*.

4 This private school argot refers, respectively, to La Salle Taft and Green Hills (where the preponderance of Spanish mestizos meant that English and Tagalog were liberally laced with Spanish, especially cuss words), Assumption Convent (a school for the daughters of the wealthy and the aspirational middle class, where a characteristically precious sing-song type of Taglish emerged), the Ateneo de Manila University (the Jesuit school of Rizal and other notable Filipino intellectuals, which, once taken over by American Jesuits, became the site for the emergence of an American English that pretentiously sought to approximate standard American pronunciation), and Xavier School and Immaculate Concepcion (the Catholic-run Chinese schools where Mandarin was required alongside English and, by the 1970s, Tagalog, but where Hokkien and Cantonese were also spoken by the students). A history of this creolized milieu from the 1950s to the 1970s is yet to be written.

5 See chapter 2 for a more extended discussion of postwar urban speech.

6　See, for example, the foundational text of the Maoist Communist Party of the Philippines, Guerrero, *Philippine Society and Revolution*.

7　For autobiographical accounts of youth politics in the years just prior to and after Martial Law, see Quimpo and Quimpo, *Subversive Lives*; Llanes, *Tibak Rising*.

8　This, at least, is what I understand from Derrida when he says, "I have only one language, and it is not mine," in *Monolingualism of the Other*, 1. See also Siegel, *Solo in the New Order*.

9　Further on: "The establishment of 'subjectivity' in language creates the category of the person—both in language and, we believe, outside of it as well." Benveniste, "Subjectivity in Language" (originally published in 1958), in *Problems in General Linguistics*, 223–30. The quotation appears on 224–25. See also "The Nature of Pronouns," 217–22 in the same volume. I thank James T. Siegel for first introducing me more than three decades ago to Benveniste's work, as well as to many of the theorists whose works I cite in what follows.

10　There is, however, another side to the reciprocal making of persons and that has to do with language itself. As that which sets forth personal pronouns, language necessarily *precedes* the category of the person. It is what sets the condition for the activation of the sense of a subject who speaks and who is in turn spoken to. Hence, in the translative relationship between I and *you*, there is some other thing that is always already at work: neither I nor *you*, but *it*. It is precisely this *it*—what we might consider to be the impersonal force of language as such—that underwrites the making of the person and yet stands outside and before it. The very possibility of transforming and translating I into *you* and vice versa is thus predicated on this *it*. Yet it remains fundamentally foreign and untranslatable into the dialogical domain of the person. Exceeding dialogical recognition, it is nonetheless the agency that generates the discursive agents of such recognition. Prior to communication, there is language. And language becomes communicative only in and through the performative effects of translation, when personal pronouns I and *you* (and *we*) are used. At the same time, this dialogical relationship between the first and the second issues from an impersonal force, a third term that resists translation yet underwrites its effects. It is the workings of this third impersonal force that is picked up throughout the chapters that follow.

11　Khatibi, *Love in Two Languages*, 48–49.

12　Jakobson, "On the Linguistic Aspects of Translation," 126–31.

13　Jakobson, "On the Linguistic Aspects of Translation," 128.

14　Jakobson, "On the Linguistic Aspects of Translation," 129.

15　Jakobson, "On the Linguistic Aspects of Translation," 130.

16　See, for example, Rafael, *Contracting Colonialism*.

17　On the topic of the gift as a kind of speech that is always already in circulation, see the classic work by Marcel Mauss, *The Gift*. See also the important but quite different glosses on this work by Lévi-Strauss, *Introduction to the*

Works of Marcel Mauss; Bataille, *The Accursed Share*; Derrida, *Given Time*. For a compelling description of the coming of the gift as the experience of the uncanny that suggests a power that is beyond the social as much as it is resistant to translation, see James T. Siegel, "False Beggars: Marcel Mauss, the Gift, and Its Commentators."

18 Benveniste, "Subjectivity in Language," 230.

19 Benedict Anderson's classic term "imagined communities" has often been quickly conflated with the nation, eliding the tension and arbitrary relationship between "imagination" and "community." Yet a careful reading of the book shows that the question of "imagination" is tied primarily to language conceived not simply as a medium for communicating the will of its speakers but as the very condition for forging that will. That something like the "nation" emerges in the process is due to a series of myriad other determinations, including the emergence of new technologies of production and reproduction, the rise of capitalist markets, the expansion of empires and the formation of particular racialized and gendered subjects, for example, American or Filipino creoles, who will begin to speak of themselves as if they were part of a community of Europeans, but whose fantasies of assimilation would be dashed, leading to the reconfiguration of their identities as "we Americans" or "we Filipinos" distinct from "you Europeans." Other sorts of communities could have easily emerged (and did), given different kinds of forces at play. The coming of the nation form as we recognize it today was far from inevitable, and even today its existence is constantly contested and challenged. The contingency of the nation is thus tied to the essential open-endedness of imagination grounded in what I have been calling the insurgency of language. See Anderson, *Imagined Communities*.

20 See Derrida, "Faith and Knowledge." See also Foucault's *Security, Territory, Population*, which situates Christian practices at the nodal point of the emergence of regimes of power and knowledge—for example, in pastoral and disciplinary practices—so important in the formation of Western and, eventually, globalized practices of power. See also Foucault, *The History of Sexuality*.

21 New Testament, Acts of the Apostles, 2:3–4, King James Version. Further on, at 2:37–39: "Now when they heard this, they were pricked in their heart, and said unto Peter and to the rest of the apostles, 'Men and brethren, what shall we do?' Then Peter said unto them, 'Repent, and be baptized every one of you in the name of Jesus Christ for the remission of sins, and ye shall receive the gift of the Holy Ghost. For the promise is unto you, and to your children, and to all that are afar off, even as many as the Lord our God shall call.'"

22 The link between conversion and translation is all the more apparent in the Pentecost since it marks the rebaptism of the Apostles as well as the beginning of their move—literally their translation—as founders of the Church

from Jerusalem to Rome. See also Rafael, *Contracting Colonialism*, especially chapter 1; Rafael, "Betraying Empire."

23 I thank Sandra Joshel for alerting me to the complex train of associations that underlie the etymology of the word *translation*. It is derived from the Latin *translatus*, the past participle of *transferre*, which in turn is from *transfero*, "to transfer, carry, bring, or convey over, to bear." It is formed by coupling *trans*, "across, through," and so on, with *fero*, which, aside from bearing all the other meanings of *transfero*, can also mean "to carry off, take away by force, as a robber, etc.: to plunder, spoil, ravage" (Lewis and Short, *A Latin Dictionary*). There is, then, an underlying violence to translation involving the conquest and conversion of words and things, something borne out by the planetary history of Christian expansion. For the violence of translation, see especially Berman, "Translation and the Trials of the Foreign." See also Nietzsche, "Translation," which talks about the ethos of conquest that animated the Roman translation or, better yet, capture of Greek classics, subjugating the original to suit their needs.

24 Rafael, *Contracting Colonialism*, chapter 6.

25 Derrida, "What Is Relevant Translation?," 366. As we shall see in chapters 4 and 5, such powerful fantasies of communication at a distance that is thought to lead to the end of translation and therefore the end of the otherness of the other is consistently played out in the U.S. attempt to assimilate immigrants and target insurgents and civilian populations in occupied territories.

26 Jakobson, "On the Linguistic Aspects of Translation," 129–30.

27 Venuti, introduction; Venuti, "Genealogies of Translation Theory."

28 The phrase is from Nabokov, "Problems of Translation."

29 Kofman, "Beyond Aporia?," 13. I am indebted to Kofman's essay for the following discussion.

30 Kofman, "Beyond Aporia?," 10.

31 Cited in Kofman, "Beyond Aporia?," 13.

32 Kofman, "Beyond Aporia?," 16.

33 Plato, *Philebus*, cited in Kofman, "Beyond Aporia?," 14.

34 For a discussion of mercy in connection to conversion and translation, see Derrida, "What Is Relevant Translation?"

35 Poros, the way out, could, however, just as easily lead back to aporia. This much is suggested by a passage in Plato's *Symposium* about Poros (in Greek, "resource," "plenty") son of Metis (wisdom, skill) and with Penia (poverty), parent of Eros: "On the birthday of Aphrodite there was a feast of the gods, at which the god Poros (Expediency), who is the son of Metis (Wisdom), was one of the guests. When the feast was over, Penia (Poverty), as the manner is on such occasions, came about the doors to beg. Now Poros who was the worse for nectar (there was no wine in those days), went into the garden of Zeus and fell into a heavy sleep, and Penia considering her own straitened

circumstances, plotted to have a child by him, and accordingly she lay down at his side and conceived Eros (Love), who partly because he is naturally a lover of the beautiful, and because Aphrodite is herself beautiful, and also because he was born on her birthday, is her follower and attendant. And as his parentage is, so also are his fortunes. In the first place he is always poor, and anything but tender and fair, as the many imagine him; and he is rough and squalid, and has no shoes, nor a house to dwell in; on the bare earth exposed he lies under the open heaven, in the streets, or at the doors of houses, taking his rest; and like his mother he is always in distress. Like his father too, whom he also partly resembles, he is always plotting against the fair and good; he is bold, enterprising, strong, a mighty hunter, always weaving some intrigue or other, keen in the pursuit of wisdom, fertile in resources; a philosopher at all times, terrible as an enchanter, sorcerer, sophist." Plato, *Symposium*, in *Lysis. Symposium. Gorgias*, trans. by W. R. M Lamb, Loeb Classics (Cambridge, MA: Harvard University Press, 1925), 178.

Chapter 1: Welcoming What Comes

An earlier version of this chapter appeared as "Welcoming What Comes: Translating Sovereignty in the Revolutionary Philippines," *Comparative Studies in Society and History* 52, no. 1 (2010): 157–79.

The significance of this chapter's title will become evident in the last section. For now it is worth noting that "welcoming what comes" is my rough translation of a common Tagalog saying, "*Bahala na*" (Come what may). It is usually said in response to conditions of extreme uncertainty that nonetheless call for urgent action. One acts without knowing exactly what one will do, or what effects such actions will have, or what will become of one at the end of an act. How does one manage without a job and with four children to feed, pass an exam without enough time to study, embark on a job in a foreign country whose language and customs are entirely alien from one's own? "*Bahala na*," would be the first but certainly not the last response. It thus signifies a willingness to expose oneself to chance, to face the unknown which is yet to have a face, and to open oneself up to the other from another place and in another time, thus to be free for a future that is yet to come. With *bahala na*, we begin to get a sense of what the vernacular notion of sovereignty might be like, which is one of the topics of this essay.

1 The historiography of the Philippine Revolution is extensive. The classic accounts remain those by Agoncillo, *Revolt of the Masses* and *Malolos*. For works relating the historical background of the Revolution and its aftermath, see the seminal books by Schumacher: *The Propaganda Movement*, *Revolutionary Clergy*, and *The Making of a Nation*. See also Fast and Richardson, *Roots of Dependency*; Guerrero, "Luzon at War"; Ileto, *Pasyon and Revolution*; Richardson, *The Light of Liberty*.

2　Much of the Western, specifically North American, academic interest in
sovereignty has emerged in the wake of the Cold War, but especially after
the events of 9/11 and the assertion of broad executive powers in the United
States during the run-up to the Second Gulf War in 2003. The reasons for
these are various and call for explanation, but such a project is outside the
scope of this essay. The work of Carl Schmitt has been at the forefront of this
renewed interest in sovereignty, as it has been the focus of extensive critique
by such thinkers as Derrida, Agamben, Jean-Luc Nancy, and Judith Butler,
among many others. See, for example, the wide-ranging essays in de Vries
and Sullivan, *Political Theologies*; and in Cheah and Guerlac, *Derrida and the Time
of the Political*. Among the numerous recent studies that have sought to situate
these debates on sovereignty in specific historical and cultural contexts, one
can consult the collection of essays in Hansen and Stepputat, *Sovereign Bodies*;
and the same editors' very useful survey, "Sovereignty Revisited." See also
the essays on Schmitt's concepts of the political and the partisan in a special
issue of CR: *New Centennial Review* 4, no. 3 (2004); and the essays organized
around the topic "Taking Exception to the Exception," edited by Frank and
McNulty.

3　Schmitt, *Political Theology*, 5. See also Balakrishnan, *The Enemy*.

4　Bodin, *On Sovereignty*, 3. See also the essays in Frank and McNulty, "Taking
Exception to the Exception."

5　Bodin, *On Sovereignty*, 8–11.

6　See Phelan, *The Hispanization of the Philippines*; Elliott, *Imperial Spain*; Rafael,
Contracting Colonialism, chapter 4; Kamen, *Spain*.

7　For a discussion of the Patronato Real, see de la Costa, "Church and State in
the Philippines during the Administration of Bishop Salazer"; Phelan, "Some
Ideological Aspects of the Conquest of the Philippines"; Elliott, *Empires of the
Atlantic World*, 68–69, 198.

8　In a similar vein, the Laws of the Indies (http://geoanalyzer.britannica.com
/ebc/topic?idxStructId=493769&typeId=13, *Recopilación de las leyes de los reinos
de Indias*, 1681) were meant not only to address and synthesize the adminis-
trative complexity of empire. They were also cast as the positive encoding
of natural law, which in turn was thought to derive from Divine Law. The
first law of Recopilación, for example, situates colonization as the work of
evangelization. It lays out the law as if it were continuous with the confession
of the Faith: "God, our Lord, through His infinite Mercy and Goodness has
designed to give us, unworthy as we are, such a great portion of His Dominion in this world, and having joined in our Royal person the great kingdoms
of our glorious progenitors . . . has obligated us further to . . . employ all the
forces and power that He has given us to work so that He may be known and
adored all over the world as the true God, as in fact He is, and the Creator
of all that is visible and invisible; and desiring the glory of the Holy Roman
Catholic Church among the Heathen and Nations that inhabit the Indies,

Islands and Other Lands of the Oceans as well as other parts subject to our dominion, and so that everyone universally shall enjoy the admirable beneficence of the Resurrection through the Blood of Christ our Lord, we pray and entreat the native of our Indies who may not have yet received the Faith, since our end is to provide and to deliver to them Teachers and Preachers, for the purpose of their conversion and salvation, that they should receive and listen benignly to and believe totally in the doctrine of the Faith. And we command that all natives and Spaniards and other Christians of the various Provinces and Nations . . . firmly believe and simply confess the Mystery of the Blessed Trinity, Father, Son and Holy Ghost, three distinct persons and one True God, the Articles of the Faith, and all that is taught and preached by the Holy Mother Roman Catholic Church." (Translation mine.) See Elliott, *Empires of the Atlantic World*, 128.

9 On this conception of imperialism see, for example, the nineteenth-century notions of "manifest destiny," and "benevolent assimilation" in the case of the United States, or Operation Iraqi Freedom in our own time.

10 For a detailed discussion of the linguistic basis of Spanish colonial rule, see Rafael, *Contracting Colonialism*. For an overview of the structure of the Spanish colonial bureaucracy, see Phelan, *Hispanization of the Philippines*.

11 Critiques of the Western notions of sovereignty include Derrida, *The Politics of Friendship and Rogues*; Nancy, *The Creation of the World*, 96–107. See also Frank and McNulty, "Taking Exception to the Exception"; Cheah and Guerlac, *Derrida and the Time of the Political*.

12 See, for example, de la Costa, "Church and State in the Philippines during the Administration of Bishop Salazer"; Schumacher, *Father Jose Burgos*; and Rafael, *Contracting Colonialism*.

13 For the most compelling studies regarding the remarkable growth of the Spanish liberal state in the wake of the collapse of the Spanish American Empire, thanks to its more efficient, flexible, but no less ruthless exploitation of its archipelagic empire of Cuba, Puerto Rico, and the Philippines, see Fradera, *Colonias para despues de un imperio* and *Filipinas, la colonia mas peculiar*. Spanish liberalism, borrowing the techniques of its Bourbon predecessors and taking its cue from the British, sought to govern the colonies as states of exception, whose racially mixed populations were seen to be inferior and unequal to Peninsular Spaniards and, especially in the case of the Philippines, consigned to become colonial subjects without any prospects of assimilation as citizens. Where the Spanish Habsburgs sought to endow colonial subjects with natural rights and wed them to the universal laws of Christianity, Spanish liberals sought (and never quite succeeded) to govern them with "special laws" designed to keep them politically subordinate and legally apart from Peninsular Spaniards even as they remained increasingly tethered to the regional economies of Spain. The point here is that contrary to much Anglo-American scholarship that sees the Spanish Empire fading

into obscurity after the 1820s, Fradera shows that it in fact went through significant reform and became revitalized in the course of the nineteenth century. See also Schmidt-Nowara, *The Conquest of History*, for the cultural consequences of these attempts at liberal absolutism.

14 For an extended discussion on the origins of Filipino nationalism, see Schumacher, *The Propaganda Movement*; and Mojares, *The Brains of the Nation*. See also Rafael, *The Promise of the Foreign*.

15 Del Pilar, *La soberania monacal en Filipinias* and *La frailocracia Filipina*.

16 A facsimile of the handwritten Spanish text of the Declaration of Independence, *Acta de la Proclamación de la independenica del pueblo Filipino*, can be found in de Ocampo, *June 12, 1898 and Related Documents*, 19–40. A printed version of the text is on pages 41–44, and my references below refer to that.

17 Ocampo, *June 12, 1898 and Related Documents* 42–43. The Spanish text reads, "Y poñiendo como testigo de la rectitud de nuestras intenciones al Supremo Juez del Universo, y bajo la protección de la poderosa y humanitaria nación, Norte Americana, proclamamos y solemnemente declaramos, en nombre y autoridad de los habitantes de las islas Filipinas que son y tienen derecho a ser libres e independientes; que este en libres de toda obediencia de la Corona de España. . . . Estado libre e independiente, tienen completa autoridad para declarar la Guerra, entrar en alianzas y regular el comercio y ejecutar todos aquellos otros actos y cosas de incumbencia de los estados independientes."

18 For a discussion of the "we" in the U.S. Constitution that proclaims "we, the people" that constitutes itself retrospectively as the author of the very text that inaugurates its existence, see Derrida, "Declarations of Independence." For an elaboration of this Derridean analysis, see Frank, "'Unauthorized Propositions.'" See also Warner, *The Letters of the Republic*, 104–8.

19 See Guerrero, "Luzon at War"; Agoncillo, *Malolos*; Ileto, *Pasyon and Revolution*.

20 See, for example, the text of Malolos Constitution, Article 2: "La Republica Filipina es libre e independiente," and Article 3, "La soberania reside exclusivamente en el pueblo." Yet the Constitution proceeded to further consolidate elite power, leaving aside the interests, much less the "voice," of the people. For the Spanish text of the Constitution, see Guevara, *The Laws of the First Philippine Republic*, 88–103. See also Agoncillo, *Malolos*; Guerrero, "Luzon at War."

21 The standard biography of Mabini is Majul, *Mabini and the Philippine Revolution*.

22 Mabini, *La Revolución Filipina*, 2: 56–57, 125, 134–35.

23 Mabini, *La Revolución Filipina*, 2: 57–59.

24 Mabini, *La Revolución Filipina*, 2: 196.

25 Mabini, *La Revolución Filipina*, 2: 53–59, 206–9, 300–325.

26 Mabini, *La Revolución Filipina*, 2: 278–79. For an extended discussion of the

significance of the blood compact in late nineteenth-century nationalist thinking, see Rafael, *The Promise of the Foreign*, chapter 7.

27   Mabini, *La Revolución Filipina*, 2: 72–74, 131, 161–67.

28   Mabini, *La Revolución Filipina*, 2: 93, 54–55.

29   Mabini was drawing, as many of his fellow ilustrados were, on the idea of natural law found in Catholic philosophy, particularly in the writings of St. Thomas Aquinas. See, for example, the selections on natural law taken from the *Summa Theologica* in Pegis, *Introduction to St. Thomas Aquinas*, 616–45. See also the useful discussion in Majul, *Mabini and the Philippine Revolution*, 79–84.

30   Mabini, *La Revolución Filipina*, 2: 48, 206, 180.

31   Mabini, *La Revolución Filipina*, 2: 66–67.

32   See Guerrero, "Luzon at War," chapter 3.

33   Mabini, *La Revolución Filipina*, 2: 68–69.

34   Mabini, *La Revolución Filipina*, 2: 69.

35   Honesto Mariano, "Popular Songs of the Revolution" (1915), cited in Ileto, *Pasyon and Revolution*, 181–82.

36   Rousseau, *The Social Contract*, 59.

37   Indeed the serial extension and open-ended inclusion of others into the nation is suggested by the formation of the word itself through the agglutinative addition of the prefixes *ka* and *ba* to the root word *bayan*.

38   My discussion of *damayan* and *kalayaan* is clearly indebted to Reynaldo Ileto's pathbreaking study of the idioms of popular revolt in the Philippines, *Pasyon and Revolution*. However, while Ileto sought to frame the affective politics of freedom, mourning, and compassion within the text of the Tagalog version of Christ's epic suffering and death (which would seem to lend to all Philippine politics a Christian colonial cast), I suggest that these notions in the context of the Filipino Revolution at once fall short and exceed whatever Christian significance we might ascribe to them. Their provenance in everyday life, as I suggest below, allows them some room to maneuver around the reductive, colonizing projects of state building and political theology while looking toward what we might think of as proto-democratic (and, more modestly, messianic) possibilities. A similar set of concerns that seeks to de-theologize, as it were, Philippine nationalist history, is implicit in my book, *The Promise of the Foreign*, especially chapter 7.

39   Alvarez, *Katipunan at ang Paghihimagsik*, 281. All translations from the Tagalog are mine.

40   Alvarez, *Katipunan at ang Paghihimagsik*, 282.

41   Aguinaldo, *Mga Gunita ng Himagsikan*, 117.

42   Aguinaldo, *Mga Gunita ng Himagsikan*, 403.

43   Laktaw, *Diccionario Tagalo-Hispano*, 203–4.

44   Aguinaldo, *Mga Gunita ng Himagsikan*, 81, 111, 117, 147.

45 Aguinaldo, *Mga Gunita ng Himagsikan*, 233–34.

46 Ileto, *Pasyon and Revolution*, 88–89.

47 One is led to think here of Derrida's revision of the classical notion of sovereignty based on ipseity, the sense of the "I can" that underlies almost all accounts of freedom as self-determination and self-mastery. He calls for a critique of ipseity beyond the terms of the self-evident autonomy of the "I" who says "I can," and for a reconsideration of freedom "that would no longer be the power of a subject, a freedom without autonomy, a heteronomy without servitude" (*Rogues*, 152). The revolutionary accounts I have been reading suggest some non-European sites for receiving and responding to these calls.

48 I am indebted to Bonnie Honig's careful analysis of Schmitt's use of the metaphor of the "miracle" to theologize the notion of exception, which for him serves as the privileged manifestation of sovereign power. See Honig, "The Miracle of Metaphor." Honig's explication of the everyday quality of the miraculous, and the miraculous because prophetic nature of the everyday, has been productive for thinking about the vernacular experience of sovereignty in the Philippine context. See also Honig's book *Democracy and the Foreigner*.

49 Bataille, "Sovereignty," in *The Accursed Share*, 3: 201.

50 To get an acute sense of the quotidian quality of popular sovereignty arising precisely from the intensification of everyday acts of pity, sharing, mourning, and pilgrimage, see Ileto's detailed description of the movement led by the revolutionary fighter Felipe Salvador, in *Pasyon and Revolution*, chapter 6.

Chapter 2: Wars of Translation

An earlier version of this chapter appeared as "The War of Translation: Colonial Schooling, American English, and Tagalog Slang," *Journal of Asian Studies* 74, no. 2 (2015), 283–302.

1 Cited in Osias, "Education and Religion," 9: 126. For a more or less critical look at the first thirteen years of colonial education, see May, *Social Engineering in the Philippines*, 77–126. See also Wesling, *Empire's Proxy*.

2 See Kramer, *The Blood of Government*.

3 Osias, "Education," 9: 126; May, *Social Engineering*, 81–83.

4 See Duffy Burnett and Marshall, *Foreign in a Domestic Sense*; Rafael, *White Love and Other Events in Filipino History*, especially chapters 1–2; Kramer, *The Blood of Government*.

5 Philippines (Commonwealth) Commission of the Census, *Census of the Philippines*, 1939.

6 Constantino, "The Mis-education of the Filipino," originally written in 1959, first published in the *Weekly Graphic*, June 8, 1966. My pagination follows the reprint. Subsequent citations appear parenthetically in the text.

7 For an example of the unreconstructed and uncritical use of Constantino's

essay in the context of Filipino American studies, see San Juan, "Inventing the Vernacular Speech-Acts," especially 152. See also Ina Alleco R. Silverio, "Removing Filipino as a Subject in College: A Betrayal in the Name of Business?," Bulatlat, 23 July 2014, http://bulatlat.com/main/2014/06/27/removing-filipino-as-a-subject-in-college-a-betrayal-in-the-name-of-business/. Accessed 14 August 2014.

8 The most engrossing and detailed biography of Renato Constantino is Ofreneo, *Renato Constantino*, especially 16–55, 70–129. The quotation is on 159. Ofreneo conducted long interviews with both Renato and his wife, Letizia Roxas, as well as with his children, Renato Jr. and Karina, and their spouses and their grandchildren. She was also afforded access to his unpublished "Memoirs," scrapbooks, letters, and family photographs.

9 Ofreneo, *Renato Constantino*, 158–84. Worth noting is a recurring feature of Constantino's life: that it was fashioned within the very structures of English-language colonial education and bourgeois privilege of which he would become a harsh critic. All three of his mother's sisters, for example, were schoolteachers in colonial public schools who spoke English and delighted in the American popular culture of their time, in contrast to his maternal grandmother, who spoke Spanish and regarded Americans with fierce hostility. Constantino attended colonial public schools, graduating from Arellano High School and continued to the University of the Philippines. Both schools had been sites of student protests: in Arellano against the racist behavior of its American principal; in UP against the conservatism and proto-fascism of Commonwealth president Manuel L. Quezon. Constantino was also the beneficiary of Filipino elite politics. His left-wing thinking occurred against the backdrop of his marriage to Roxas, whose family owned extensive properties in Manila and Aklan province, whose father was a well-known lawyer (like Constantino's), and whose uncle was no less than the former house speaker and first president of the Philippine Republic, Manuel Roxas. He owed his job at the Department of Foreign Affairs to Foreign Secretary Carlos P. Romulo, who had met him while he was a student at UP, and managed to elude jail time, unlike some of his other left-wing friends (e.g., Angel Baking), thanks to the intercession of Senator Claro M. Recto and the wealthy landlord Eugenio Lopez, and no doubt owed something to his wife's familial prominence. While he suffered from the communist witch hunts of the 1950s and early 1960s in part for his refusal to cooperate with the military, he was eventually given a job by the Lopez family, first serving as an economic researcher at the Binalbagan-Isabela Sugar Company (Biscom) in 1955, and more significantly as the curator and director of the Lopez Memorial Museum from 1960 to 1972, where he would hone his skills as a historian and write several major works revising Philippine history. See Ofreneo, *Renato Constantino*, 1–15, 36–53, 54–69, 109–57.

Constantino's life testifies to the contradictions inherent in the history of left-wing nationalist intellectuals, beginning with late nineteenth-century ilustrados. Direct beneficiaries of the economic, cultural, and political structures put in place by colonial rule, they nonetheless find in this inheritance the very resources with which to negate it, crafting a language of refusal of and resistance to its unjust workings. Ironically their ability to sustain such resistance continues to be predicated, as with other Filipino nationalist elites, on their ability to call upon the protections and patronage of the very system of colonial and neocolonial rule—and the cultural-educational system that reproduces it—on their behalf. Thus even in the darkest days of Constantino's life he was able to hide out during the Japanese Occupation in remote provincial locations, hidden by peasants working on lands owned by his family in Bulacan, or while in the midst of the anticommunist witch hunts in the 1950s, play tennis at the Philippine Columbine Club and live off rents collected from apartments he had himself designed in the Manila properties he and his wife owned, and of course eventually get jobs with the Lopez companies and museum. When Martial Law was declared in 1972, he evaded the fate of many other anti-Marcos opponents, escaping detention through the intervention of a Marcos ally, the prominent journalist Doroy Valencia, who was a good friend of his father. He was instead consigned to house arrest until 1975.

It is also worth noting that as an ilustrado male, he benefited enormously from the physical and emotional labor as well as devoted loyalty of his wife. She served in many cases as his researcher, typist, and most sympathetic reader—in many ways his coauthor, as he would belatedly acknowledge in later works. She recalls how her husband, once comfortably ensconced as director of the Lopez Museum and Library, found the thirty-minute commute to his office in his chauffeured air-conditioned car boring and, unable to read because of his car-sickness, asked her and daughter Karina to record entire books that he could listen to on the way to work. Among his favorites was a book recounting the life and struggles of Che Guevara and his brave attempts to elude capture. The irony boggles the mind. It is as if "miseducation," as Constantino called it, always harbored the means not only for its critique but also for its constant reformulation and ever-exquisite refinement.

10 See Ofreneo, *Renato Constantino*, 16–35, 70–80, to get a sense of the anti-colonial, Marxist-nationalist motifs that inform his university and postwar writings. For the American colonial influences, see my discussion below. One wonders too if its title may have owed something to the 1933 book by one of a small number of African Americans who taught in the Philippines, the historian Carter Woodson, *The Mis-education of the Negro* (Trenton, NJ: Africa World Press, 1990).

11 Saleeby, *The Language of Education of the Philippine Islands*, qtd. in Constantino,

"The Mis-education of the Filipino," 32. For a related critique of the limited utility of English, see the speech of the vice-governor and head of the Bureau of Education George C. Butte, "Shall the Philippines Have a Common Language," especially 14, 19–20.

12 Monroe, *A Survey of the Educational System of the Philippine Islands by the Board of Educational Surveys*. Subsequent citations appear parenthetically in the text.

13 Qtd. in May, *Social Engineering*, 83.

14 Atkinson, qtd. in May, *Social Engineering*, 40.

15 For a discussion of an early colonial Tagalog precedent for this linguistic practice, see Rafael, *Contracting Colonialism*, especially chapter 2.

16 Barry, "A Little Brown Language," 15, 20. Subsequent citations appear parenthetically in the text.

17 For a social history of cocheros in early twentieth-century Manila, see Pante, "The *Cocheros* of American-Occupied Manila."

18 For the most informative biographical information on Joaquin, see Mojares, "Biography of Nick Joaquin"; Lanot, *The Trouble with Nick and Other Profiles*.

19 Lanot, *The Trouble with Nick and Other Profiles*, 8.

20 Mojares, "Biography of Nick Joaquin," 5.

21 "The Language of the Streets" first appeared in 1963 and was republished in Quijano de Manila, *The Language of the Streets and Other Essays*, 3–21. Subsequent citations appear parenthetically in the text.

22 See Rafael, *The Promise of the Foreign*, chapter 6.

23 Anderson, *Why Counting Counts*, 79. See also Romanillos, "El Chabacano de Cavite." See also Nakpil's account of speaking Ermita Spanish during the 1930s in her autobiography, *Myself, Elsewhere*, 75–76.

24 Indeed, as Anderson conjectures, had the United States not arrived and had the First Republic survived, Spanish would have become one of the official languages of the state, while "a kind of Filipino Spanish would have become, de facto, either the official language or the country's lingua franca." It would have been one that, as Joaquin would say regarding Tagalog slang, was "open to everyone to adapt it, corrupt it, change it in accord with local needs." Anderson, *Why Counting Counts*, 84, 86.

25 Joaquin, like many others who have written about Tagalog slang or Taglish, elides the presence of Hokkien contributions to the lingua franca or national language in the same way that they tend to repress the profound Chinese presence in Philippine history.

26 This "venerable theory" of language, one predicated on translation as play, dates back further than the introduction of vaudeville to the Philippines. See, for example, the *awit*, songs of the sixteenth-century ladino Tomas Pinpin, a bilingual poet, printer, and translator for Spanish friars, as discussed in Rafael, *Contracting Colonialism*, chapter 2. This makes Joaquin a kind of postcolonial ladino himself.

An earlier version of this chapter appeared as "The Cell Phone and the Crowd: Messianic Politics in the Contemporary Philippines," *Public Culture* 15, no. 3 (2003): 399–425.

1 The link between telecommunication technologies and the politics of belief that I pursue here is indebted to the work of Jacques Derrida, especially in such writings as "Faith and Knowledge"; "Signature Event Context"; and *The Politics of Friendship*.

2 See the bundle entitled "Telefonos, 1885–1891" at the Philippine National Archives, Manila, for sketches of a plan to install a telephone system in the city as early as November 1885. By December 1885 the Office of Telephone Communication had been established, and the first telephone station at Santa Lucia, Manila, was operational.

3 For a more extended discussion of telegraphy and the formation of a wish for a lingua franca among the first generation of nationalists, see Rafael, *The Promise of the Foreign*.

4 For an elaboration of other modalities of these telecommunicative fantasies and their role in shaping nationalist consciousness, see Rafael, *White Love and Other Events in Filipino History*, especially chapters 4 and 8 on rumor and gossip as populist modes of communication in Philippine history; and *The Promise of the Foreign*.

5 For a useful collection of documents and newspaper articles relating to the corruption case against Estrada, see Coronel, *Investigating Estrada*.

6 Uli Schmetzer, "Cell Phones Spurred Filipinos' Coup," *Chicago Tribune*, 22 January 2001; Ederic Penaflor Eder, "Tinig ng Generation Txt" (Voice of Generation Txt), *Pinoy Times*, 8 February 2001; Malou Mangahas, "Text Messaging Comes of Age in the Philippines," *Reuters Technology News*, 28 January 2001.

7 Much of the information that follows was gathered from Wayne Arnold, "Manila's Talk of the Town Isn't Talk at All," *New York Times*, 5 July 2000, http://www.nytimes.com/2000/07/05/business/international-business-manila-s-talk-of-the-town-isn-t-talk-at-all.html; "Text Generation," special issue, especially 14–21, 28–32; Mata, *The Ultimate Text Book*, which is especially good for examples of the more common text messages that circulate among Filipino users.

8 According to official figures from 2009–11, these trends have continued. The popularity of cell phones has increased while the number of fixed landlines has steadily decreased, as more people tend to favor the former over the latter. The latest estimates show that there are approximately seven landlines to every hundred people, compared to ninety-five cell phones to every hundred. The Philippines continues to be one of the "texting capitals" of the world, with about 10 percent of the total text messages sent worldwide. Among those who have cell phones, texting is overwhelmingly popular. About 97

percent of those who have cell phones regularly use this service. By contrast, only 10 percent use Internet services on their cell phones since these are far more expensive. Indeed while Internet use is fairly widespread in the major cities of the Philippines today, the figures for Internet subscription remain way below the levels of the rest of the Asia-Pacific region. As of 2011 only 5.5 percent have a broadband connection at home. While this represents a five-fold increase from 1999, it shows that the expense of an Internet subscription still makes it difficult for most people to have their own Internet access. And even those who can afford Internet services have to contend with constant interruptions and uneven, often incompetent customer service and technical support. There is, instead, widespread recourse to computers in offices, schools, and Internet cafés. For this reason the actual use of the Internet, especially with regard to social networking, is about the global average—33 percent—even as the rate of computer ownership and Internet subscription is relatively low. No doubt this is due to the huge income gap in the country, reflected in the Philippines' stubbornly high GINI coefficient rating of 43 and poverty incidence of around 24 percent. See the National Telecommunications Commission and the National Statistics Coordination Board report, "Philippines: Fifth Progress Report on the Millennium Development Goals (MDGs)," prepared by the National Economic Development Authority and the Human Development and Poverty Reduction Cluster, 31 July 2013. I am grateful to Lila Ramos Shahani for providing me with these data.

9   For a succinct historical analysis of the Philippine state, see Anderson, "Cacique Democracy in the Philippines." See also Sidel, *Capital, Coercion, and Crime*; Hutchcroft, *Booty Capitalism*.

10 Technologies for monitoring cell phone use do exist, and there is some indication that the Philippine government is beginning to acquire them. It is doubtful, however, that cell phone surveillance technology was available to the Estrada administration in 2001.

11 The average cost of a text message today is about 1 peso, or US$0.22 in 2001, as compared to a voice call, which is about ten times more. See Arnold, "Manila's Talk of the Town Isn't Talk at All"; Mangahas, "Text Messaging Comes of Age in the Philippines"; Schmetzer, "Cell Phones Spurred Filipinos' Coup." See also Leah Salterio, "Text Power in EDSA 2001," *Philippine Daily Inquirer*, 22 January 2001; Conrado de Quiros, "Undiscovered Country," *Philippine Daily Inquirer*, 7 February 2001; Michael L. Tan, "Taming the Cell Phone," *Philippine Daily Inquirer*, 6 February 2001.

12 This article was circulated on the listservs of various nongovernmental organizations in the Philippines and bore the title "Pinoy Lifestyle." I have no knowledge of the original source of this piece, so it exists in some ways like a forwarded text message. Thanks to Tina Cuyugan for forwarding this essay to me. All translations are mine unless otherwise indicated.

13 Arnold, "Manila's Talk of the Town Isn't Talk at All."
14 Message posted by rnrsarreal@aol.com, in Plaridel (plaridel_papers @egroups.com), 25 January 2001.
15 Arnold, "Manila's Talk of the Town Isn't Talk at All."
16 Tan, "Taming the Cell Phone."
17 Tan, "Taming the Cell Phone"; de Quiros, "Undiscovered Country."
18 Arnold, "Manila's Talk of the Town Isn't Talk at All."
19 These messages were forwarded by rnrsarreal@aol.com to the Plaridel discussion group (plaridel_papers@yahoogroups.com), 25 January 2001.
20 Bart Guingona, Plaridel (plaridel_papers@yahoogroups.com), 26 January 2001. Texting is widely credited with bringing about the rapid convergence of crowds at the EDSA Shrine within approximately seventy-five minutes of the abrupt halt of the Estrada impeachment trial on the evening of 16 January. Even prior to Cardinal Sin and former president Cory Aquino's appeal for people to converge at this hallowed site, it has been estimated that over twenty thousand people had already arrived there, perhaps drawn by text messages they received. As Danny A. Gozo, an employee at Ayala Corporation, points out in his posting on Plaridel (plaridel_papers@yahoogroups .com), 23 January 2001, during the four days of EDSA II, Globe Telecom reported an average of 42 million outgoing messages and roughly an equal number of incoming ones as well, while Smart Telecom reported over 70 million outgoing and incoming messages texted through their system *per day*. He observes enthusiastically that "the interconnectedness of people, both within the country and outside is a phenomenon unheard of before. It is changing the way that we live!"
21 Eder, "Tining ng Generation Txt." The translation of this text is mine.
22 I owe this term to Siegel, *Fetish, Recognition, Revolution*.
23 Breton, cited in Benjamin, "Marseilles."
24 My remarks on Manila's streets were gleaned from the notes and observations I made during my extended visits to the city in the 1990s. On Manila's urban forms, see the excellent essay by Tadiar, "Manila's New Metropolitan Form." For a lucid portrait of Manila's fantastic street life in the 1990s, see Hamilton-Paterson's novel *The Ghosts of Manila*. Contemporary Philippine films, which often traverse the divide between rich and poor and explore their spaces of habitation, are excellent primary source materials for the study of Manila's urban forms. For a recent collection of essays on Philippine cinema, see Tolentino, *Geopolitics of the Visible*.
25 See chapter 4 of Schivelbusch's *The Railway Journey*.
26 I owe this information to David Rafael, former manager of the Glorietta shopping mall in the Ayala Center, Makati.
27 For a discussion of the historical link between linguistic and social hierarchies, see Rafael, "Taglish, or the Phantom Power of the Lingua Franca," in *White Love and Other Events in Filipino History*. See also chapter 2 of this book.

28 Here I draw from Heidegger's essay "The Question concerning Technology," in *The Question concerning Technology and Other Essays*. See also the illuminating commentary by Weber, "Upsetting the Setup: Remarks on Heidegger's 'Questing after Technics,'" in *Mass Mediauras*. My remarks on the crowd are indebted to Benjamin, *Charles Baudelaire*.

29 For a discussion of the history of this nationalist fantasy, see the introduction to Rafael, *White Love and Other Events in Filipino History*. For a comparative approach to the radical potential of nationalist ideas, see Anderson, *Imagined Communities*.

30 Flor C., Plaridel listserv (plaridel_papers@yahoogroups.com), 24 January 2001.

31 Flor C., I have subsequently learned, is Flor Caagusan, formerly editor of the Opinion page of the *Manila Times* and at one point the managing editor of the *Diliman Review*. I owe this information to the journalist Pete Lacaba. While she would be known to a small number of journalists who are part of the Plaridel discussion group, she would presumably be unknown to the majority of the group's participants.

32 See chapter 1 of this book for an extended discussion of sovereignty relevant to the crowd.

33 For a discussion of aporia, see the introduction of this book.

34 For a discussion of *damayan*, see chapter 1 of this book. See also Ileto, *Pasyon and Revolution*. See also the important work of Cannell on Bikol Province, south of Manila, *Power and Intimacy in the Christian Philippines*.

35 Flor C.'s account also recalls the experience of crowding in certain religious gatherings, notably the all-male procession of the image of the Black Nazarene that marks the high point of the fiesta of Quiapo, a district of Manila, on 9 January. For a description of the 1995 procession that conveys some sense of the dangers and pleasures experienced by onlookers and practitioners alike in the experience of crowding, see Laya, "The Black Nazarene of Quiapo," in *Letras y Figuras*, 86–90.

36 Derrida, "Faith and Knowledge," 56–57. The relationship among politics, promise, and technology intimated by Derrida is, of course, a key preoccupation of this essay. Promises arguably lie at the basis of the political and the social. The possibility of making and breaking pledges, of bearing or renouncing obligations, of exchanging vows and taking oaths forges a sense of futurity and chance, allowing for an opening to otherness. It is this possibility of promising that, Derrida has argued, engenders the sense of something to come, of events yet to arrive. But promises can be made and broken only if they can be witnessed and sanctioned, confirmed and reaffirmed. They must, in other words, be repeatable and citable, capable of being performed again and again. Repetition underlies the making of promises and thus the practices of politics. We can gloss this iterative necessity as the workings of the technical and the mechanical that inhere in every act of promising. Tech-

nology as the elaboration of the technical, including the technics of speech and writing, is then not merely an instrument for engaging in politics. It is that without which the political and the futures it claims to bring forth would simply never emerge, along with the very notion of emergence itself.

37 See, for example, the news reports and opinion columns of the *Philippine Daily Inquirer* from 26 April to 5 May 2001 for coverage of "Poor People Power," or, as others have referred to it, "People Power III." In particular see the following: Alcuin Papa, Dave Veridiano, and Michael Lim Ubac, "Estrada Loyalists Overwhelm Cops on Way to Malacañang," 2 May 2001; Amando Doronila, "The State Defends Itself," 2 May 2001; Amando Doronila, "Now the Fight over Semantics," 4 May 2001; "Exchanges on EDSA III," 3 May 2001; Blanche S. Rivera and Christian Esguerra, "EDSA Reclaimed by EDSA II Forces," 2 May 2001; Blanche Gallardo, "Tears of Joy for Tears of Sadness," 6 May 2001. See also Jarius Bondoc, "Gotcha," *Philippine Star*, 1 May 2001; Howie G. Severino, "The Hand That Rocks the Masa," *Filipinas Magazine*, June 2001, 70–72; Pete Lacaba, "EDSA Puwersa," *Pinoy Times*, 29 April 2001.

38 See, for example, Conrado de Quiros, "Lessons," *Philippine Daily Inquirer*, 29 April 2001; Walden Bello, "The May 1st Riot: Birth of Peronism RP Style?" *Philippine Daily Inquirer*, 8 May 2001; La Liga Policy Institute (Quezon City), "Poor People Power: Preludes and Prospects," filipino-studies@yahoogroups .com, 6 May 2001; Ferdinand Llanes, "EDSA at Mendiola ng Masa," filipino -studies@yahoogroups.com, 3 May 2001.

39 Papa et al., "Estrada Loyalists Overwhelm Cops."

40 *Horde* comes from the Turkish *ordi/ordu*, meaning "camp," and originally re-ferred to "troops of Tartar or other nomads dwelling in tents or wagons and moving from place to place for pasturage or for war and plunder," according to the *Oxford English Dictionary*.

41 See Rivera and Esguerra, "EDSA Reclaimed by EDSA II Forces," which reports, among other things, how those involved in People Power II "brought their own towels, sponges, and scrubs" to clean the garbage that had been left behind by the pro-Estrada crowd, hosing down "the filth from the ground" and "disinfecting" the shrine with chlorine. Estrada's supporters had "heaped mounds of garbage, sang and danced lustfully over the EDSA shrine marker, rammed a truck into the landscape and directed huge loud-speakers to the shrine door," according to the shrine rector Monsignor Soc Villegas.

42 One further postscript: as of 2015 no other mass urban uprisings or successful coup attempts have materialized. Instead Macapagal-Arroyo eventually issued a presidential pardon to former president Estrada, who then proceeded to run for president in the elections of 2010, which he lost to Benigno "Noynoy" Aquino III, the son of Cory and Ferdinand Marcos's old political rival, Ninoy Aquino. Meanwhile former president Macapagal-Arroyo has herself been accused of massive corruption and is currently under

hospital arrest awaiting trial. For his part Estrada was elected as the mayor of Manila, and his sons were elected to the Senate (though one is under arrest for corruption). The restoration of Estrada (along with the return of the Marcoses to local and national offices, with son Ferdinand Jr. planning to run for the presidency in 2016) have convinced nearly everyone in the Philippines today of the futility of launching another mass uprising or any other extraconstitutional attempt at regime change. Instead middle-class politics have shifted decisively in the direction of parliamentary contests and judicial venues, alongside work in the numerous nongovernmental organizations. As for the masses, the attraction of the communist New People's Army has tended to wane, even as the NPA continues to exercise considerable influence in remote rural areas, especially among the Indigenous Peoples. Those who can, migrate abroad and confront the harsh conditions of overseas work to send home remittances that have long kept the islands' economy afloat, while still others engage intermittently in grassroots organizing with the noncommunist left groups. Most have fallen back on the conventional practices of patronage politics. This helps to explain the return of Estrada and the political fortunes of another of Estrada's friends and former running mate, the current vice president and presidential aspirant Jejomar "Jojo" Binay.

Chapter 4: Translation, American English, and the National Insecurities of Empire

An earlier version of this chapter appeared as "Translation, American English, and the National Insecurities of Empire," *Social Text* 101, 27, no. 4 (2009): 1–24.

1 Michael Janofsky, "Bush Proposes Broader Language Training," *New York Times*, 6 January 2006. For more details on the National Security Language Initiative, see http://exchanges.state.gov/us/program/national-security -language-initiative-youth-nsli-y, American Council on the Teaching of Foreign Languages, "National Security Language Initiative." It is unclear, however, how much of the funding for this program has actually been released as of the date of this writing. I am grateful to Mary Pratt for referring me to this story on President Bush's language initiative.

2 For the Spanish Empire, see, for example, MacCormack, *Religion in the Andes*; Rafael, *Contracting Colonialism*. For the British Empire, see Cohn, *An Anthropologist among Historians and Other Essays*. For Central Africa, see Fabian, *Language and Colonial Power*.

3 The logocentrism that frames this American notion of translation predicated on the reorganization of foreign languages into a hierarchical relationship to American speech is comparable to that of sixteenth-century Spanish missionaries' ideas about translation: they regarded all languages as gifts from God. They were thus available for the conversion of their native speakers, a process that, among other things, entailed the translation of native speech

into vessels for carrying and conveying Christ, the Word of God. All words at all times and all places were thus mere derivatives of the divine lingua franca. For an extended discussion of this Spanish history of colonial translation, see Rafael, *Contracting Colonialism*, especially chapter 1. See also Rafael, "Betraying Empire."

4 United States, *Lost in Translation*, 2, 40. See also United States, Department of Defense, "Defense Language Transformation Roadmap."

5 For the text of the National Defense Education Act, see the appendix in Clowse, *Brain Power for the Cold War*, 162–65. See also Bigelow and Legters, NDEA. For critical examinations of area studies in the wake of the Cold War, see Miyoshi and Harootunian, *Learning Places*.

6 See Shell, "Babel in America"; Lepore, *A Is for American*, 27–29; Dodd, *Historical Statistics of the States of the United States*; Heath, "Why No Official Tongue?"; Sagarin and Kelly, "Polylingualism in the United States of America"; Fishman, *Language Loyalty in the United States*.

7 See Gomez, *Exchanging Our Country Marks*, 170–84; Lepore, *A Is for American*, 120–21; Dillard, *Black English*.

8 Shell, "Babel in America," 105. The contemporary hegemony of English notwithstanding, the persistence of linguistic diversity in the United States remains impressive. See, for example, Modern Language Association, "MLA Language Map," and Ashman's remarkable interactive "Full-Scale Dialect Map."

9 Hamilton et al., *The Federalist Papers*, 6.

10 Webster, *Dissertation on the English Language*, 178.

11 Adams, cited in Crawford, *Language Loyalties*, 26–27, 32.

12 Adams, cited in Crawford, *Language Loyalties*, 26–27.

13 Nebrija, *Gramatica de la lengua castellana*. See also Lodares, "Languages, Catholicism, and Power in the Hispanic Empire."

14 Howe, *Language and Political Meaning in Revolutionary America*, 15.

15 For an insightful discussion of eighteenth-century projects for reforming English, see Howe, *Language and Political Meaning in Revolutionary America*, 13–27. The quotations in this paragraph are taken from these pages.

16 Webster, "Author's Preface," in *An American Dictionary of the English Language*, xiii.

17 Webster, *Dissertation on the English Language*, 21.

18 Webster, *Dissertation on the English Language*, 21. See also Webster, *An American Dictionary of the English Language*, xiii.

19 Webster, *An American Dictionary of the English Language*, xiv; Webster, *A Grammatical Institute of the English Language*, 14–15.

20 Webster, *An American Dictionary of the English Language*, xi.

21 Webster, *A Grammatical Institute of the English Language*, 6–7. First published in 1783, Webster's blue-backed spellers sold close to 10 million copies by 1823 and were the most commonly used books for teaching American children

how to read until the later nineteenth century. Frederick Douglass credits Webster spellers with helping him to gain fluency in the national language. Indeed sales of the books experienced one of their most dramatic spikes shortly after the Civil War, when freedmen sought them out in order to acquire the literacy that had been forbidden to them as slaves. See Lepore, *A Is for American*, 6, 125–26.

22 Webster, *Dissertation on the English Language*, 19.

23 Webster, *Dissertation on the English Language*, 20.

24 See, for example, Jakobson, "On the Linguistic Aspects of Translation"; Derrida, *Monolingualism of the Other* and "What Is Relevant Translation?" See also Emad, "Thinking More Deeply into the Question of Translation." Indeed much of Heidegger's writings exemplify the inescapable task of translating within the same language. For a brilliant ethnographic study of the poetics and politics of intralingual translation in the context of Javanese, see Siegel, *Solo in the New Order*.

25 Webster, *Dissertation on the English Language*, 103–22.

26 Heath, "Why No Official Tongue?"; Sagarin and Kelly, "Polylingualism in the United States."

27 For the texts of various Official English amendments to state constitutions, see "State Official Language Statutes and Constitutional Amendments," in Crawford, *Language Loyalties*, 132–35.

28 Gray, *New World Babel*.

29 Sagarin and Kelly, "Polylingualism in the United States," 42; Solarz, "Official English," 124—27, "The English Plus Alternative," 151–53, and "Native American Language Act," 155–57, all in Crawford, *Language Loyalties*. Indeed the Native American Language Act of 1990, which provides official encouragement (though not funding) for the learning and preservation of native languages, including Hawaiian, designates these languages as "foreign," so studying them allows students to fulfill credits toward the satisfaction of a foreign-language requirement.

30 Atkins, *Report of the Secretary of the Interior*, 2: 18–19. For the vicissitudes of Indian language policies under the U.S. government, see Jon Reyhner, "Policies toward American Indian Languages: A Historical Sketch," in Crawford, *Language Loyalties*, 41–46.

31 Roosevelt, "Children of the Crucible," 35, 45–46; I also cite the shorter version that appears in Crawford, *Language Loyalties*, 84–85. See also Theodore Roosevelt, "The Children of the Crucible," *Outlook*, 19 September 1917, 80.

32 See, for example, Ryan Lizze, "The Return of the Nativist," *New Yorker*, 17 December 2007, 48. For accounts of nativist insistence on English as a touchstone of assimilation, see Higham, *Strangers in the Land*; Kellor, *Straight America*.

33 See chapter 2 of this book for an example of how this project of monolingual citizenship is applied, and fails, in the U.S. colony of the Philippines.

34 For a genealogy of American "exceptionalism," see Rogers, "Exceptionalism." For an indispensable critique of exceptionalism as it relates to American imperialism, see Go, *Patterns of Empire*. See also Elliott, *Empires of the Atlantic World*, 184–218.

35 Cited in Shell, "Babel in America," 104.

36 Cited in Crawford, *Language Loyalties*, 100.

37 Weber has discussed in detail the complications of the word *babel* in his essay "A Touch of Translation." For an important explication of Babel, see Derrida, "Des Tours des Babel." See also Gray, *New World Babel*, 3–27.

38 See, for example, the case of Captain James Yee, who had converted to Islam and, fluent in Arabic, was assigned to serve as a chaplain to detainees in Guantánamo. In 2003 he was arrested on charges of espionage, though he was convicted of much lesser charges a few years later. Yee's example is discussed in Pratt, "Harm's Way."

39 Deborah Amos, "Iraqi Interpreters Grateful for U.S. Troops' Support," National Public Radio, 17 October 2007; Joseph B. Frazier (for Associated Press), "Oregon Guardsman Returns the Favor for His Iraqi Interpreter," *Seattle Post-Intelligencer*, 24 December 2007; Michael Breen, "The Debt We Owe Iraqi Interpreters," *Christian Science Monitor*, 8 December 2008.

40 John Koopman, "Interpreter's Death Rattles Troops," *San Francisco Chronicle*, 1 August 2004; Moni Basu, "Iraqi Interpreters Risk Their Lives to Aid GIs," *Cox News Services*, 2 November 2005; Howard LaFranci, "Remembering Allan: A Tribute to Jim Carroll's Interpreter," *Christian Science Monitor*, 6 March 2006.

41 Charles Levinson, "Iraq's 'Terps' Face Suspicions on Both Sides," *Christian Science Monitor*, 17 April 2006; Nick Wadhams, "Iraqi Interpreters Face Death Threats from Countrymen, Alienation from U.S. Troops," Associated Press, 23 January 2006.

42 Levinson, "Iraq's 'Terps' Face Suspicions on Both Sides." See also Ann Scott Tyson, "Always in Hiding, an Iraqi Interpreter's Anguished Life," *Christian Science Monitor*, 15 September 2004.

43 John M. Glionna and Ashraf Khalil, "'Combat Linguists' Battle on Two Fronts," *Los Angeles Times*, 5 June 2005; Matthew D. LaPlante, "Speaking the Language; A Vital Skill; Interpreters in High Demand in Iraq," *Salt Lake Tribune*, 13 October 2005; C. Mark Brinkley, "Translators' Fears Disrupt Vital Lines of Communication," *Army Times*, 8 December 2004.

44 Amos, "Iraqi Interpreters Grateful for U.S. Troops' Support."

45 Amos, "Iraqi Interpreters Grateful for U.S. Troops' Support."

46 David Washburn, "Dangerous Work of Contractors in Iraq," *San Diego Union-Tribune*, 22 November 2006.

47 The phrase "foreign [to the United States] in a domestic sense" comes from the concurring opinion of Supreme Court Justice Edward Douglas White describing the "unincorporated territories" held by the United States in the

wake of the wars of 1898—the Philippines, Puerto Rico, and Guam—in *Downes v. Bidwell*, one in a series of decisions collectively known as the Insular Cases of 1901. See Duffy Burnett and Marshall, *Foreign in a Domestic Sense*, especially 1–17. For a sustained inquiry into this notion of foreignness that at once conjures and troubles the domestic, see Kaplan, *The Anarchy of Empire in the Making of U.S. Culture*. My own attempt to specify foreignness as the recurrence of untranslatability amid the imperative to translate can be found in Rafael, *The Promise of the Foreign*.

48 Levinson, "Iraq's 'Terps' Face Suspicions on Both Sides."

49 Friedrich Nietzsche, "Use and Abuse of History," in *Untimely Observations*, cited in Weber, "Wartime," 91.

50 Weber, "Wartime," 92.

Chapter 5: Targeting Translation

An earlier version of this chapter appeared as "Targeting Translation: Counterinsurgency and the Weaponization of Language," *Social Text* 113, 30, no. 4 (2012): 55–80.

1 Ellen Nakashima and Craig Whitlock, "With Air Force's New Drone 'We Can See Everything,'" *Washington Post*, 2 January 2011, washingtonpost.com/wp -dyn/content/article/2011/ 01/ 01/AR2011010102690.html.

2 I have found most useful the critical terms for thinking about the technical transformation of the world into a visual picture targeted for expropriation by humans laid out by Heidegger in "The Age of the World Picture," in *The Question Concerning Technology and Other Essays*, 115–54. Weber, *Targets of Opportunity*, offers an extended gloss on Heidegger. For an analysis of weaponization, see Deleuze and Guattari, *A Thousand Plateaus*, especially 395–403; de Landa, *War in the Age of Intelligent Machines*, 11–126. For a discussion of the conversion of visual perception into a military weapon, see Chow, *The Age of the World Target*, 25–44.

3 For the dangers of data overload, see Thom Shankel and Matt Richtel, "In New Military, Data Overload Can Be Deadly," *New York Times*, 16 January 2011, nytimes.com/2011/ 01/17/technology/17brain.html?src=me&ref=homepage. For one of the most insightful sites for critically tracking the development of drone technology and the continuous militarization of spatial relations, see Derek Gregory's blog, "Geographical Imaginations."

4 Nakashima and Whitlock, "With Air Force's New Drone."

5 See United States, Department of the Army, *The US Army/Marine Corps Counterinsurgency Field Manual*.

6 See Anderson, "Winning the Nation-Building War."

7 See Gumz, "Reframing the Historical Problematic of Insurgency," 561–62. See also Sarah Sewall, "Introduction to the University of Chicago Press

Edition: A Radical Field Manual," in United States, Department of the Army, *Counterinsurgency Field Manual*.

8   John A. Nagl, cited in Gumz, "Reframing the Historical Problematic of Insurgency," 562.

9   United States, Department of the Army, *Counterinsurgency Field Manual*, tables 5–6: 173.

10 United States, Department of the Army, *Counterinsurgency Field Manual*, xliii, 151–97. The notion of the United States as "the indispensible nation" comes from former secretary of state Madeleine Albright and has been echoed by counterinsurgent theorists such as John Nagl and more recently by President Obama in his 2012 State of the Union speech. See also Mckelvey, "The Cult of Counterinsurgency," 11.

11 The literature on counterinsurgency is extensive and varied. See, for example, Ucko, *The New Era of Counterinsurgency*; Bacevich, *Washington Rules*; Kilcullen, *The Accidental Guerrilla*; Nagl, *Counterinsurgency Lessons from Malaysia and Vietnam*; Cassidy, *Counterinsurgency and the Global War on Terror*; Kelly et al., *Anthropology and Global Counterinsurgency*; Price, *Anthropological Intelligence*; Masco, *The Theater of Operations*; Mirzoeff, "War Is Culture"; Gregory, "The Rush to the Intimate."

12 See Heidegger, "The Question Concerning Technology," in *The Question Concerning Technology and Other Essays*, especially 16. See also Weber, "Upsetting the Setup: Remarks on Heidegger's 'The Questing after Technics,'" in *Mass Mediauras*, 55–74.

13 An examination of the Defense Language Institute Foreign Language Center would require a separate essay. For now, it is perhaps enough to say that its mission stems from the directives of the Department of Defense: to furnish "culturally-based foreign language education" in order to "enhance the security of the nation," and to do so "at the point of need." See their website at http://www.dliflc.edu/. As with the language program I describe below, the Center's approach to languages amounts to their conversion into a standing reserve, as weapons for securing the American imperial order under the sign of "national security."

14 Tunnell, "Developing a Unit Language Capability for War."

15 United States, Department of Defense, "Defense Language Transformation Roadmap."

16 Tunnell, "Developing a Unit Language Capability for War," 115.

17 Tunnell, "Developing a Unit Language Capability for War," 116.

18 Pratt, "Harm's Way."

19 See "AJK" comment on Joshua Foust, "Unfit Interpreters," Registan, 23 July 2009, accessed 14 November 2009. http://registan.net/2009/07/23/unfit-interpreters/.

20 For a critique of this Aristotelian notion of media and mediation, see Stiegler, *Technics and Time*.

21 See de Landa, *War in the Age of Intelligent Machines*, 206–15; Slocum, "A Survey of Machine Translation."

22 United States, Defense Advanced Research Projects Agency, "Babylon Program."

23 Garamone, "Joint Vision 2020 Emphasizes Full-Spectrum Dominance."

24 The company is called Voxtec. See "Phraselator P2," Voxtec, http://www .voxtec.com/. See Harrison, "Machines Not Lost in Translation." For an astute critique of the Phraselator, see Pratt, "Harm's Way," 1519.

25 See Juang and Rabiner, "Automatic Speech Recognition."

26 See Hanlon, "Mobile Technology"; Mieszkowski, "How Do You Say 'Regime Change' in Arabic?"

27 See Waibel et al., "Speechalator." Also see Gao, "Speech-to-Speech Translation."

28 See Juang and Rabiner, "Automatic Speech Recognition," 12–21.

29 See chapter 4 of this book.

30 United States, Department of the Army, *Counterinsurgency Field Manual*, Section C-19: 340.

31 Moss, "The Hidden Engagement."

32 On the militarization of anthropology, see Kelly et al., *Anthropology and Global Counterinsurgency.* For one of the more illuminating anthropological critiques of counterinsurgency and the war on terror, see Masco, *The Theater of Operations.*

33 United States, Department of the Army, *Counterinsurgency Field Manual*, Section C-19: 340.

34 See Moss, "The Hidden Engagement," 4; Chatterjee, "Outsourcing Intelligence in Iraq."

35 United States, Department of the Army, *Counterinsurgency Field Manual*, Section C-7–8: 337, C-8: 337.

36 Center for Army Lessons Learned, "How to Communicate Effectively through Interpreters."

37 See especially Derrida's critique of logocentrism in *Of Grammatology* and *Limited, Inc.*

38 United States, Department of the Army, *Counterinsurgency Field Manual*, Section C-12: 338, C-33: 343, Table C-1: 342.

39 United States, Department of the Army, *Counterinsurgency Field Manual*, Section C-32: 343.

40 United States, Department of the Army, *Counterinsurgency Field Manual*, Section C-37: 344.

41 United States, Department of the Army, *Counterinsurgency Field Manual*, Section Table C-2: 346.

42 United States, Department of the Army, *Counterinsurgency Field Manual*, Section Table C-2: 346.

43 It is as if the authors of these military protocols had read Benveniste on

pronouns. See "Subjectivity in Language," in *Problems in General Linguistics*, 223–30, and the introduction of this book.

44 United States, Department of the Army, *Counterinsurgency Field Manual*, Section C-38: 344.

45 United States, Department of the Army, *Counterinsurgency Field Manual*, Section C-39–44: 344–45.

46 Alissa J. Rubin and Sangar Rahimi, "Nine Afghan Boys Collecting Firewood Killed by NATO Helicopters," *New York Times*, 2 March 2011, accessed 4 March 2011. nytimes.com/2011/03/03/world/asia/03afghan.html?_r =1&scp=1&sq=afghanistan%20killings&st=cse. The killing of civilians by manned and unmanned aircraft has been all too familiar and frequent in the U.S. war in Afghanistan and Pakistan. See Kathy Kelly, "Incalculable," *Huffington Post*, 4 March 2011, accessed 6 March 2011. huffingtonpost.com /kathy-kelly/afghanistan-war-asualties_b_831190.html.

47 Rubin and Rahimi, "Nine Afghan Boys Collecting Firewood Killed by NATO Helicopters."

48 Rubin and Rahimi, "Nine Afghan Boys Collecting Firewood Killed by NATO Helicopters."

49 Benjamin, "The Task of the Translator," especially 82.

50 Rubin and Rahimi, "Nine Afghan Boys Collecting Firewood Killed by NATO Helicopters."

51 Benjamin, "The Task of the Translator," 81–82. For Benjamin the exemplar of interlinear translation is the Septuagint scriptures, where the books of the Old Testament appear with a Greek translation situated between the lines of the Hebrew. Insofar as interlinear translation opens the way for more interpretation and more translation without limits, it plays out, as I imply below, the aporetic nature of translation that I discuss in the introduction of this book.

52 Rubin and Rahimi, "Nine Afghan Boys Collecting Firewood Killed by NATO Helicopters."

53 Rubin and Rahimi, "Nine Afghan Boys Collecting Firewood Killed by NATO Helicopters"; Patrick Quinn, "Karzai Rejects U.S. Apology for Killing of Nine Afghan Boys," *Huffington Post*, 6 March 2011, accessed 8 March 2011. huffingtonpost.com/2011/03/06/karzai-rejects-us-apology-afghanistan-boys -killed_n _831972.html.

54 Samuel Johnson, cited in *Oxford English Dictionary* for the definition of the verb to *linger*.

Chapter 6: The Accidents of Area Studies

An earlier version of this chapter appeared as "The Accidents of Area Studies," *American Historical Review* 104, no. 4 (1999): 1208–20.

1 The literature on post–Cold War area studies is extensive. See, for example,

Miyoshi and Harootunian, *Learning Places*; Sears, *Knowing Southeast Asian Subjects*; Hirschman et al., *Southeast Asia in the Balance*; Rafael, "The Culture of Area Studies in the United States."

2 Kahin's story appears in Anderson, *The Specter of Comparisons*, 18–19. Thanks to examples set by founding figures such as Kahin and Harry Benda at Yale, Southeast Asian scholars for the most part have tended to be skeptical of, if not militantly opposed to, U.S. interventions in Southeast Asia.

3 This is the story told by Judith Becker, professor of ethnomusicology at the University of Michigan, about the genesis of her interest in Southeast Asian music.

4 Here I am thinking of such scholars as Anna Tsing, Gail Hershatter, Laurie Sears, Nancy Florida, Barbara Andaya, Ann Laura Stoler, and Peggy Choy, who were kind enough to relate their stories to me.

5 This story was told to me by Gerard Finin.

6 See, for example, Thompson et al., *Sentimental Imperialists*; Kaplan and Pease, *Cultures of United States Imperialism*; Espiritu, *Five Faces of Exile*; Rafael, *White Love and Other Events in Filipino History*.

7 Said, *Orientalism*, 78.

8 See also the section entitled "Personal Vectors" in Anderson, *The Specter of Comparisons*, 18–20.

9 Anderson, *Language and Power*, 1.

10 See Holt, *Art in Indonesia*. For a fuller biography of Holt, see Burton, *Sitting at the Feet of Gurus*.

11 Anderson, *Language and Power*, 10.

12 See, for example, "The Idea of Power in Javanese Culture," "Old State, New Society: Indonesia's New Order in Comparative Historical Perspective," "The Languages of Indonesian Politics," "Cartoons and Monuments: The Evolution of Political Communication under the New Order," all of which are in Anderson, *Language and Power*.

13 Anderson, *Language and Power*, 6, 14. See also the dedication of *The Specter of Comparisons*.

14 Appadurai's serious fascination with objects in circulation is apparent in an earlier volume he edited, *The Social Life of Things*.

15 Appadurai, *Modernity at Large*, 18.

16 Appadurai, *Modernity at Large*, 1.

17 Appadurai, *Modernity at Large*, 2.

18 Siegel, *Objects and Objections of Ethnography*, 1–2.

19 On the first-person pronoun as inherently divided between the self that speaks and the language that is spoken, see the introduction of this book, with reference to Benveniste, "The Nature of Pronouns" and "Subjectivity in Language," both in *Problems in General Linguistics*, 217–22 and 223–30, respectively.

Chapter 7: Contracting Nostalgia

What follows is the text of a talk given in a panel honoring Renato Rosaldo at the American Anthropological Association Meetings, San Jose, CA, 18 November 2006.

1   Rosaldo, *Ilongot Headhunting*, v.
2   Rosaldo, *Culture and Truth*, 69, 70.
3   Rosaldo, *Ilongot Headhunting*, 86.
4   Rosaldo, *Ilongot Headhunting*, 87, 289.
5   For a critique of U.S. colonial photography in the Philippines, see Copozolla, "Photography and Power in the Colonial Philippines," http://ocw.mit.edu /ans7870/21f/21f.027/photography_and_power_02/dwo2_essay01.html, accessed 29 July 2015.
6   For an analysis of the conventions of portraiture in Western art, see Simmel, "The Aesthetic Significance of the Face." And for a deconstructive commentary on this essay, see Siegel, "Georg Simmel Reappers: The Aesthetic Significance of the Face," in *Objects and Objections of Ethnography*, 3–20.
7   Rosaldo, *Culture and Truth*, 5–6.
8   Rosaldo, *Culture and Truth*, 6.
9   Rosaldo, *Knowledge and Passion*, 34–35. For a related discussion of nostalgia, see the classic essay by Kathleen Stewart, "Nostalgia—A Polemic."
10 Nancy, *Being Singular-Plural*, xiii.

Chapter 8: Language, History, and Autobiography

An earlier version of this chapter appeared as "Becoming Reynaldo Ileto: Language, History and Autobiography," *Philippine Studies: Historical and Ethnographic Viewpoints* 62, no. 1 (2014): 115–32.

1   Reynaldo Ileto, preface to the Japanese translation of *Pasyon and Revolution*, unpaginated manuscript, Singapore, March 2005. I thank the author for furnishing me a copy of this manuscript.
2   See also chapter 1 of this book for a discussion of these concepts.
3   Ileto, "Father and Son in the Embrace of Uncle Sam," 80. I have also consulted a slightly different manuscript version of this essay from 2010, graciously provided to me by Ileto.
4   Ileto, *Pasyon and Revolution*, 2–3. On Renato Constantino, see chapter 2 of this book.
5   My understanding of proper nouns and proper names as heterogeneous and therefore untranslatable elements in language, which, like signatures, survive their referents, owes much to the following books by Derrida: *The Ear of the Other*, *Writing and Difference*, and *Acts of Religion*, among other works.
6   Ileto, *Pasyon and Revolution*, 12.
7   See, for example, Rafael, *Contracting Colonialism* and *The Promise of the Foreign*.

8 For a detailed account of Wolters's colonial and scholarly careers, see Craig J. Reynolds, "The Professional Lives of O. W. Wolters," in Wolters, *Early Southeast Asia*, 1–38.

9 Agoncillo, *A History of the Filipino People*. Having gone through numerous revisions and editions, the latest in 2012, Agoncillo's is still the most widely used textbook in Philippine history for colleges and universities in the Philippines.

10 Ileto, "Father and Son in the Embrace of Uncle Sam," 121.

11 See Ileto, "Reflections on Teodoro Agoncillo's *Revolt of the Masses* and the Politics of History" and "Scholarship, Society and Politics in Three Worlds." There is as yet no critical biography of Agoncillo, but see the instructive interviews by Ambeth Ocampo, *Talking History*.

12 It is worth noting that as much as Ileto initially rebels against Wolters's injunction to "not write" like Agoncillo, Ileto's work will come to rely on notions of Southeast Asian power developed by Wolters, especially in such books as Wolters, *History, Culture and Region in Southeast Asian Perspectives*.

13 Ileto, "Father and Son in the Embrace of Uncle Sam," 100–101. It is worth noting that Jesuit historians such as Fr. John Schumacher, Fr. Mario Francisco, and Fr. Jose Cruz were some of the earliest and, in most cases, enthusiastic readers of Ileto's work. Fr. Schumacher had taught Ileto's work while it was still a dissertation and has through the years incorporated many of its insights into his own work.

14 Ileto, *Pasyon and Revolution*, 4.

15 Ileto, *Pasyon and Revolution*, 5.

16 Rafael Ileto was part of the Alamo Scouts of the Sixth U.S. Army responsible for the spectacular rescue of American prisoners of war in Cabanatuan, Nueva Ecija, on 30 January 1945.

17 Rafael Ileto's service included founding the first special forces unit, the Scout Rangers, in 1950, and serving as operating chief of the National Intelligence Coordinating Agency, commanding general of the Philippine Army under Marcos (with whom he would break), and secretary of national defense under Cory Aquino in 1986. He also served as ambassador to Iran, Turkey, Thailand, Cambodia, and Laos at various times. I thank Rey Ileto for providing me with these details.

18 The best account of the Huks is still Kerkvliet, *The Huk Rebellion*. See also the important history of women's participation in the Huk Rebellion by Vina Lanzona, *Amazons in the Huk Rebellion*.

19 Ileto, "Father and Son in the Embrace of Uncle Sam," 100.

20 Ileto, "Father and Son in the Embrace of Uncle Sam," 77–79.

21 Ileto, "Father and Son in the Embrace of Uncle Sam," 81.

22 Ileto, "Father and Son in the Embrace of Uncle Sam," 111.

23 Ileto, "Father and Son in the Embrace of Uncle Sam," 113.

24 Deleuze, "Control and Becoming."

25 See chapter 1 of this book.

26 See chapters 1, 2, and 3 of this book for examples of my ongoing conversations with Rey Ileto's work.

Chapter 9: Interview

1 See chapter 5 of this book.
2 See the introduction of this book.
3 See chapter 4 of this book.
4 Berman, *The Experience of the Foreign* and "Translation and the Trials of the Foreign."
5 See chapter 2 of this book.
6 See chapter 2 of this book.
7 Deleuze, "He Stuttered," in *Essays: Critical and Clinical*, 107–14.

BIBLIOGRAPHY

....

Acta de la Proclamacion de la independenica del pueblo Filipino. In June 12, 1898 and Related
    Documents, edited by Esteban de Ocampo. Manila: National Historical Com-
    mission, 1972, 19–40.
Agoncillo, Teodoro. A History of the Filipino People. Quezon City: RP Garcia, 1960.
———. Malolos: The Crisis of the Republic. Quezon City: University of the Philip-
    pines Press, 1960.
———. Revolt of the Masses: The Story of Bonifacio and the Katipunan. Quezon City:
    University of the Philippines Press, 1956.
Aguinaldo, Emilio. Mga Gunita ng Himagsikan. Cavite (?): Cristina Aguinaldo
    Suntay, 1964.
Alvarez, Mariano. Katipunan at ang Paghihimagsik. Translated by Paula Carolina
    Malay as The Katipunan and the Revolution: Memoirs of a General. Quezon City:
    Ateneo de Manila University Press, 1992.
American Council on the Teaching of Foreign Languages. "National Security
    Language Initiative." 5 January 2006. www.actfl.org/i4a/pages/index.cfm
    ?pageid= 4249. Accessed 20 July 2009.
Anderson, Benedict. "Cacique Democracy in the Philippines." In The Specter of
    Comparison: Nationalism, Southeast Asia and the World. London: Verso, 1998.
———. Imagined Communities: Reflections on the Origins and Spread of Nationalism.
    Revised edition. London: Verso, 2006.
———. Language and Power: Exploring Political Cultures in Indonesia. Ithaca: Cornell
    University Press, 1990.
———. The Specter of Comparisons: Nationalism, Southeast Asia and the World. London:
    Verso, 1998.
———. Why Counting Counts: A Study of Forms of Consciousness and Problems of Lan-

guage in the *Noli me tangere* and *El Filibusterismo*. Quezon City: Ateneo de Manila University Press, 2009.

Anderson, George E., III. "Winning the Nation-Building War." *Military Review,* September–October 2004, 47–50.

Appadurai, Arjun. *Modernity at Large: Cultural Dimensions of Globalization*. Minneapolis: University of Minnesota Press, 1996.

———. *The Social Life of Things: Commodities in Cultural Perspective*. Cambridge: Cambridge University Press, 1986.

Ashman, Rick. "Full-Scale Dialect Map." North American English Dialects, Based on Pronunciation Patterns. 9 December 2014. http://aschmann.net /AmEng/#LargeMap. Accessed 21 December 2014.

Atkins, J. D. *Report of the Secretary of the Interior, in 50th Session, House of Congress.* 5 vols. Washington, DC: Government Printing Office, 1887.

Bacevich, Andrew. *Washington Rules: America's Path to Permanent War*. New York: Metropolitan Books, 2010.

Balakrishnan, Gopal. *The Enemy: An Intellectual Portrait of Carl Schmitt*. London: Verso, 2000.

Barry, Jerome. "A Little Brown Language." *American Speech* 3, no. 1 (1927): 14–20.

Bataille, Georges. *The Accursed Share: An Essay on General Economy*. 3 vols. Translated by Robert Hurley. New York: Zone Books, 1988.

Bautista, Maria Lourdes, and Kingsley Bolton, eds. *Philippine English: Linguistic and Literary Perspectives*. Hong Kong: Hong Kong University Press, 2008.

Beer, William R., and James E. Jacob. *Language Policy and National Unity*. Totowa, NJ: Rowman and Allanheld, 1985.

Benjamin, Walter. *Charles Baudelaire: A Lyric Poet in the Era of High Capitalism*. London: Verso, 1997.

———. "Marseilles." In *Reflections: Essays, Aphorisms, Autobiographical Writings*. Edited by Peter Demetz. Translated by Edmund Jephcott. New York: Schocken Books, 1986, 131–36.

———. "The Task of the Translator." In *Illuminations*. Translated by Harry Zohn. New York: Schocken Books, 1969, 69–82.

Benveniste, Emile. *Problems in General Linguistics*. Translated by Mary Elizabeth Meek. Coral Gables: University of Miami Press, 1973.

Berman, Antoine. *The Experience of the Foreign: Culture and Translation in Romantic Germany*. Translated by S. Hayvaert. Albany: State University of New York Press, 1992.

———. "Translation and the Trials of the Foreign." Translated by Lawrence Venuti. In *Translation Studies Reader*, edited by Lawrence Venuti. 3rd edition. New York: Routledge, 2012, 240–55.

Bigelow, Donald, and Lyman Legters. NDEA: *Language and Area Center. A Report on the First Five Years*. Washington, DC: Government Printing Office, 1964.

Bodin, Jean. *On Sovereignty: Four Chapters from Six Books on the Commonwealth*. Translated and edited by Julian H. Franklin. Cambridge: Cambridge University Press, 1992.

Breton, André. *Nadja*. Translated by Richard Howard. New York: Grove Press, 1994 (originally published 1928).

Burton, Deena. *Sitting at the Feet of Gurus: The Life and Dance Ethnography of Claire Holt*. Philadelphia: Xlibris, 2009.

Butte, George C. "Shall the Philippines Have a Common Language." Manila: Bureau of Printing, 1931.

Cannell, Fenella. *Power and Intimacy in the Christian Philippines*. Cambridge: Cambridge University Press, 1999.

Cassidy, Robert. *Counterinsurgency and the Global War on Terror: Military Culture and Irregular War*. Westport, CT: Praeger, 2006.

Center for Army Lessons Learned. "How to Communicate Effectively through Interpreters: A Guide for Leaders." *News from the Front*, November–December 2003. au.af.mil/au/awc/awcgate/army/using_interpreters.htm. Accessed 15 March 2005.

Chatterjee, Pratap. "Outsourcing Intelligence in Iraq: A *Corp Watch Report* on 1-3/ Titan." Corp Watch. 9 December 2008. corpwatch.org/article.php?id=15253. Accessed 10 January 2009.

Cheah, Pheng, and Suzanne Guerlac, eds. *Derrida and the Time of the Political*. Durham: Duke University Press, 2009.

Chow, Rey. *The Age of the World Target: Self-Referentiality in War, Theory, and Comparative Work*. Durham: Duke University Press, 2006.

Clowse, Barbara Barksdale. *Brain Power for the Cold War: The Sputnik Crisis and the National Defense Education Act of 1958*. Westport, CT: Greenwood Press, 1981.

Cohn, Bernard. *An Anthropologist among Historians and Other Essays*. New York: Oxford University Press, 1987.

Constantino, Renato. "The Mis-education of the Filipino." 1959. *Journal of Cotemporary Asia* 1, no. 1 (1970): 20–36.

Copozolla, Christopher. "Photography and Power in the Colonial Philippines: Dean Worcester's Ethnographic Images of Filipinos (1898–1912). http://ocw .mit.edu/ans7870/21f/21f.027/photography_and_power_02/dw02_essay01 .htm. Accessed 29 July 2015.

Coronel, Sheila, ed. *Investigating Estrada: Millions, Mansions and Mistresses*. Manila: Philippine Center for Investigative Journalism, 2000.

Crawford, James, ed. *Language Loyalties: A Source Book on the Official English Controversy*. Chicago: University of Chicago Press, 1992.

de la Costa, Horacio, SJ. "Church and State in the Philippines during the Administration of Bishop Salazer, 1581–1594." *Hispanic American Historical Review* 30 (3 August 1950): 314–35.

de Landa, Manuel. *War in the Age of Intelligent Machines*. New York: Zone Books, 1991.

Deleuze, Gilles. "Control and Becoming." In *Negotiations: 1972–1990*. Translated by Martin Joughin. New York: Columbia University Press, 1995, 169–76.

———. *Essays: Critical and Clinical*. Translated by Daniel W. Smith and Daniel Greco. London: Verso 1998.

Deleuze, Gilles, and Félix Guattari. *A Thousand Plateaus: Capitalism and Schizophrenia*. Translated by Brian Massumi. Minneapolis: University of Minnesota Press, 1987.

del Pilar, Marcelo. *La frailocracia Filipina*. Barcelona: Imprenta Iberica de Francisco Fossas, 1888.

———. *La soberania monacal en Filipinias*. Barcelona: Imprenta Iberica de Francisco Fossas, 1888.

de Ocampo, Esteban, ed. *June 12, 1898 and Related Documents*. Manila: National Historical Commission, 1972.

Derrida, Jacques. *Acts of Religion*. Edited by Gil Anidjar. New York: Routledge, 2001.

———. "Declarations of Independence." *New Political Science* 15 (1986): 7–17.

———. *The Ear of the Other*. Translated by Peggy Kamuf. Lincoln: University of Nebraska Press, 1985.

———. "Faith and Knowledge: The Two Sources of 'Religion' at the Limits of Reason Alone." Translated by Samuel Weber. In *Acts of Religion*, edited by Gil Anidjar. New York: Routledge, 2002, 40–101.

———. *Given Time: Counterfeit Money*. Translated by Peggy Kamuf. Chicago: University of Chicago Press, 1992.

———. *Limited, Inc.* Translated by Samuel Weber. Evanston, IL: Northwestern University Press, 1988.

———. *Monolingualism of the Other, or The Prosthesis of Origin*. Translated by Patrick Mensah. Stanford: Stanford University Press, 1998.

———. *Of Grammatology*. Translated by Gayatri Chakravorty Spivak. Baltimore: Johns Hopkins University Press, 1976.

———. *The Politics of Friendship*. Translated by George Collins. London: Verso, 1997.

———. *Rogues: Two Essays on Reason*. Translated by Pascale-Anne Brault and Michael Naas. Stanford: Stanford University Press, 2005.

———. "Signature Event Context." In *Margins of Philosophy*, translated by Alan Bass. Chicago: University of Chicago Press, 1982.

———. "Des Tours des Babel." Translated by Joseph Graham. In *Acts of Religion*, edited by Gil Anidjar. New York: Routledge, 2002, 102–34.

———. "What Is Relevant Translation?" Translated by Lawrence Venuti. In *Translation Studies Reader*, edited by Lawrence Venuti. 3rd edition. New York: Routledge, 2012, 365–88.

———. *Writing and Difference*. Translated by Alan Bass. Chicago: University of Chicago Press, 1978.

de Vries, Hent, and Lawrence C. Sullivan, eds. *Political Theologies: Public Religions in a Post-Secular World*. New York: Fordham University Press, 2006.

Dillard, J. L. *Black English: Its History and Usages in the United States.* New York: Vintage, 1973.

Dodd, Don. *Historical Statistics of the States of the United States: Two Centuries of the Census, 1790–1990.* Westport, CT: Greenwood Press, 1993.

Duffy Burnett, Christina, and Burke Marshall, eds. *Foreign in a Domestic Sense: Puerto Rico, American Expansion and the Constitution.* Durham: Duke University Press, 2001.

Elliott, J. H. *Empires of the Atlantic World: Britain and Spain in America, 1492–1830.* New Haven: Yale University Press, 2006.

———. *Imperial Spain, 1469–1716.* New York: New American Library, 1963.

Emad, Parvis. "Thinking More Deeply into the Question of Translation." In *Reading Heidegger: Commemoration,* edited by John Sallis. Bloomington: Indiana University Press, 1993, 323–40.

Espiritu, Augusto. *Five Faces of Exile: The Nation and Filipino American Exiles.* Stanford: Stanford University Press, 2005.

Fabian, Johannes. *Language and Colonial Power: The Appropriation of Swahili in the Former Belgian Congo, 1880–1938.* Berkeley: University of California Press, 1986.

Fast, Jonathan, and Jim Richardson. *Roots of Dependency: Political and Economic Revolution in 19th Century Philippines.* Quezon City: Foundation of Nationalist Studies, 1979.

Fishman, Joshua. *Language Loyalty in the United States: The Maintenance and Perpetuation of Non-English Mother Tongues by American Ethnic and Religious Groups.* The Hague: Mouton, 1966.

Foucault, Michel. *The History of Sexuality, Vol. 1.* Translated by Robert Hurley. New York: Vintage, 1990.

———. *Security, Territory, Population: Lectures at the Collège de France 1977–1978.* Translated by Graham Burchell. New York: Palgrave, 2008.

Fradera, Josep. *Colonias para despues de un imperio.* Barcelona: Edición Bellaterra, 2005.

———. *Filipinas, la colonia mas peculiar: La hacienda publica en la definición de la politica colonial, 1762–1868.* Madrid: Consejo Superior de Investigaciones Cientificas, 1999.

Frank, Jason. "'Unauthorized Propositions': The Federalist Papers and Constituent Power." *Diacritics* 37, nos. 2–3 (2007): 103–20.

Frank, Jason, and Tracy McNulty, eds. "Taking Exception to the Exception." Special issue of *Diacritics* 37, nos. 1–2 (2007).

Gao, Yuging. "Speech-to-Speech Translation." IBM Research, 2003. domino.research.ibm.com/comm/research.nsf/pages/r.uit.innovation.html. Accessed 4 April 2006.

Garamone, Jim. "Joint Vision 2020 Emphasizes Full-Spectrum Dominance." U.S. Department of Defense, 2 June 2000. defense.gov/news/newsarticle.aspx?id = 45289. Accessed 4 February 2004.

Go, Julian. *Patterns of Empire: The British and the American Empires, 1688 to the Present.* Cambridge: Cambridge University Press, 2012.

Gomez, Michael A. *Exchanging Our Country Marks: The Transformation of African Identities in the Colonial and Antebellum South*. Chapel Hill: University of North Carolina Press, 1998.

Gonzalez, Andrew S. *Language and Nationalism: The Philippine Experience Thus Far*. Quezon City: Ateneo de Manila University Press 1980.

Gray, Edward G. *New World Babel: Languages and Nations in Early America*. Princeton: Princeton University Press, 1999.

Gregory, Derek. "Geographical Imaginations: War, Space and Security." http://geographicalimaginations.com/.

———. "The Rush to the Intimate: Counterinsurgency and the Cultural Turn." *Radical Philosophy*, no. 150 (July–August 2008). radicalphilosophy.com/article/'the-rush-to-the-intimate'. Accessed 5 March 2009.

Guerrero, Amado (Jose Maria Sison). *Philippine Society and Revolution*. Manila: Ta Kung Pao, 1971.

Guerrero, Milagros. "Luzon at War: Contradictions in Philippine Society, 1898–1902." PhD dissertation, University of Michigan, 1977.

Guevara, Sulpicio, ed. *The Laws of the First Philippine Republic, 1898–1899*. Manila: National Historical Commission, 1972.

Gumz, Jonathan. "Reframing the Historical Problematic of Insurgency: How the Professional Military Literature Created a New History and Missed the Past." *Journal of Strategic Studies* 32, no. 4 (2009): 553–88.

Hamilton, Alexander, James Madison, and John Jay. *The Federalist Papers: A Collection of Essays Written in Support of the Constitution of the United States*. Edited by Roy P. Fairfield. Garden City, NY: Anchor, 1966.

Hamilton-Paterson, James. *The Ghosts of Manila*. New York: Vintage, 1995.

Hanlon, Mike. "Mobile Technology: PDA Based Translator for Field Use." *Gizmag*, 4 June 2004. gizmag.com/go/1833. Accessed 8 November 2006.

Hansen, Thomas Blom, and Finn Stepputat, eds. *Sovereign Bodies: Citizens, Migrants and States in the Postcolonial World*. Princeton: Princeton University Press, 2005.

———. "Sovereignty Revisited." *Annual Review of Anthropology* 35 (2006): 295–315.

Harrison, Ann. "Machines Not Lost in Translation." *Wired*, 9 March 2005. http://archive.wired.com/science/discoveries/news/2005/03/66816?currentPage=all. Accessed 10 November 2006.

Heath, Shirley Brice. "Why No Official Tongue?" In *Language Loyalties: A Source Book on the Official English Controversy*, edited by James Crawford. Chicago: University of Chicago Press, 1992, 20–30.

Heidegger, Martin. *The Question concerning Technology and Other Essays*. Translated by William Lovitt. New York: Harper and Row, 1977.

Higham, John. *Strangers in the Land: Patterns of American Nativism, 1860–1925*. New Brunswick, NJ: Rutgers University Press, 1955.

Hirschman, Charles, Joint Committee on Southeast Asia, ACLS-SSRC, et al.

Southeast Asia in the Balance: Reflection from America. Ann Arbor, MI: Association of Asian Studies, 1992.

Holt, C. Art in Indonesia: Continuity and Change. Ithaca: Cornell University Press, 1967.

Honig, Bonnie. Democracy and the Foreigner. Princeton: Princeton University Press, 2001.

———. "The Miracle of Metaphor: Rethinking the State of Exception with Rosenzweig and Schmitt." Diacritics 37, nos. 1–2 (2007): 78–102.

Howe, John. Language and Political Meaning in Revolutionary America. Amherst: University of Massachusetts Press, 2004.

Hutchcroft, Paul D. Booty Capitalism: The Politics of Banking in the Philippines. Ithaca: Cornell University Press, 1998.

Ileto, Reynaldo. "Father and Son in the Embrace of Uncle Sam." Philippine Studies: Historical and Ethnographic Viewpoints 62, no. 1 (2014): 67–114.

———. Pasyon and Revolution: Popular Movements in the Philippines, 1840–1910. Quezon City: Ateneo de Manila University Press, 1979.

———. "Reflections on Teodoro Agoncillo's Revolt of the Masses and the Politics of History." Southeast Asian Studies 49, no. 3 (2011): 496–520.

———. "Scholarship, Society and Politics in Three Worlds: Reflections of a Filipino Sojourner, 1965–95." In Decentering and Diversifying Southeast Asian Studies: Perspectives from the Region, edited by Goh Beng-Lan. Singapore: Institute of Southeast Asian Studies, 2011, 105–28.

Jakobson, Roman. "On the Linguistic Aspects of Translation." 1959. In The Translation Studies Reader, edited by Lawrence Venuti. 3rd edition. New York: Routledge, 2012, 126–31.

Juang, B. H., and Lawrence R. Rabiner. "Automatic Speech Recognition: A Brief History of the Technology Development." 8 October 2004. http://www.idi.ntnu.no/~gamback/teaching/TDT4275/literature/juang_rabiner04.pdf. Accessed 1 August 2012.

Kamen, Henry. Spain, 1469–1714: A Society in Conflict. London: Longman, 1983.

Kaplan, Amy. The Anarchy of Empire in the Making of U.S. Culture. Cambridge, MA: Harvard University Press, 2002.

Kaplan, Amy, and Donald Pease, eds. Cultures of United States Imperialism. Durham: Duke University Press, 1994.

Kellor, Frances. Straight America: A Call to National Service. New York: Macmillan, 1916.

Kelly, John, Beatrice Jauregui, Sean T. Mitchell, and Jeremy Walton, eds. Anthropology and Global Counterinsurgency. Chicago: University of Chicago Press, 2010.

Kerkvliet, Benedict Tria. The Huk Rebellion: A Study of Peasant Revolt in the Philippines. Berkeley: University of California Press, 1977.

Khatibi, Abdelkebir. Love in Two Languages. Translated by Richard Howard. Minneapolis: University of Minnesota Press, 1990.

Kilcullen, David. *The Accidental Guerrilla: Fighting Small Wars in the Midst of a Big One*. New York: Oxford University Press, 2009.

Kofman, Sarah. "Beyond Aporia?" Translated by David Macey. In *Post-structuralist Classics*, edited by Andrew Benjamin. New York: Routledge, 1988, 7–44.

Kramer, Paul. *The Blood of Government: Race, Empire, the United States and the Philippines*. Chapel Hill: University of North Carolina Press, 2006.

Laktaw, Pedro Serrano. *Diccionario Tagalo-Hispano. Segunda parte*. Manila: Santos y Bernal, 1914.

Lanot, Maara. *The Trouble with Nick and Other Profiles*. Quezon City: University of the Philippines Press, 1999.

Lanzona, Vina. *Amazons in the Huk Rebellion: Gender, Sex and Revolution in the Philippines*. Madison: University of Wisconsin Press, 2009.

Laya, Jaime C. *Letras y Figuras: Business in Culture, Culture in Business*. Manila: Anvil, 2001.

Lepore, Jill. *A Is for American: Letters and Other Characters in the Newly United States*. New York: Knopf, 2002.

Lévi-Strauss, Claude. *Introduction to the Works of Marcel Mauss*. Translated by Felicity Baker. London: Routledge and Keegan Paul, 1987.

Lewis, C. T., and C. Short. *Latin Dictionary: Based on Andrews's Edition of Freund's Latin Dictionary*. New York: Oxford University Press, 1963.

Lizze, Ryan. "The Return of the Nativist." *New Yorker*, 17 December 2007. http://www.newyorker.com/magazine/2007/12/17/return-of-the-nativist. Accessed 20 December 2007.

Llanes, Ferdinand, C., ed. *Tibak Rising: Activism in the Days of Martial Law*. Manila: Anvil, 2012.

Lodares, Juan R. "Languages, Catholicism, and Power in the Hispanic Empire (1500–1750)." In *Spanish and Empire*, edited by Nelsy Echavez-Solano and Kenya C. Dworkin y Mendez. Nashville, TN: Vanderbilt University Press, 2007, 3–31.

Mabanglo, Ruth Elynia, and Rosita S. Galang, eds. *Essays on Philippine Language and Literature*. Manila: Anvil, 2010.

Mabini, Apolinario. *La Revolución Filipina*. 2 vols. Manila: Bureau of Printing, 1931.

MacCormack, Sabine. *Religion in the Andes: Vision and Imagination in Early Colonial Peru*. Princeton: Princeton University Press, 1991.

Majul, Cesar Adib. *Mabini and the Philippine Revolution*. Quezon City: University of the Philippines Press, 1960.

Masco, Joseph. *The Theater of Operations: National Security Affect from the Cold War to the War on Terror*. Durham: Duke University Press, 2014.

Mata, Elvira. *The Ultimate Text Book*. Quezon City: Philippine Center for Investigative Journalism, 2000.

Mauss, Marcel. *The Gift: Forms and Functions of Exchange in Archaic Societies*. Translated by Ian Gunnison. New York: Norton, 1967.

May, Glenn. *Social Engineering in the Philippines*. Westport, CT: Greenwood Press, 1980.

Mckelvey, Tara. "The Cult of Counterinsurgency." *American Prospect* (November 2008): 19–22.

Mieszkowski, Katherine. "How Do You Say 'Regime Change' in Arabic?" *Salon*, 7 April 2003. http://www.salon.com/2003/04/07/phraselator/. Accessed 10 May 2010.

Mirzoeff, Nicholas. "War Is Culture: Global Counterinsurgency, Visuality, and the Petraeus Doctrine." *PMLA* 124, no. 5 (2009): 1737–746.

Miyoshi, Masao, and Harry Harootunian, eds. *Learning Places: The "Afterlives" of Area Studies*. Durham: Duke University Press, 2002.

Modern Language Association. "MLA Language Map." www.mla.org/map_main. Accessed 10 June 2009.

Mojares, Resil. "Biography of Nick Joaquin." Ramon Magsaysay Award Foundation. 1996, https://filipinoscribbles.wordpress.com/2010/09/15/biography-of-nick-joaquin-1917-2004/. Accessed 20 March 2011.

———. *Brains of the Nation: Pedro Paterno, T. H. Pardo de Tavera, Isabelo de los Reyes, and the Production of Modern Knowledge*. Quezon City: Ateneo de Manila University Press, 2008.

Monroe, Paul. *A Survey of the Educational System of the Philippine Islands by the Board of Educational Surveys: Created under Acts 3162 and 3196 of the Philippine Legislature*. Manila: Bureau of Printing, 1925.

Moss, Don. "The Hidden Engagement: Interpreters." *Small Wars Journal*, 17 May 2010. 1–4, http://smallwarsjournal.com/jrnl/art/the-hidden-engagement-interpreters. Accessed 18 July 2010.

Nabokov, Vladimir. "Problems of Translation: Onegin in English." In *Translation Studies Reader*, edited by Lawrence Venuti. 3rd ed. New York: Routledge, 2012, 113–25.

Nagl, John. *Counterinsurgency Lessons from Malaysia and Vietnam: Learning to Eat Soup with a Knife*. Westport, CT: Praeger, 2002.

Nakpil, Carmen Guerrero. *Myself, Elsewhere*. Manila: Circe Communications, 2006.

Nancy, Jean-Luc. *Being Singular-Plural*. Translated by Richard D. Richardson and Anne E. O'Byrne. Stanford: Stanford University Press, 2000.

———. *The Creation of the World, or Globalization*. Translated by François Raffoul and David Pettigrew. Albany: State University of New York Press, 2007.

Nebrija, Antonio de. *Gramatica de la lengua castellana*. Edited by Ig. Gonzalez-Llubera. London: Oxford University Press, 1926.

Nietzsche, Friedrich. "Translation." In *Translation Studies Reader*, edited by Lawrence Venuti. 3rd edition. New York: Routledge, 2012, 67–68.

Ocampo, Ambeth. *Talking History: Conversations with Teodoro Agoncillo*. Manila: De La Salle University Press, 1995.

Ofreneo, Rosalinda Pineda. *Renato Constantino: A Life Revisited*. Quezon City: Foundation for Nationalist Studies, 2001.

Osias, Camilio. "Education and Religion." In *Encyclopedia of the Philippines*, edited by Zoilo M. Galang. 20 vols. Manila: E. Floro, 1950–58, 9: 126.

Pante, Michael D. "The *Cocheros* of American-Occupied Manila: Representations and Persistence." *Philippine Studies: Historical and Ethnographic Viewpoints* 60, no. 4 (2012): 429–62.

Paz, Octavio. *The Labyrinth of Solitude*. New York: Grove Press, 1985.

Pegis, Anton C., ed. *Introduction to St. Thomas Aquinas*. New York: Random House, 1945.

Phelan, John Leddy. *The Hispanization of the Philippines: Spanish Aims and Filipino Responses, 1565–1700*. Madison: University of Wisconsin Press, 1967.

———. "Some Ideological Aspects of the Conquest of the Philippines." *Americas* 13, no. 3 (1957): 221–39.

Philippines (Commonwealth) Commission of the Census. *Census of the Philippines, 1939*. 5 vols. Manila: Bureau of Printing, 1940–43.

Pratt, Mary Louise. "Harm's Way: Language and the Contemporary Arts of War." *PMLA* 124, no. 5 (2009): 1515–31.

Price, David. *Anthropological Intelligence: The Deployment and Neglect of American Anthropology in the Second World War*. Durham: Duke University Press, 2008.

Quijano de Manila (Nick Joaquin). *The Language of the Streets and Other Essays*. Manila: National Bookstore, 1980.

Quimpo, Susan F., and Nathan Q. Quimpo, eds. *Subversive Lives: A Family Memoir of the Marcos Years*. Manila: Anvil, 2012.

Rafael, Vicente L. "Betraying Empire: Translation and the Ideology of Conquest." *Translation Studies* 8, no.1 (2014): 1–11. http://dx.doi.org/10.1080/14781700.2014.928649.

———. *Contracting Colonialism: Translation and Christian Conversion in Tagalog Society under Early Spanish Rule*. Durham: Duke University Press, 1993.

———. "The Culture of Area Studies in the United States." *Social Text* 41 (Winter 1994): 91–111.

———. *The Promise of the Foreign: Nationalism and the Technics of Translation in the Spanish Philippines*. Durham: Duke University Press, 2005.

———. *White Love and Other Events in Filipino History*. Durham: Duke University Press, 2000.

Recopilación de las leyes de los reinos de Indias. 4th edition. 1681. Facsimile. Madrid: Consejo de Hispanidad, 1943.

Richardson, Jim. *The Light of Liberty: Documents and Studies on the Katipunan, 1892–1897*. Quezon City: Ateneo de Manila University Press, 2013.

Rizal, Jose. *Por Telefono*. 1889. In *Miscellaneous Writings*. Manila: R. Martinez and Sons, 1959.

Rogers, Daniel. "Exceptionalism." In *Imagined Histories: American Historians Interpret the Past*, edited by Anthony Molho and Gordon S. Wood. Princeton: Princeton University Press, 1998, 21–40.

Romanillos, Emmanuel Luis. "El Chabacano de Cavite: Crepusculo de un Criollo Hispano-Filipino?" *Linguae et Litterae* 1 (December 1992): 9–14.

Roosevelt, Theodore. "Children of the Crucible." In *Annals of America*, vol. 14, 1916–1928. Chicago: Encyclopedia Britanica, 1968, 129–31.

Rosaldo, Michele. *Knowledge and Passion: Ilongot Notions of Self and Social Life.* Cambridge: Cambridge University Press, 1980.

Rosaldo, Renato. *Culture and Truth: The Remaking of Social Analysis.* Boston: Beacon Press, 1993.

———. *Ilongot Headhunting, 1883–1974: A Study in Society and History.* Stanford: Stanford University Press, 1980.

Rousseau, Jean-Jacques. *The Social Contract.* Translated by M. Cranston. New York: Penguin, 1968.

Sagarin, Edward, and Robert J. Kelly. "Polylingualism in the United States of America: A Multitude of Tongues amid a Monolingual Majority." In *Language Policy and National Unity*, edited by William R. Beer and James E. Jacob. Totowa, NJ: Rowman and Allanheld, 1985, 20–44.

Said, Edward. *Orientalism.* New York: Vintage, 1979.

Saleeby, Najib Mitry. *The Language of Education of the Philippine Islands.* Manila: n.p., 1924.

San Juan, E., Jr. "Inventing the Vernacular Speech-Acts: Articulating Filipino Self-Determination in the United States." *Socialism and Democracy* 19, no. 1 (2005): 136–54.

Schivelbusch, Wolfgang. *The Railway Journey: The Industrialization of Time and Space in the 19th Century.* Berkeley: University of California Press, 1986.

Schmidt-Nowara, Christopher. *The Conquest of History: Spanish Colonialism and National Histories in the Nineteenth Century.* Pittsburgh: University of Pittsburgh Press, 2006.

Schmitt, Carl. *Political Theology: Four Chapters on the Concept of Sovereignty.* Translated by George Schwab. Chicago: University of Chicago Press, 2005.

Schumacher, John. *Father Jose Burgos: A Documentary History.* Quezon City: Ateneo de Manila University Press, 1999.

———. *The Making of a Nation: Essays on Nineteenth-Century Filipino Nationalism.* Quezon City: Ateneo de Manila University Press, 1991.

———. *The Propaganda Movement, 1880–1895: The Creators of a Filipino Consciousness, the Makers of Revolution.* Manila: Solidaridad, 1973.

———. *Revolutionary Clergy: The Filipino Clergy and the Nationalist Movement, 1850–1903.* Quezon City: Ateneo de Manila University Press, 1981.

Sears, Laurie, ed. *Knowing Southeast Asian Subjects.* Seattle: University of Washington Press, 2007.

Severino, Howie G. "The Hand That Rocks the Masa." *Filipinas Magazine*, June 2001, 70–72.

Shell, Marc. "Babel in America: The Politics of Language Diversity in the United States." *Critical Inquiry* 20 (1993): 103–27.

Sidel, John. *Capital, Coercion, and Crime: Bossism in the Philippines.* Stanford: Stanford University Press, 1999.

Siegel, James T. "False Beggars: Marcel Mauss, *The Gift*, and Its Commentators," *diacritics* 41, no. 2 (2013): 60–79.

———. *Fetish, Recognition, Revolution.* Princeton: Princeton University Press, 1997.

———. "Georg Simmel Reappears." *diacritics* 29, no. 2 (1999): 100–113.

———. *Objects and Objections of Ethnography.* New York: Fordham University Press, 2011.

———. *Solo in the New Order: Language and Hierarchy in an Indonesian City.* Princeton: Princeton University Press, 1986.

Simmel, Georg. "The Aesthetic Signifiance of the Face," in *Georg Simmel, 1858–1918: A Collection of Essays and a Bibliography,* edited by Kurt H. Wolff. Columbus: Ohio State University Press, 1959, 276–81.

Slocum, Jonathan. "A Survey of Machine Translation: Its History, Current Status, and Future Prospects." In *Machine Translation Systems,* edited by Jonathan Slocum. Cambridge: Cambridge University Press, 1988, 1–48.

Stewart, Kathleen. "Nostalgia—A Polemic." *Cultural Anthropology* 3, no. 3 (1988): 227–41.

Stiegler, Bernard. *Technics and Time.* Vol. 1: *The Fault of Ephimetheus.* Translated by Richard Beardsworth and George Collins. Stanford: Stanford University Press, 1998.

Tadiar, Neferti X. "Manila's New Metropolitan Form." In *Discrepant Histories: Translocal Essays on Filipino Cultures,* edited by Vicente L. Rafael. Philadelphia: Temple University Press, 1995, 285–313.

"Text Generation." Special issue of *I: The Investigative Reporting Magazine* 8, no. 2 (2002).

Thompson, James, Jr., Peter C. Stanley, and John Curtis Perry. *Sentimental Imperialists: The American Experience in East Asia.* New York: Harper and Row, 1981.

Tolentino, Rolando, ed. *Geopolitics of the Visible: Essays on Philippine Film Cultures.* Quezon City: Ateneo de Manila University Press, 2000.

Tunnell, Harry D., IV. "Developing a Unit Language Capability for War." *JFQ: Joint Forces Quarterly,* no. 51 (October 2008): 114–16.

Ucko, David H. *The New Era of Counterinsurgency.* Washington, DC: Georgetown University Press, 2008.

United States. Defense Advanced Research Projects Agency. "Babylon Program." http://www.thelivingmoon.com/45jack_files/03documents/Darpa_Fact_File .html. Accessed 26 July 2015.

———. Department of the Army. *The U.S. Army/Marine Corps Counterinsurgency Field Manual (FM 3–24).* Chicago: University of Chicago Press, 2007.

———. Department of Defense. "Defense Language Transformation Roadmap." January 2005. www.defense.gov/news/Mar2005/d20050330roadmap.pdf. Accessed 10 April 2006.

———. *Lost in Translation: A Review of the Federal Government's Efforts to Develop a*

Foreign Language Strategy. Washington, DC: U.S. Government Printing Office, 2007.

Venuti, Lawrence. "Genealogies of Translation Theory: Jerome." In Translation Studies Reader, edited by Lawrence Venuti. 3rd edition. New York: Routledge, 2012, 483–501.

———. Introduction to The Translation Studies Reader, edited by Lawrence Venuti. 3rd edition. New York: Routledge, 2012, 1–10.

———, ed. The Translation Studies Reader. 3rd edition. New York: Routledge, 2012.

Waibel, Alex, et al. "Speechalator: Two-Way Speech-to-Speech Translation on a Consumer PDA." Eurospeech 2003. cs.cmu.edu/~awb/papers/eurospeech 2003/speechalator.pdf. Accessed 10 April 2006.

Warner, Michael. The Letters of the Republic: Publication and the Public Sphere in Eighteenth-Century America. Cambridge, MA: Harvard University Press, 1990.

Weber, Samuel. Mass Mediauras: Form, Technics, Media. Stanford: Stanford University Press, 1996.

———. Targets of Opportunity: On the Militarization of Thinking. New York: Fordham University Press, 2005.

———. "A Touch of Translation: On Walter Benjamin's 'Task of the Translator.'" In Nation, Language and the Ethics of Translation, edited by Sandra Bermann and Michael Wood. Princeton: Princeton University Press, 2005, 65–78.

———. "Wartime." In Violence, Identity, and Self-Determination, edited by Hent de Vries and Samuel Weber. Stanford: Stanford University Press, 1997, 92.

Webster, Noah. An American Dictionary of the English Language. 1826. Revised and enlarged edition. Springfield, MA: Merriam, 1862.

———. Dissertation on the English Language. Boston: Thomas, 1789.

———. A Grammatical Institute of the English Language. Facsimile of the 1783 edition. Menston, England: Scholar, 1968.

Wesling, Meg. Empire's Proxy: American Literature and U.S. Imperialism in the Philippines. New York: New York University Press, 2011.

Wolters, O. W. Early Southeast Asia: Selected Essays. Edited by Craig J. Reynolds. Ithaca: Cornell University, Southeast Asian Program Publications, 2008.

———. History, Culture and Region in Southeast Asian Perspectives. Ithaca: Cornell University, Southeast Asian Program Publications, 1999.

INDEX

....

accidents, agency of, 152–56
Adams, John, 104–5, 107
Afghanistan, U.S. occupation of, 122–24, 142–46
Agoncillo, Teodoro, 178–82
Aguinaldo, Emilio, 21, 27–28, 38–42, 60, 178
Akaka, Daniel, 101–3
Alvarez, Santiago, 37–42
American English: dominance in Philippines of, 43–44, 203n4; global significance of, 100–103, 221n3; historical evolution of, 103–8; nationalism linked to, 108–15; systematic privileging of, 109–15
American Revolution: American English after, 104; Philippine Revolution and, 30
American slang, 57–58
Anderson, Benedict, 63, 192, 205n19, 215n24; area studies and, 156–61
Anderson, Perry, 157–61
anonymity: of crowding, 85–92; military protocols for interpreta-

tion and, 131–37; in photography, 166–72; sociality and, 73–74; texting and, 79–82
anti-Americanism in Philippines, 46–50; Reynaldo Ileto and, 183–87
aporia of translation: elusiveness of, 12–14, 206n35; limits of counter-insurgency and, 141–46; meta-language and, 8–12
Appadurai, Arjun, 149, 158–61
Aquino, Cory, 168, 231n17
Arabic language: U.S. invasion of Iraq and translation of, 115–19; U.S. military language training in, 125–26
area studies: Cold War ideology, 149–50; language and, 149–61; post–Cold War influences on, 150–56; role of translation in, 15–18
Ateneo de Manila University, 178, 203n4
Atkinson, Fred, 53
authorship, authority and, 177–80
autobiography, 16–17; Ileto's use of, 177–80

automatic translation systems, 126–31
awa (pity), popular sovereignty and, 36–42

Babel, Tower of, 112–13; monolingualism and metaphor of, 111–15
Babylon Program, 127–31
Bahala na (Come what may), as Tagalog response to uncertainty, 207
balikbayan (Filipino expatriate), 74–75
barkada (friends), 65–66
Barry, Jerome, 56–58
Bataille, George, 21, 42
Battle of Manila (1945), 83–84
benevolent assimilation, 45–46
Benjamin, Walter, 143, 228n51
Benveniste, Emile, 6–7
bilingualism, assimilation and, 109–10
Bodin, Jean, 22
Bonifacio, Andres, 179–80
Breton, André, 70, 83
British English: American English and, 104–5; linguistic reforms in, 105–6
Bush, George W., 99

Caagusan, Flor (Flor C), narrative of, 88–92, 219n31
Catholic Church: Catholic conversion and, 20–23, 122; Filipino revolt against, 179–80; inter- and intra-linguistic vernaculars and, 3–4; Patronato Real of, 23–27; Revolution of 1896 as challenge to, 34–35; texting and, 79–80
cell phones: EDSA II and impact of, 72–74, 86–96; Filipino mania for, 74–82; introduction in Philippines of, 72–74; statistics on popularity of, 216n8; surveillance technology for, 217n10; texting and, 74–82
Center for Army Lessons Learned, 134–37

Chinese languages: in Filipino schools, 3–4, 203n4; presence in Philippine history of, 215n25
Christianity: American nationalism linked to, 112–15; conversion using local languages and, 100–103; impact on Ilongots of, 168–72; metalinguistics and, 10–12, 205n20; political theology of empire and, 22–27
citizenship, monolingualism linked to, 111–15
Civil Rights movement, area studies and, 152–56
class politics: cell phone use and, 72–74; Constantino's work and, 213n9; crowding and, 85–92; democratization and dissolution of, 83–92; English in public schools and, 45–46; fetishization of communication and, 70–71; Filipino slang and, 64–69; Filipino sovereignty and, 21–42; *ilustrados* and, 26–27; Poor People Power movement and, 93–96; translation and, 15
cocheros (coach drivers), linguistic versatility of, 59–61
Cold War ideology: American policy in Philippines and, 46–50; area studies and, 149–50; language as weapon in, 14–15
colonialism: Filipino dependency on U.S. and, 46–50; gender and, 186–87; hegemony of English and, 43–44; linguistic hierarchy and, 198–201; nostalgia and, 163–72; political theology of empire and, 22–27; telecommunications technology and, 71–72; U.S. counterinsurgency as, 122–24
communication: with dead, 168–72;

middle-class fetishization of, 70–71; military approaches to, 127–31; military protocols for interpretation and, 132–37; war of translation and, 56–58

Communist Party: Patriotic Youth (*Kabataang Makabayan*), 4; in postwar Philippines, 181–87

Constantino, Renato, 178, 213n8; family and education of, 213n9; on miseducation in English, 44–50, 65–69, 174, 184; on vernacular languages, 50–51, 63–69

counterinsurgency: colonial education as, 44–46, 54–58; interpreters in U.S. invasion of Iraq and, 115–19; language of, 121–24; limitations of, 141–46; popular sovereignty and, 28–35; U.S. surveillance technology and, 120–24; weaponization of language and, 120–48

counterterrorism, U.S. counterinsurgency and, 122–24

crowding: as political technology, 82–92; at religious gatherings, 219n35; saving power of, 89–90

damayan (joining with the other), 37–42, 211n28; crowding and, 90–92

Declaration of Independence, 28

Defense Advanced Research Projects Agency (DARPA), 127

Defense Language Institute Foreign Language Center, 125–26, 226n13

"Defense Language Transformation Roadmap," 101, 125–26

de la Costa, Horacio, 178

Deleuze, Gilles, 186

dependency on translation, in U.S. invasion of Iraq and risks of, 115–19

Derrida, Jacques, 1, 11–12, 204n8, 206n25, 208n2, 212n47; on messianism, 91–92; on politics and promise, 219n36

drone surveillance, U.S. monitoring of Afghanistan-Pakistan border with, 120–24

drug culture, in Filipino slang, 64–69

Dryden, John, 105

Echols, John, 156

Eder, Ederic Peñaflor, 80–81

EDSA II uprising, 70; backlash against, 93–96; cell phone use during, 72–74; class heterogeneity during, 91–92; crowding technology during, 78–82; telecommunications technology and, 72; texting as tool during, 78–82, 218n20

education policy: American English and, 46–50; assessment of, 51–58; as colonial conquest, 46–50; as counterinsurgency, 44–46; foreign language education in U.S. military and, 125–26; linguistic hierarchy and, 198–201; linguistic war in, 43–44; national security linked to, 99–103

English language: adoption in public schools of, 44–46; Cold War ideology and, 14–15; Constantino on miseducation as result of, 46–58; privileging of, in Philippines, 1–18, 43–44; Tagalong slang and, 61–69, 173–77; texting and condensation of, 77–82; as tool of colonial conquest, 46–50

español de Parian, 63–64

Estrada, Joseph ("Erap"), 70, 72–73, 80, 92–93, 220n42

evangelization, political theology of empire and, 23–27

exceptionalism, monolingualism and, 112–15

The Federalist, 104
filibusteros (subversives), 26–27
Filipino-American War of 1899–1902, 2, 44–46
First Republic of Philippines, 38–39
foreign languages: imperialism and, 99–103, 223n29; militarization of, 125–26
Fort Lewis Foreign Language Training Center, 125–26
Franco-Prussian War, 118–19
Franklin, Benjamin, 103–4
freedom. See kalayaan (freedom)
French Revolution, Philippine Revolution and, 30
friendship, translation and, 59–69

Generation Txt, 77–82
generosity during Revolution, 37–42
German language, history in U.S. of, 103–4
Globe network, 74
Gorgon Stare surveillance system, 120–24, 130
grammar, texting and rearticulation of, 77–82
Great Recession of 2008, 123–24
Guam, U.S. colonization of, 103
Guingona, Bart, 78–80

Hayakawa, S. I., 112
headhunting tradition, Rosaldo's study of, 163–72
Heidegger, Martin, 123, 223n24
hierarchy: authorship and, 177–80; crowding and suspension of, 85–92; military protocols for interpreters and, 135–37
Hokkien Chinese: in Filipino schools, 3–4, 203n4; postcolonial amalgamation of, 63, 215n25

Holt, Claire, 156
Huk rebellion, 46, 181

identity: area studies and, 155–56; crowding and erasure of, 85–92; insurgency of language and, 137–41; military protocols for interpreters and issues of, 132–37; nationalism and, 160–61; nostalgia and, 166–72; pronouns and, 6–7, 204n10; Rafael and Reynaldo Ileto and issues of, 180–87
Ileto, Loolee Carandang, 174–77, 182–87
Ileto, Olga Clemeña, 148, 184–87
Ileto, Rafael, 180–87; military service of, 231nn16–17; Renaldo Ileto's memories of, 180–87
Ileto, Reynaldo, 17–18, 40–42, 148, 173–88, 211n38; memories of father, 180–87; on Tagalog and English, 173–77; use of autobiography, 177–80
Ilonggo culture and language, 2–3, 162–72
ilustrados (Filipino bourgeoisie), 26–28; Agoncillo's history of, 179–80; Constantino and, 213n9
immigrants, monolingualism and marginalization of, 109–15
imperialism: counterinsurgency as, 121–24; Ileto father and son and experiences with, 180–87; language education and, 99–103; nostalgia and legacy of, 165–72; sovereignty and political theology of empire, 22–27, 209n9; translation, power and, 8–12, 14–18
indigenous peoples: monolingualism and marginalization of, 109–10
indios, Spanish imperialists and, 31–35
insurgency of language, translation and, 18, 137–41

interlinear translation, limits of counterinsurgency and, 143–46, 228n51
Internet use in Philippines, statistics
on, 216n8
interpreters: automatic translation
systems vs., 130–31; insurgency
of language and, 137–41; military
protocols for conduct of, 131–37;
simultaneous protection and policing of, 132–37; U.S. invasion of Iraq
and role of, 115–19
intralingual translation, 5; insurgency
of language and, 140–41
Iraq, U.S. invasion and occupation of,
115–19, 122–24

Jakobson, Roman, 7–12
Japanese Occupation of Philippines,
64, 180–87, 213n9
Jay, John, 104
Joaquin, Nick, 59–69
Johnson, Samuel, 106
Jones, William, 165
Jones Law of 1916, 51
justice, crowding as promise of,
85–92

Kahin, George, 151, 156–57
kalayaan (freedom): crowding as,
90–92; in Tagalog revolutionary
discourse, 35, 40–42, 211n38
Kapampangan language, 2–3
Katipunan (revolutionary society),
26–27, 179–80
Khatibi, Abdelkebir, 7
Kofman, Sarah, 12–13

language: counterinsurgency and
weaponization of, 120–48; failure of
counterinsurgency conversion of,
141–46; history and autobiography
and, 16–18, 173–88; as instrument
of empire, 105–8; insurgency of, 18,

137–41; as software, 127–31; texting
and condensation of, 77–82
Laws of the Indies, 23–27, 208n8
linguistic militarization, foreign language education and, 125–26
linguistic pluralism: monolingualism
and marginalization of, 110–15;
persistence in U.S. of, 104–15,
222n8; in Philippines, 1–18; pronouns in, 6–7

Mabini, Apolinario, 28–35, 41–42,
178
Macapagal-Arroyo, Gloria, 80, 92–94,
220n42
MacArthur, Arthur (Gen.), 44
MacArthur, Douglas (Gen.), 181
Malolos Republic, 33, 38–39; Constitution of, 210n18
Marcos, Ferdinand, 70, 168, 231n17
McKinley, William, 45
media politics: backlash against
EDSA II uprising and, 93–96; cell
phone use and, 72–74; class divisions and, 71–96; crowding and,
82–92; texting and, 74–82
Mencken, H. L., 62
middle classes: crowding and, 82–92;
fetish of communication for, 70–71;
political tactics of, 220n42; telecommunications technology and, 71–72;
texting and, 78–82
missionaries, use of local languages
by, 100–103, 221n3
monolingualism: history of American
English and, 104–8; military language training in context of, 125–26;
nationalism linked to, 108–15
Monroe, Paul, 51

Nancy, Jean-Luc, 172, 208n2
National Defense Education Act,
101–3

nationalism: Anderson's discussion of,
157–61; Appadurai's view of, 158–61;
colonial linguistic legacy and,
45–46; Constantino's and, 213n9;
education policy in Philippines and,
46–50, 64–65; foreign language
education and, 101–3; media politics
and, 71–74; monolingualism and,
108–15; popular sovereignty and,
31–35

national security: interpreters in
U.S. invasion of Iraq and, 115–19;
language education and, 99–103;
military protocols for interpretation
and, 131–37

National Security Language Initiative
(U.S.), 99–103

Native Americans: languages of, 103;
monolingualism and marginalization of, 109–10, 223n29

natural law, popular sovereignty and,
31–35, 211n29

Nebrija, Antonio de, 104

neocolonialism in Philippines, American education policy and, 46–50

neoliberalism, U.S. counterinsurgency
and conversion to, 122–24

Nergaard, Siri, 189–201

Nietzsche, Friedrich, 118–19

nostalgia, language and, 162–72

Official English constitutional amendment proposal, 111

Orientalism, area studies and, 152–56

otherness: area studies and role of,
152–56; Ileto's research on, 173–77;
monolingualism and marginalization of, 110–15

pacto de sangre (blood compact), 31–35

pag-iibigan (love), 39

Patronato Real (Royal Patronage),
23–27

Paz, Octavio, 1, 6

Peace Corps, area studies and influence of, 150–56

Pentecost, 10–12

People Power II. See Epifanio de los
Santos Avenue (EDSA II) uprising

People Power revolt (1986), 70

Petraeus, David, 142

Philippine Collegian magazine, 46–50

Philippine Long Distance Company,
73

Philippines: independence proclaimed
in, 15; linguistic pluralism in,
1–5; U.S. occupation of, 21, 31–35,
64–69, 103–4, 224n47

photography: experiences registered
through, 87–92; nostalgia and,
165–72

Phraselator device, 129

Pilar, Marcelo H. del, 26–27

Pinoy Times, 80

Plaridel (online discussion group), 76,
78–79, 86

Plato, 13–14, 206n35

political movements: crowding and,
82–92; decline of, 220n42; telecommunications technology and, 71–74;
texting and, 74–82

political theology of empire: Mabini
and, 32–35; sovereignty and,
22–27

Poor People Power movement, backlash against middle class of, 93–96

popular sovereignty, emergence of,
27–35, 40–42, 212n50

postcolonialism: area studies and,
153–56; nostalgia and, 165–72

power: cell phone as instrument of,
73–74; translation and, 1, 7–12

Pratt, Mary Louise, 125–26

prayer, 11–12

Proclamation of Independence, Philippines, 27–35

promise, politics and, 91–92, 219n36

pronouns, personhood and, 6–7, 204n10

pronunciation, American English and standardization of, 107

public school system, U.S. military establishment of, 44–46

Quezon, Manuel L., 64, 213n9

Quijano de Manila. *See* Joaquin, Nick

racism: Filipinized English and, 54–58; political theology of empire and, 26–27; Reynaldo Ileto's memories of, 182–87; Spanish denial of Filipino parliamentary representation and, 209n13; in U.S. colonial policy, 45–46

radio in the Philippines, political impact of, 72, 79

Rapid Multilingual Support program, 127–31

Recto, Claro M., 46, 178, 213n9

Revolution of 1896, 2–3; historiography, 207n1; popular sovereignty and, 27–35; translation of sovereignty after, 21; vernacular discourse concerning, 35–42

Rianzares Bautista, Ambrosio, 28

Rizal, Jose, 46, 59, 71–72, 178

Romulo, Carlos P., 153, 213n9

Roosevelt, Theodore, 110–12

Rosaldo, Michelle, 164–65, 168–71

Rosaldo, Renato, 17–18, 162–72

Rousseau, Jean-Jacques, 36

Rush, Benjamin, 103

Said, Edward, 154–56

Sakay, Macario (Gen.), 36

Saleeby, Najeeb, 50

Salvador, Felipe, 174

Schlesinger, Arthur, 112

Schmitt, Carl, 22, 41, 208n2

Schumacher, John (Fr.), 187–88, 231n13

settler colonialism, monolingual citizenship and, 111

Siegel, James T., 149, 160–61, 192

slang: insurgency of language and, 133–41; Joaquin's analysis of, 62–69; Taglish and, 4, 15–18, 203nn3–4

slavery in U.S.: evolution of American English and, 103–4; literacy and, 222n21

Smart network, 74

soberanía monacal (monastic sovereignty), 26–27

Sophists, 13–14

Southeast Asian Studies, 151–61

sovereignty: political theology of empire and, 22–27; popular sovereignty, 27–35; translation and, 21–42; Western conceptions of, 208n2

space, war and concepts of, 118–19

Spanish Empire: Catholic conversion and, 122; denial of Filipino representation in Spain and, 26, 209n13; *indios* and, 31–35; revolution of 1896 and, 23–27

Spanish language: in early United States, 103, 105; historical legacy of, 62–63, 215n24; imperialism and imposition of, 99–103; Philippine elite use of, 15; in Philippines, 3–4, 44; popular sovereignty and use of, 27–35

Speechalator, 129–31

street: cell phone use linked to, 73–74; emergence of slang in, 16, 43–44; Joaquin on language of, 62–69; linguistic versatility in, 58–60; social mixing in, 70–71, 83–84, 218n24

Stutterheim, William, 157

Supreme Court of U.S., 45–46; Insular Cases of 1901 before, 224n47 surveillance technology: cell phones and, 217n10; drone surveillance, 120–24; mechanization of translation and, 126–31; use in retail space of, 84–85, 89–92

Survey of the Educational System in the Philippines, 51

Swift, Jonathan, 105

Tagalog language, 2–5; American English and (Taglish), 16–18, 64–69; English and, 173–77; Ileto and, 174–77, 182–87

Taglish: crowding and use of, 86–92; evolution of, 4, 15–18, 203nn3–4; texting in, 74–82

telephones, introduction in Philippines of, 71–72

texting: costs of, 217n11; politics of, 74–82, 217n20; statistics on popularity of, 216n8

time, war and concepts of, 118–19

Titan private contractor, 132–33

traffic in Manila, 83–96

translation: aporia of, 1–18; autobiography and, 16–17, 180–87; automatization of, 126–31; colonial education as war of, 54–58; communication across social space and, 70–96; conversion and, 123–24, 205n22; etymology of, 206n23; foreign language handicap and, 53–58; imperialism and, 99–103; insurgency of language and, 18, 137–41; interpreters' role in, 115–19; Joaquin's analysis of slang and, 59–69; limits of counterinsurgency and, 141–46; linguistic reform and, 107–8; military mobilization of, 125–26; military protocols for conduct of, 131–37; monolingualism and, 110–15; power and, 1, 7–12; Spanish missionaries' ideas about,

221n3; in U.S. invasion of Iraq and risks of, 115–19; U.S. notion of, 100–103; weaponization of language and, 125–48

Treaty of Guadalupe (1848), 103

Treaty of Paris (1899), 31

United States: evolution of American English in, 103–8; Filipino dependency on, 46–50; as "indispensible nation," 226n10; National Security Language Initiative in, 99–103; notion of translation of, 100–103; occupation of Philippines by, 21, 31–35, 64–69, 103–4; persistence of linguistic pluralism in, 104–15, 222n8

untranslatability, 12, 18; insurgency of language and, 137–41; war and experience of, 115–16, 224n47

urban space, Manila, 83–96

U.S. military: governance of postwar Philippines by, 44–46, 104; interpreters in U.S. invasion of Iraq and, 115–19; language-enabled soldier in, 125–26

The U.S. Army/Marine Corps Counterinsurgency Field Manual of 2006, 131–41

vernacular languages: in colonial U.S., 105; evolution of slang and, 64–69; friendship and translation and, 59–60; Ileto's research on, 174–77, 188; Joaquin's writing on, 60–69; marginalization of, 2–18; nationalism and, 15–18; Revolution of 1896 and, 35–42; tenacity of, 50–58

virtue, popular sovereignty and, 30–35

war: area studies and influence of, 150–56; insurgency of language and, 133–39; limits of counterinsurgency and, 141–46; surveillance technology during, 120–24; translation and, 14–18, 101–3, 115–19, 195–201

weaponization of language, 124–48; automation of translation and, 126–31; insurgency of language and, 137–41; limitations of, 141–46; military foreign language education and, 124–26; military protocols for interpretation and, 131–37; U.S.

counterinsurgency initiatives and, 120–24

weaponization of vision, 120–24

Weber, Samuel, 119

Webster, Noah, 104, 106–8, 112, 222n21

Wheeler, Joseph (Gen.), 29

Wolters, Oliver, 178–80, 184, 231n12

women: area studies and, 151–56; in nationalist historiography, 186–87

Worcester, Dean C., 165